TRADING THE
FUNDAMENTALS

TRADING THE FUNDAMENTALS

Revised Edition

THE TRADER'S GUIDE TO INTERPRETING ECONOMIC INDICATORS AND MONETARY POLICY

MICHAEL P. NIEMIRA

GERALD F. ZUKOWSKI

McGRAW-HILL
New York   San Francisco   Washington, D.C.   Auckland   Bogotá
Caracas   Lisbon   London   Madrid   Mexico City   Milan
Montreal   New Delhi   San Juan   Singapore
Sydney   Tokyo   Toronto

Library of Congress Cataloging-in-Publication Data

Niemira, Michael P.
    Trading the fundamentals / Michael P. Niemira and Gerald F.
    Zukowski.—rev ed.
        p.   cm.
    ISBN 0-7863-1100-2
    1. Investments—United States—Handbooks, manuals, etc.
2. Economic indicators—United States.   3. Monetary policy—United
States.   4. Economic forecasting—United States.   I. Zukowski,
Gerald F.   II. Title.
HG4521.N477   1998
332.6—dc21   97-30364
                                                                CIP

McGraw-Hill

A Division of The **McGraw·Hill** Companies

Copyright © 1998 by The McGraw-Hill Companies, Inc. All rights reserved. Printed in the
United States of America. Except as permitted under the United States Copyright Act of
1976, no part of this publication may be reproduced or distributed in any form or by any
means, or stored in a data base or retrieval system, without the prior written permission
of the publisher.

1 2 3 4 5 6 7 8 9 0 DOC/DOC 9 0 2 1 0 9 8 7

The sponsoring editor for this book was Stephen Isaacs, the editing supervisor was John
M. Morriss, and the production supervisor was Suzanne W. B. Rapcavage. It was set in
Times Roman by North Market Street Graphics.

Printed and bound by R. R. Donnelley & Sons Company.

McGraw-Hill books are available at special quantity discounts to use as premiums and
sales promotions, or for use in corporate training programs. For more information, please
write to the Director of Special Sales, McGraw-Hill, 11 West 19th Street, New York, NY
10011. Or contact your local bookstore.

Information contained in this work has been obtained by The McGraw-Hill Companies, Inc.
("McGraw-Hill") from sources believed to be reliable. However, neither McGraw-Hill nor its authors guarantee the accuracy or completeness of any information published herein, and neither
McGraw-Hill nor its authors shall be responsible for any errors, omissions, or damages arising out
of use of this information. This work is published with the understanding that McGraw-Hill and
its authors are supplying information but are not attempting to render engineering or other professional services. If such services are required, the assistance of an appropriate professional
should be sought.

 This book is printed on recycled, acid-free paper containing a minimum of 50%
recycled de-inked fiber.

Dedicated to Our Families

Lottie Zukowski and Kathleen, Alexis, Sarah, and Keith

and

Anne, Henry, Shirley, and Andrew Niemira

Table of Contents

Preface

Investors today are more savvy than ever about the interaction of the economy and monetary policy. News reporting is faster, more detailed, and more analytical; investors are compelled to understand more thoroughly the intricacies of the economic data and the conduct of monetary policy. It is the intent of this revised edition to update analytical information about the economic indicators and the conduct of monetary policy since the first edition was printed, to provide references to Internet sources of information, and to help fill in and expand investors' understanding of the fundamentals that ultimately drive the financial markets. Finally, given the rapidity of change in and delivery of our economic statistics, readers should look to the Internet—at the address indicated—to update information contained in each of the chapters.

Michael P. Niemira
Gerald F. Zukowski

Section 1

Analyzing Business Conditions

Chapter 1

More Than a Numbers Game

The Five C's of Economic News

Every economic indicator has a story to tell. The role of the trader, dealer, or investor of fixed-income instruments, stocks, options, futures, and foreign currency is to determine quickly that story and the significance of a move in the indicator. In most cases, the market reaction to an economic news report is determined by: (1) the background economic theme, (2) the reliability and comprehensiveness of an economic indicator, (3) the market consensus forecast, (4) the significance of the data revisions in previous periods, and (5) the perception of how important the indicator is to policy makers. These are the five C's—*concept, coverage, consensus, changes,* and *consequence*—that are needed to understand how the financial markets may react to economic news.

Economic Concepts ("Concepts"): The financial markets tend to be sensitive to background concepts or themes—recessions, booms, inflation, foreign trade deterioration, dollar strength or weakness, strengthening or weakening cyclical sectors, and so on, and any incoming economic data generally are evaluated against a broader economic issue. The paramount economic theme will change for the financial markets over time and through the business cycle. Moreover, in recent years, the news media have helped to shape those background issues with stories citing the concern of Federal Reserve officials about this or that issue. Well-timed release of those news stories also can have a market impact as the key background issue is challenged, reinforced, or shifted.

Data Coverage ("Coverage"): Some economic indicators tend to have a greater market impact than other series because of their breadth in coverage, depth of detail, and timeliness. In most cases, the market's technical indicators along with global political factors play an important role in determining how significant a market reaction will be and whether the financial market reaction is "as expected" or just the reverse. As a rough guide to how the financial markets react to the economic news, Figure 1-1 illustrates the "normal" market reaction.

Consensus Forecasts ("Consensus"): Numerous surveys of the major economic indicator forecasts exist, and there is a good deal of overlap in who participates in the forecast surveys. Most major firms participate in most of the consensus surveys. Some of the more widely followed consensus takers are Bloomberg Business News, Bridge News, Dow-Jones Capital Markets, Market News Service, Money Market Services, MCM's MoneyWatch, and Technical Data Corporation.

Data Revisions ("Changes"): Sometimes the data revisions are more important in assessing the financial reaction than the current month's data. If the current month's reading is about as expected but the recent data tell a very different story about the strength or weakness of the economy, then that story may be more significant and overshadow the most recent data.

FIGURE 1–1   Assessing Financial Market Impact of Economic News

Market	Stronger/Larger than Expected		Weaker/Lower than Expected	
	Business Conditions	Inflation	Business Conditions	Inflation
Fixed Income (prices)	↓	↓	↑	↑
U.S. Equity (prices)	↑	↓	↓	↑
Foreign Exchange (dollar)	↑	↑	↑	↓

Policy Significance ("Consequence"): There is no clearer reflection of the power and importance of these economic news reports than in witnessing how the information is guarded and who is privy to the information before the official release. Only the president of the United States through the chair of the Council of Economic Advisers (CEA) is given the full contents of a government-issued economic report prior to its official release time. Generally, the president is informed of the economic news on the evening before the scheduled release. In turn, the president's representative—the CEA chairperson or a CEA-designated person—as a courtesy, advises the chairperson of the Federal Reserve Board of Governors about the essence of the economic report. Thus, the government's highest fiscal and monetary policy makers are privy to the information before the public is notified. In a broad sense, the fixed-income and exchange rate markets tend to react more directly to the economic news than the stock market, which also is dependent on specific company and industry fundamentals. The fixed-income markets focus more heavily on the pace of economic growth and inflation; the foreign exchange markets tend to worry about the pace of world economic growth, worldwide inflation and interest rates, and foreign trade imbalances; the stock market is interested in earnings, which are driven by economic growth and the asset allocation implications from changes in interest rates. But all the financial markets are linked, and at times the linkage can be strong.

Economic and Financial Linkages

To truly appreciate the individual economic news reports, it is important to have a framework for analysis. Our perspective is twofold: (1) a theoretical view of the linkage between sectors and (2) an empirical business cycle view. These two perspectives go hand in hand in putting together the economic indicator mosaic. It is not sufficient just to have a technical knowledge of the data or of Federal Reserve operations, but one also must have a "big picture" view of how the parts fit together.

Although it is not our intention to summarize macroeconomic theory, it is helpful to provide a thumbnail sketch of some strands of theory, which could be helpful in understanding how the economic indicator pieces of news might fit together. To this end, we will rely on a compact discussion by Frederic S. Mishkin, the former director of research at the Federal Reserve Bank of New York, on four common and competing types of theories linking the financial and consumer and business sectors of the economy. The main theories can be called: (1) the "interest rate channel," (2) the "exchange rate channel," (3) the "equity share price channel," and (4) the "credit channel."[1] Mishkin also offers some simple flow diagrams, which we rely upon to summarize each of these theories.

The Interest Rate Channel: The standard Keynesian economics model of a contraction in monetary policy works like this: when monetary policy (M) tightens, real interest rates rise (i), and investment (I) goes down, which causes a decline in output or income (Y). This framework is shown in the schematic diagram, as offered by Mishkin:

$$M \downarrow \Rightarrow i \uparrow \Rightarrow I \downarrow \Rightarrow Y \downarrow$$

Investment is considered to be business investment, residential investment, and consumer durable goods expenditures. For a monetary policy ease, the up-down arrows, which indicate the direction of change in the measure, are reversed.

The Exchange Rate Channel: With growing international monetary policy coordination and central bank concern about exchange rates, a second possible framework for analysis could be through the exchange rate channel. This schematic diagram for a tightening in monetary policy and its impact on the real sector might look like this:

$$M \downarrow \Rightarrow i \uparrow \Rightarrow E \uparrow \Rightarrow NX \downarrow \Rightarrow Y \downarrow$$

where a monetary policy tightening again leads to higher real interest rates, and in turn causes the exchange rate (E) to strengthen and net exports (NX) to decline—as exports weaken and imports strengthen, which ultimately causes a decline in output. Similarly, for a monetary policy ease, the directions of the arrows are reversed.

The Equity Share Price Channel: Another channel of influence on the economy is through the equity and other asset markets—including land and property values. Two competing views of this

---

1   Frederic S. Mishkin, "Symposium on the Monetary Transmission Mechanism," *Journal of Economic Perspectives,* Vol. 9, No. 4, Fall 1995, pp. 3–10.

model show monetary policy impacts working through: (1) investment (Tobin's q) and/or (2) the wealth effect on consumption. The equity price-investment channel is shown in the following diagram:

$$M \downarrow \Rightarrow P_e \downarrow \Rightarrow q \downarrow \Rightarrow I \downarrow \Rightarrow Y \downarrow$$

Under this framework, a monetary policy tightening puts downward pressure on equity prices (P_e), which leads to a decline in q, which is the ratio market value of capital assets (durable assets) to the replacement value of those assets. In turn, that decline in the market value of assets relative to their book value causes a decline in investment, which then results in a lower national output.

Alternatively, the life cycle consumption model suggests that when stock prices fall, wealth declines, which in turn causes consumption to weaken and national income with it. This monetary policy transmission scheme is diagrammed as follows:

$$M \downarrow \Rightarrow P_e \downarrow \Rightarrow \text{wealth} \downarrow \Rightarrow C \downarrow \Rightarrow Y \downarrow$$

where wealth represents all financial wealth, and C indicates consumption. There are other variants on this consumption chain, and the investment and consumption approaches need not be viewed as mutually exclusive. As is the case with all the monetary channels presented, the directions of the up-down arrows are reversed for a monetary policy ease.

The Credit Channel: There are two basic approaches under the credit channel: (1) the bank lending approach and (2) the balance sheet approach. The bank lending view suggests that monetary policy changes work through the banking system and the ability of banks to lend. When the Federal Reserve tightens policy, this causes a decrease in bank reserves and bank deposits, which curtails lending. This can be diagrammed as:

$$M \downarrow \Rightarrow \text{bank deposits} \downarrow \Rightarrow \text{bank loans} \downarrow \Rightarrow I \downarrow \Rightarrow Y \downarrow$$

Empirically, this view has been challenged in the literature and has led to another credit channel, the balance sheet approach. This framework suggests that changes in monetary policy cause changes in the net worth of business firms or consumer balance sheets, which in turn impact output. Two variants of this view for the business sector are:

(a) $M \downarrow \Rightarrow P_e \downarrow \Rightarrow$ lending risk $\uparrow \Rightarrow$ lending $\downarrow \Rightarrow I \downarrow \Rightarrow Y \downarrow$

(b) $M \downarrow \Rightarrow i \uparrow \Rightarrow$ lending risk $\uparrow \Rightarrow$ lending $\downarrow \Rightarrow I \downarrow \Rightarrow Y \downarrow$

where the differences in (a) and (b) are whether the impact is through equity prices or interest rates acting through the banks' increased risk of lending, which causes banks to tighten credit standards, which in turn curtails lending and investment. Another credit channel theory is tied to consumer credit availability, where an increase in interest rates and/or a decrease in equity prices results in an increase in lending risk to consumers, which in turn triggers a cutback in consumer lending. With the availability of consumer credit diminished, consumption is pared and with it national income, which is diagrammed below:

$$M \downarrow \Rightarrow i \uparrow \text{ and/or } P_e \downarrow \Rightarrow \text{lending risk } \uparrow$$

$$\Rightarrow \text{consumer lending } \downarrow \Rightarrow C \downarrow \Rightarrow Y \downarrow$$

In reality, no one of these frameworks is totally correct or totally wrong, and numerous variants exist. The differences between most theories of the impact of a change in monetary policy on the economy lie more with the emphasis on what is deemed the most crucial factor for the economy. Each theory sheds some light on the inner workings of the economy—all, of course, in a simplified manner. And to some extent, all of these theories have some validity—as well as the same ultimate impact on output. Whatever perspective one takes, it is useful to be aware of the other approaches and the empirical support for and popularity of each of these hypotheses.

Mishkin correctly noted that the importance of understanding how monetary policy works through the economy is "crucial to answering a broad range of policy questions. What is the appropriate monetary policy in different business cycle episodes? What should be the appropriate role for monetary policy? What is the correct choice of a tradeoff between output variability and inflation variability? Would a fixed rather than a flexible exchange rate regime produce better inflation and output outcomes?"[2]

For their part, the financial markets are more eclectic in their collective view of the economic linkages and importance of any

---

2   Ibid., pp. 9–10.

particular theory. *Theories de jour* exist and are made popular by the financial press such as *Barron's, Business Week, Forbes, Fortune, Investors Business Daily,* the *Wall Street Journal,* the *Financial Times,* and so on. Traders are easily swayed by the view of the day since it is the "tradable idea" that is important to their business and not always whether the view is correct.

Economic Indicators over the Business Cycle

The second perspective is based on business cycle measurement and is devoid of any particular theory. Looking at the data over the business cycle provides one of the best vantage points to understand the economy and the implication for monetary and fiscal policy changes. It also allows one to empirically reject or accept a theory. However, it is generally not very easy in a real-time world to tell which phase of the business cycle one is in— even with sophisticated statistical methods. Of course, with the benefit of hindsight, those cycle phases are much more obvious.

A business cycle is simply the way that growth takes place. Recessions are triggered when imbalances in the cost-price-profit relationship occur, which often are caused by a shock or cumulative excess in the economy. Recoveries are phases of the cycle delineated from the economy's low point or trough until the economy recaptures its lost output. Expansions are cyclical phases that begin when the economy expands beyond its prior cyclical high through to the next recession. But expansions also include periods of accelerating and decelerating growth, which are called *growth cycles* (also popularly known as *mini-cycles* or *growth rate cycles*). The National Bureau of Economic Research, which is the arbiter of the official business cycle turning-point dates, also has produced a growth cycle chronology.

Our perspective is to divide the business cycle into three phases—recession, recovery, and expansion.[3] (See Figure 1-2.) We then subdivide the expansion into two stages—the rapid-growth and slow-growth expansion phases. The slow-growth

---

3   See Daniel E. Sichel, "Inventories and the Three Phases of the Business Cycle," *Journal of Business & Economic Statistics,* Vol. 12, No. 3, July 1994, pp. 269–277. Also see Kenneth M. Emery and Evan F. Koenig, "Forecasting Turning Points: Is a Two-State Characterization of the Business Cycle Appropriate?" Research Paper, Federal Reserve Bank of Dallas, September 1992.

FIGURE 1–2   Phases of the Business Cycle Based on Payroll Employment

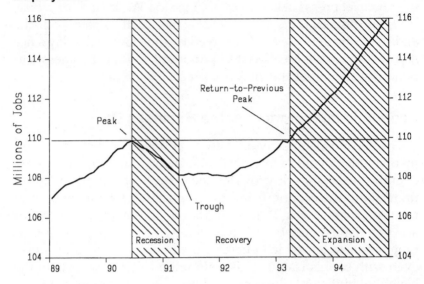

phase also corresponds to "growth cycle slowdowns" during an expansion period. The expansion phase—either the rapid- or slow-growth phase—then turns into the next recession, and the sequence continues, though the duration of each phase may vary. A schematic diagram of this business cycle framework would look like this:

Recession ⇒ Recovery ⇒ Expansion ⇒ Next Recession

and

Expansion = Rapid Expansion ↔ Slow Expansion

Expansions typically are characterized by an initial rapid-growth phase followed by a slow-growth phase, which often has led to a recession. However, this pattern is less predictable and consistent; some recessions have followed the rapid-growth phase, and some business cycle expansions have contained more than one rapid-growth or slow-growth phase. Moreover, not all economic indicators show a statistical difference between the rapid- and slow-growth phases of the cycle, which will be clear from the tables with each indicator. Still, the alternating phases of slow and rapid growth provide another level of analysis to understand the dynamic within the business cycle expansion, which can encompass many years.

For purposes of our analysis, the indicator's performance during recessions is calculated from the month following the peak in the business cycle to the trough; the recovery is defined from the trough to the return-to-the-previous peak as measured in the composite coincident indicator (a composite indicator of employment, sales, and production); the expansion begins in the month following the return-to-the-previous peak through the next peak. The rapid-growth phase of the expansion is determined from the coincident indicator growth rates and delineated for periods when growth exceeded its previous long-term trend (which generally was 4 percent or stronger through the 1970s, 3½ percent through the 1980s, and 3.25 percent thereafter), while slow-growth phases were the remaining periods of the expansion. The dates for each of those periods are shown in Table 1-1.

Typical News Flow

As a general rule, the National Association of Purchasing Management's Purchasing Managers' Index is the first nationwide indicator for the prior month, followed by monthly chain store sales and car sales; and on the first Friday of the month, the employment report is released. The price indexes—the U.S. Consumer Price Index (CPI) and the Produce Price Index (PPI)—tend to be released late in the second or early in the third week of the month. The real gross domestic product (GDP), personal income and consumption, the index of leading indicators, and factory orders reports all tend to be reported late in the month, with most other economic reports in the third week of the month. In December, U.S. government statistical agencies under the coordination of the Office of Management and Budget announce scheduled release dates for the upcoming year, and for the most part those dates are not changed. When a release date is changed for some unforeseen reason, the statistical agency alerts data users of the change as soon as possible. (See Box 1-1 for a glimpse of what it is like to be present at some of these releases.)

Several financial publications, such as the *Wall Street Journal* and *Business Week,* show a week-ahead economic calendar; and

TABLE 1–1   U.S. Business Cycle Stages, 1948–1997

Recession	Recovery	Expansion	Rapid-Growth Expansion Phase	Slow-Growth Expansion Phase
December 1948–October 1949	November 1949–May 1950	June 1950–July 1953	June 1950–April 1951	May 1951–August 1952
			September 1952–July 1953	
August 1953–May 1954	June 1954–May 1955	June 1955–August 1957	June 1955–January 1956	February 1956–August 1957
September 1957–April 1958	May 1958–April 1959	May 1959–April 1960	May 1959–September 1959	October 1959–April 1960
May 1960–February 1961	March 1961–November 1961	December 1961–December 1969	December 1961–July 1962	August 1962–September 1963
			October 1963–April 1966	May 1966–December 1967
			January 1968–December 1968	January 1969–December 1969
January 1970–November 1970	December 1970–January 1972	February 1972–November 1973	February 1972–April 1973	May 1973–November 1973
December 1973–March 1975	April 1975–June 1977	July 1977–January 1980	July 1977–February 1979	March 1979–January 1980
February 1980–July 1980	August 1980–March 1981	April 1981–July 1981	April 1981–July 1981	
August 1981–November 1982	December 1982–April 1984	May 1984–July 1990	May 1984–August 1984	September 1984–October 1986
			November 1986–July 1988	August 1988–July 1990
August 1990–March 1991	April 1991–September 1992	October 1992–	October 1992–April 1995	May 1995–May 1996
			June 1996–April 1997 (*t*)	

t = tentative.

some, such as *Barron's* and *Futures*, publish a month-ahead calendar. Additionally, the newswires, as well as the Internet sites of
the newswires and financial publications, make available the
dates of release for major economic indicators both domestically
and internationally.

BOX 1–1   Informing the Public: The Press Lockup

*Jon E. Hilsenrath**

When Adren Cooper first came to the Commerce Department in 1966, there was little structure to the government's release of economic data. Cooper says President Lyndon Johnson sometimes announced upbeat reports himself, in speeches. But more sleepy reports could sit on tables for hours on release dates, untouched by reporters.

Twenty-seven years later, journalists from newswires around the world crowd into the fifth-floor Commerce Department press room, scrambling to get out as many numbers as financial markets can digest. Cooper now runs these so-called lockups for Commerce.

The Commerce Department and Labor Department, both driven by fears and rumors of leaks in recent years, have taken to locking reporters into their press rooms for key reports, giving them 30 minutes to prepare stories for release. Reporters come to these lockups armed with editors and statisticians to help put together tables, headlines and stories. Between 8 AM and 8:30 AM, the door is closed behind them and their phones are disconnected from the outside world.

During more complex reports, like the 20-page unemployment report, lockup rooms can become hectic, as reporters search for nuances in the data and dozens of stat people read out numbers from tables. According to Labor Department officials, as many as 25 organizations may be present at key lockups, including representatives from French, German, English and Japanese agencies.

Still concerned about leaks of the data, both Commerce and Labor attach unusual rules to their lockups. Emergency trips to the bathroom require a government escort. When phone lines are opened at 8:29 AM to connect to copy desks, all conversations must be in English. And that conversation cannot concern the data until the Naval Observatory deems it is exactly 8:30 Eastern time.

In a global marketplace, releasing a few numbers just isn't that simple anymore.

---

*   Jon Hilsenrath was formerly with Knight-Ridder Financial News in Washington, D.C., and attended those press lockups.

What's Ahead in the Book

In the following pages, each economic indicator is discussed in sections that allow for easy reference. The placement of the economic indicator chapters was based on an alphabetical listing of the indicators and not on their market importance or their typical release schedule during the month. Over time, the market significance of some economic indicators has shifted, given broader global, political, and economic concerns. For example, in the early 1980s the money supply was riding high in its importance for the markets, but by the end of the 1980s this was no longer true due to the unstable short-term empirical link between money, growth, and inflation. A shift in market focus also occurred for the international trade report, which was a very significant market mover in the late 1980s, but its importance dwindled as the trade gap narrowed due to the impact of and market preoccupation with the 1990–1991 recession.

Each indicator discussion addresses several key questions, such as what it measures, why look at it, how it is used, and how the markets tend to react to the data. Any market reaction discussion is only suggestive, since, as previously noted, external factors play a role in determining the strength and type of market reaction. Additionally, a data performance table is included with each indicator. The series performance shows the average change or level and normal bounds for each stage of the business cycle, which should help the user evaluate quickly the strength or weakness of an indicator's reading. Because all data are noisy, a normal high and normal low band is presented. "Normal" is defined as the average plus or minus one-half of the standard deviation. A wide normal band should alert the user to very high volatility in the series, which can alternatively be measured directly by the standard deviation, which is also presented.

Through the Internet Looking Glass—Finding the Data

The Internet is fast becoming the one source of information, including financial and economic data and news. Throughout the pages of this book, we have included an Internet address—generally for the Commerce Department or Labor Department—

BOX 1–2   Stock and Bond Prices
over the Business Cycle

As you read through the chapters of this book, it is helpful to keep in mind that the financial markets react to the economic news differently in different phases of the business cycle. Tables 1-2 and 1-3 provide empirical support for that view and offer some background on the historical returns for the stock and bond markets over the phases of the business cycle. Of course, a more detailed analysis would be to look at the individual episodes within each cycle and cross-reference them with the phase of the inflation cycle, but that is left to the reader. Moreover, because of the lead-lag timing relationship between the financial markets and the business cycle, the turning points in the stock or bond markets often occur prior to the business cycle. Hence, this may obscure the bear markets in stocks when presented as a postwar average, which suggests another reason to examine the individual episodes in more detail.

Nonetheless, these summary measures still can provide some useful insight into the typical performance of these financial sectors over the business cycle. The stock market tends to perform best during the slow-growth and recovery phases of the business cycle, while the bond market tends to perform best during the slow-growth and recession phases of the cycle. The average yield curve performance (as reflected by the 10-year government note yield minus the three-month Treasury bill rate on a coupon equivalent)

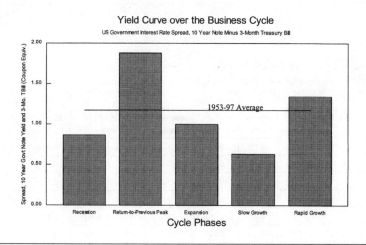

Yield Curve over the Business Cycle

over the course of the business cycle is also portrayed in the figure below—keep in mind that although the yield curve may invert at times, that occurred in only 13.4 percent of the months between April 1953 and June 1997, with the median monthly inversion lasting only three months (the longest span lasted 18 months). Moreover, the financial markets clearly are sensitive to the phase of the cycle, which underscores the approach taken within this book.

to find the economic data, but these data exist in other Internet sites and formats—in their entirety or in digest form. New sites are popping up continually. Bank and brokerage research departments are making available their commentary on the econ-

TABLE 1–2   10-Year Government Note Price

(May 1953–December 1996, % Change from Prior Month, Total Return)

		Normal Bounds				Series Characteristics	
Phase	Historic Low	Normal Low	Average	Normal High	Historic High	Standard Deviation	Share of Total Observations
Expansion	−14.7% in Jul 1981	−1.6%	−0.2%	1.3%	+13.4% in Jun 1981	3.0 pp	319	61.2%
Rapid Phase	−14.7% in Jul 1981	−2.0%	−0.5%	0.9%	+13.4% in Jun 1981	3.0 pp	160	30.7%
Slow Phase	−11.5% in Oct 1979	−1.2%	0.2%	1.7%	+10.7% in Mar 1986	2.9 pp	159	30.5%
Recession	−21.1% in Feb 1980	−2.8%	1.4%	5.6%	+47.3% in Nov 1981	8.4 pp	117	22.5%
Recovery	−13.6% in Nov 1980	−2.0%	−0.4%	1.1%	+4.8% in Dec 1970	3.1 pp	85	16.3%
All Phases	−21.1% in Feb 1980	−2.2%	0.0%	2.2%	+47.3% in Nov 1981	4.4 pp	521	100.0%

TABLE 1–3   S&P 500 Price Index

(January 1948–December 1996, % Change from Prior Month)

		Normal Bounds				Series Characteristics	
Phase	Historic Low	Normal Low	Average	Normal High	Historic High	Standard Deviation	Share of Total Observations
Expansion	−12.5% in Nov 1987	−0.9%	0.7%	2.2%	+8.8% in Aug 1984	3.0 pp	354	61.7%
Rapid Phase	−12.5% in Nov 1987	−1.2%	0.5%	2.1%	+8.8% in Aug 1984	3.3 pp	179	31.2%
Slow Phase	−7.1% in Nov 1973	−0.6%	0.8%	2.2%	+6.9% in Nov 1962	2.7 pp	175	30.5%
Recession	−11.5% in May 1970	−2.0%	0.3%	2.5%	+11.7% in Sep 1982	4.6 pp	96	16.7%
Recovery	−7.3% in Aug 1975	0.0%	1.3%	2.6%	+9.2% in Jan 1976	2.6 pp	124	21.6%
All Phases	−12.5% in Nov 1987	−0.9%	0.7%	2.4%	+11.7% in Sep 1982	3.3 pp	574	100.0%

omy to their clients and sometimes to the public. Even news organizations are making available summaries and economic data through the Internet. Table 1-4 lists a few web sites that might be of interest to readers of this book.

TABLE 1–4 Financial and Economic Internet Sites

Newswires, Financial Publications, and Other Sources		Internet Location
Newswires	Market News Service	http://www.economeister.com
	Reuters	http://www.reuters.com
	Dow Jones	http://bis.dowjones.com
	Bloomberg Business News	http://www.bloomberg.com
Publications	The Wall Street Journal	http://update.wsj.com
	Barron's	http://www.barrons.com
	The Financial Times	http://www.ft.com
	The New York Times	http://www.nytimes.com
	The Washington Post	http://www.washingtonpost.com
	Futures	http://www.futuresmag.com
Media	CNN	http://www.cnn.com
	MSNBC	http://www.msnbc.com
Central Banks	Federal Reserve Board	http://www.bog.frb.fed.us
	Bank of Canada	http://www.bank-banque-canada.ca
	Bank of England	http://bankofengland.co.uk
	Bank of Japan	http://www.boj.go.jp
	Deutsche Bundesbank	http://www.bundesregierung.de
Federal Reserve Banks	FRB of Boston	http://www.bos.frb.org
	FRB of New York	http://www.ny.frb.org
	FRB of Philadelphia	http://www.phil.frb.org
	FRB of Cleveland	http://www.clev.frb.org
	FRB of Richmond	http://www.rich.frb.org
	FRB of Atlanta	http://www.frbatlanta.org
	FRB of Chicago	http://www.frbchi.org
	FRB of St. Louis	http://www.stls.frb.org
	FRB of Minneapolis	http://www.woodrow.mpls.frb.fed.us

	FRB of Kansas City	http://www.kc.frb.org
	FRB of Dallas	http://www.dallasfed.org
	FRB of San Francisco	http://www.frbsf.org
Newswires, Financial Publications, and Other Sources		**Internet Location**
U.S. *Government*	U.S. Department of Commerce	http://www.doc.gov
	U.S. Bureau of the Census	http://www.census.gov
	U.S. Department of Labor	http://www.dol.gov
	U.S. Bureau of Labor Statistics	http://www.bls.gov
	Employment & Training Admin.	http//www.dol.eta.gov
	U.S. Department of Agriculture	http://econ.ag.gov
	Joint Economic Committee	http://townhall.org/places/ jec/hearing
	U.S. Bureau of Transportation Statistics	http://www.bts.gov
Other Financial *Data Sources*	Investment Company Institute (mutual fund data)	http://www.ici.org
International *Organizations*	United Nations	http://www.unsystem.org
	European Union	http://europa.eu.int
	OECD	http://www.oecd.org
	IMF	http://www.imf.org
	World Bank	http://www.worldbank.org
Foreign *Statistical* *Sources*	Australian Bureau of Statistics	http://www.statistics/gov.au
	Statistics Canada	http://www.statcan.ca
	German Federal Statistics Office	http://www.statistik-bund.de
	Japan Economic Trade Organization	http://www.jetro.go.jp
	Japan Economic Planning Agency	http://www.epa.go.jp
	U.K. Office of National Statistics	http://www.ons.gov.uk

Many of these web sites provide the users with links to other sources of data. The German Federal Statistics and the European Union web pages are particularly useful for links to other statistical and governmental information around the world. Clearly, this list is just a starting point for international data and news.

Chapter 2

Business Inventories

General Description

Business inventory data are collected from three sources: manufacturing, merchant wholesaler, and retail trade reports. Inventory calculations at all levels are based on book values of merchandise held at the end of each month. (See Table 2-1.)

Economic Indicator Information at a Glance

Market Significance	Low
Typical Release Time	8:30 AM Eastern Time Tenth Business Day of the Month
Released By	Commerce Department Census Bureau
Period Covered	Two Months Prior
Web Site	http://www.census.gov/svsd/www/ mtistext.html

The data are broken into inventories, sales, and the inventory-to-sales (I/S) ratio. A breakdown is also available at each level for durable and nondurable sectors. At the time of release for total business inventories and sales data, only the retail inventory portion is not known. Manufacturing inventories and sales (shipments) were available about two weeks prior, the merchant wholesale sales and inventory components were released about

TABLE 2–1   Business Inventories and Sales Percentage Share: End of 1996*

	Inventories	Sales
Manufacturing	43%	43%
Merchant Wholesalers	29%	31%
Retail Trade	28%	25%

* Total may not add to 100 due to rounding.

five business days prior, and the retail *sales* portion was released close to a month ahead of this release.

It would be difficult to analyze properly the inventory data without stepping back and understanding how inventory management has changed in the last decade. The level of inventories that companies now choose to hold relative to sales has dropped to historic lows. Just-in-time inventory management techniques have been adopted, and every manager on every level of business tries to keep inventories as low as possible without harming the flow of production or sales. This micro-tracking makes it difficult to put inventory information into historical perspective. Leads and lags are shorter, and the data themselves are not likely to suffer the extremes of the past. Where, in the past, inventories were used to absorb temporary shocks to demand, they now play a significantly lessened role as a buffer for fluctuations in economic activity.

Even with this in mind, inventories and the I/S ratio still conform to a basic pattern; they are lagging indicators, particularly in a cyclical context. Sales are the component that drives the business cycle and drives the I/S ratio at the same time. Inventory adjustment is a lagging indicator of the fall in sales; and in a sense, it is a second step in the recessionary process and the recovery stage. It is an initial drop in demand that initiates a recession and a resurgence in demand that restarts growth.

Analyzing the Data

With more than 70 percent of the inventory and 100 percent of the sales information already available, one can go into the release having a pretty good idea of what the inventory data will show. That having been said, retail inventories are the most volatile component of inventories, causing major swings in the overall series. Jumps or large drops in the I/S are one thing to keep an eye on, if only because the market still insists that they are important. Realistically there is no rule of thumb that says that increases (decreases) in inventories or the I/S ratio are good (bad) for fixed-income markets or bad (good) for equity markets. One of the reasons is the need to distinguish between unwanted and desired inventory swings. Unfortunately there is no quantitative way to ascertain this. Today, it would seem any increase in the I/S ratio would be considered unwanted, but that is too simplistic a concept. If business is growing, there are reasons to rebuild inventories and to have a higher ratio. One should not expect the I/S ratio to move only in a two- or three-hundredths of a point range or view any increase in the inventory level or I/S ratio as bad for business in subsequent months.

One place to start to determine if a given inventory change might be positive or negative for the markets, and in so doing, appraising whether it might be unwanted or desired, is to place it within its cyclical context. For example, a decline in inventories takes on a different story if it happens during a slowdown or during the latter stages of a recovery. A drop in inventories during a recession, especially early in the cycle stage, normally alludes to business wanting to reduce stocks. In so doing, production and output need to be cut. But a decline during the recovery stage takes on a more positive light. It may be desired, initially, as excess inventories are worked off (remember, they are a lagging indicator of a recovery), but over time a drop in inventories during a recovery stage can be construed as unwanted and therefore subsequently cause gains in output and production.

Another way to analyze or use inventory data is to consider their potential contribution to upcoming or already released GDP estimates. Inventory data are one of the key swing sectors of the GDP accounts; and the Department of Commerce's monthly inventory data, after much massaging, are one of the sources the Bureau of Economic Analysis (BEA) uses to estimate real, end of quarter inventory levels. As much as one can create a fundamental, underlying inventory story with the numbers, the data's potential statistical impact on a yet-to-be-released GDP estimate can be just as important as, if not more so than, any story. GDP estimates are a critical concept for the market, and if monthly inventory data point to GDP coming in significantly different than expected, they hold important information. This angle also is relevant after the initial GDP release, a release that includes only an estimate of inventories for the final month of the quarter. The subsequent inventory number for the final month can be quite different than what was estimated and can result in a fairly pivotal change in a quarter's GDP.

As important as the relationship between monthly inventory data and GDP is, the translation between the two data sets immediately brings to mind the phrase "there is much slip twixt cup and lip." The monthly data are massaged and tweaked to such an extent that even directional changes have at times been different for the two inventory series. The BEA's adjustment for consistent accounting practices and inflation, especially, has created situations in which large swings in the monthly inventory data have not shown up in the GDP accounts.

Business Inventories over the Business Cycle

Business inventories are a critical part of the business cycle, with their large swings masked by cycle averages. It is clear,

FIGURE 2–1   Business Inventories

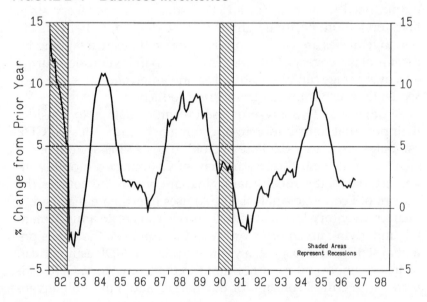

TABLE 2–2 Business Inventories

January 1981–April 1997, Month-to-Month Percentage Change

| Phase | Historic Low | Normal Bounds | | | Historic High | Series Characteristics | |
		Normal Low	Average	Normal High		Standard Deviation	Share of Total Observations
Recession	−1.0% in Mar 1991	−0.4%	0.4%	1.2%	7.1% in Jan 1982	1.5 pp.	12.2%
Recovery	−0.8% in Jan 1983	−0.1%	0.2%	0.5%	1.3% in Feb 1984	0.5 pp.	19.4%
Expansion	−0.7% in Dec 1986	0.2%	0.4%	0.6%	1.3% in Oct 1987	0.4 pp.	68.4%
Slow Phase	−0.4% in Sep 1986	0.2%	0.3%	0.5%	1.2% in Dec 1988	0.3 pp.	35.2%
Rapid Phase	−0.7% in Dec 1986	0.3%	0.5%	0.7%	1.3% in Oct 1987	0.4 pp.	33.2%
All Phases	−1.0% in Mar 1991	0.1%	0.4%	0.7%	7.1% in Jan 1982	0.6 pp.	100.0%

based on averages, that inventories grow faster during recessions than they do during recoveries and match the pace of accumulation during expansions. (See Figure 2-1 and Table 2-2.) But beneath the surface a lot is going on. Both the historic low and high rates of inventory change were registered during the recessionary phase of a business cycle. In the early stages of a recession, inventories are accumulated at their greatest rate since demand sinks before business is aware of the change. It is only then that the sharpest drop in inventory levels occurs as business reacts swiftly to the unwanted accumulation. The recovery phase of the business cycle actually shows a slower average rate of inventory building than the expansion. Not only is demand outpacing the ability of business to keep shelves stocked, but also the confidence that business needs to rebuild inventories only comes about after a sustained period of heightened activity.

Chapter 3

Car and Truck Sales

General Description

Car and truck sales are reported individually by the manufacturers and importers. The Commerce Department seasonally adjusts the major segments of monthly motor vehicle sales, which are expressed at seasonally adjusted annual rates. These data are one of the most timely measures of durable goods demand.

Economic Indicator Information at a Glance

Market Significance	Moderate
Typical Release Time	Between the First and Third Business Day of the New Month
Released By	Motor Vehicle Manufacturers and Importers
Period Covered	Prior Month
Web Site	http://stat-usa.gov/

Analyzing the Data

Car and truck sales are a consumer and an investment good depending on the purchaser. As of the fourth quarter of 1996, the share of new cars purchased by consumers accounted for 52 percent of the total units sold, business demand accounted for 46 percent of the units sold, while the remainder were purchased by federal, state, and local governments. For that same period, 47 percent of the total number of trucks sold went to consumers, about 51 percent went to business, and the remainder were purchased by governments.

Total new motor vehicle sales equals the sum of: (1) domestic car sales, (2) imported car sales, (3) light-truck sales, (4) medium-truck sales, and (5) heavy-truck sales. The light-medium-heavy designation is an industry classification based on vehicle weight. Medium- and heavy-weight vehicle sales are a relatively tiny share of the total and hence do not matter much in the aggregate or for the financial markets.

A sale of a *domestically produced* vehicle is, by definition, a sale of a vehicle produced in North America and not just the United States. Overall domestic company sales, such as those reported by General Motors, include *captive imports,* which are foreign-produced vehicles (outside of North America) sold under the domestic company's nameplate. These captive imports are not included in the aggregate tally of domestically produced vehicles by the Commerce Department.

The overall financial markets evaluate the vehicle data based on total vehicle market strength or weakness—though individual stock prices of the manufacturers may be impacted by market share issues. Moreover, the only macroeconomic interest in the vehicle weight categories is from the standpoint of how the end users of the individual segments of the vehicle market are doing, which includes demand from individuals to heavy industry.

The automotive industry has been one of the most vocal industries in objecting to foreign exchange movements that are seen as hurting the industry's competitive position vis-à-vis the Asian and European vehicle imports. Due to the industry's dollar sensitivity, motor vehicle industry officials are usually among the first to complain about the impact of exchange rate fluctuation on their sales

The keys to interpreting the motor vehicle data report for overall financial markets include:

- Recognize the **consumers' long-run preference shift** from passenger cars to mini-vans and sports utility vehicles (light trucks). The share of passenger cars being purchased by the consumer has dwindled sharply. For example, over the last 25 years the consumer share of the car market peaked in September 1968 at 77.1 percent (but on trend had been around 75 percent of the market at the time) and reached an all-time low in September 1996 at 40.3 percent.

- Focus upon the most timely monthly data reported, which are **total domestic light-vehicle sales.** (See Figure 3-1.) For calendar-year 1996, domestic light-vehicle sales accounted for 94.5 percent of the total vehicle sales. Sales of foreign-produced cars as well as imported and medium- and heavy-truck sales tend to have little impact on how the financial markets perceive these data.

- Be aware that a secondary issue that is often examined is **shifts in market share** between the "big three" manufacturers (General Motors, Ford, and Chrysler), the Asian transplants (Honda, Mazda, Mitsubishi, Nissan, Subaru, Suzuki, and Toyota), and the European transplants (Volkswagen and BMW). However, despite whether a vehicle is produced and sold in the United States by one of the big-three manufacturers or by a "transplanted" manufacturer, there is no economic difference. In calendar-year 1996, the big-three domestic manufacturers accounted for 72.8 percent of total domestic light-vehicle sales, the Asia-brand total accounted for 23.7 percent, and the Europe-brand total accounted for 3.5 percent.

- Take into consideration the fact that **vehicle incentives** often sway monthly sales. A detailed listing of incentives can be found in *Automotive News*, while a summary measure for average vehicle incentives is compiled by CNW Marketing/Research of Bandon, Oregon. The CNW Marketing/Research measure is a timely and useful barometer to monitor.

- Recognize that the **affordability** of new vehicles always has been an important driving factor behind sales. In 1996, leasing as a source of financing accounted for just a tad below a third of all industry sales. The rise of leasing has created a more predictable demand pattern within the industry and over time should dampen the sectors' cyclicality. On the other hand, it has created a ballooning used car market.

- Understand that **used car sales** have become an increasing force to reckon with. Not only are used car sales by franchised new car dealers growing as a share of the total market, but new "used car superstores" are providing another source to shop. However, comprehensive statistics on the used car market are hard to come by. Used car sales by franchised dealers of the big-three manufacturers are reported by the American Motor Vehicle Manufacturers Association, and some industry estimates exist from CNW Marketing/Research and R. L. Polk. Used car sales are difficult to pin down precisely. R. L. Polk reported that in 1996 there were 35 million used cars sold—not much of a change in 15 years—but other industry sources dispute that claim. The used truck market most recently is about a fifth of the size of the used car market. The used vehicle market is generally tracked through vehicle registration data.

- Keep in mind that, as of 1996, **vehicle fleet** demand accounted for 18 percent of all sales (compared with 21 percent in 1992). Rental fleet demand (from Hertz, Avis, Budget, etc.) accounted for the lion's share of those sales— 11 percent in 1996 (compared with 12 percent in 1992). There is some flexibility when a manufacturer includes rental fleet sales, which creates more volatility in the monthly sales pattern.

Motor Vehicle Sales over the Business Cycle

The Commerce Department has classified motor vehicle sales as a leading indicator of the business cycle, but in recent years it has become more coincident and far more influential as a "swing factor" in the economy. Car and truck sales have a typical-cycle pattern, with the strongest gains in the recovery phase of the cycle. On average, car sales increase by 1.5 percent per month during the recovery and then moderate to a 0.2 percent pace during the expansion. Truck sales typically increase by 0.9 percent per month during the recovery and slow to a gain of 0.3 percent per month thereafter. During recessions, car sales tend to decline by 1.0 percent per month, but truck sales tend to hold up—growing at a 0.7 percent pace. That in part reflects a secular shift toward light-truck demand and away from the passenger car. (See Figure 3-1 and Table 3-1.)

FIGURE 3–1   Light-Vehicle Sales

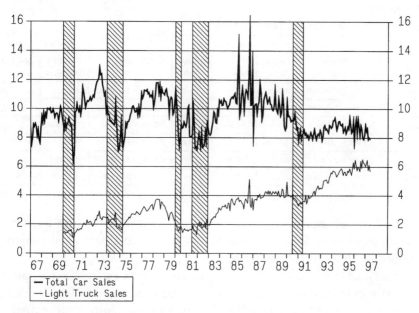

- —Total Car Sales
- —Light Truck Sales

Relationship with Other Series

CNW Marketing/Research publishes a 10-day tally of motor vehicle deliveries, which grew out of the industry tradition of reporting 10-day vehicle sales. The CNW tally of motor vehicle deliveries can be used to track the underlying performance of the market, but those data often do not mirror the monthly sales pattern. There are numerous differences between sales and deliver-

TABLE 3–1   U.S. Car Sales (Domestic and Foreign)
Jan 1960–Jun 1997, Number of Units

Phase	Historic Low	Normal Bounds			Historic High	Series Characteristics	
		Normal Low	Average	Normal High		Standard Deviation	Share of Total Observations
Recession	6.4 mn. in Nov 1970	7.8 mn.	8.3 mn.	8.8 mn.	10.5 mn. in Feb 1980	1.0 unit	14.9%
Recovery	5.2 mn. in Sep 1961	8.3 mn.	9.0 mn.	9.8 mn.	11.5 mn. in Sep 1971	1.5 units	20.7%
Expansion	5.4 mn. in Jan 1960	8.8 mn.	9.5 mn.	10.3 mn.	15.1 mn. in Sep 1986	1.5 units	64.4%
Slow Phase	5.4 mn. in Jan 1960	8.8 mn.	9.5 mn.	10.3 mn.	15.1 mn. in Sep 1986	1.5 units	30.4%
Rapid Phase	6.3 mn. in Mar 1962	8.9 mn.	9.6 mn.	10.4 mn.	12.8 mn. in Mar 1973	1.5 units	34.0%
All Phases	5.2 mn. in Sep 1961	8.5 mn.	9.2 mn.	10.0 mn.	15.1 mn. in Sep 1986	1.5 units	100.0%

TABLE 3–2   U.S. Truck Sales (Domestic and Foreign, Light, Medium, and Heavy)

January 1976–June 1997, Number of Units

Phase	Historic Low	Normal Bounds			Historic High	Series Characteristics	
		Normal Low	Average	Normal High		Standard Deviation	Share of Total Observations
Recession	1.9 mn. in Dec 1981	2.5 mn.	2.9 mn.	3.3 mn.	4.5 mn. in Sep 1990	0.8 unit	11.6%
Recovery	2.2 mn. in Dec 1980	3.2 mn.	3.6 mn.	4.0 mn.	5.2 mn. in Sep 1992	0.8 unit	23.6%
Expansion	2.2 mn. in Jul 1981	4.6 mn.	5.1 mn.	5.7 mn.	7.5 mn. in Mar 1997	1.1 units	64.7%
Slow Phase	3.1 mn. in Jan 1980	4.6 mn.	5.1 mn.	5.7 mn.	7.3 mn. in Feb 1996	1.1 units	31.0%
Rapid Phase	2.2 mn. in Jul 1981	4.5 mn.	5.0 mn.	5.6 mn.	6.8 mn. in Nov 1994	1.1 units	33.7%
All Phases	1.9 mn. in Dec 1981	3.9 mn.	4.5 mn.	5.2 mn.	7.5 mn. in Mar 1997	1.3 units	100.0%

ies, although most sales are delivered within the same month. This, however, does not necessarily apply to fleet sales, which could be delivered later.

Car and truck sales are used directly in the Commerce Department's compilation of personal consumption data. These data also provide a window on the Census Bureau's automotive dealers retail sales. There are numerous measurement differences between unit car sales and the value of automotive dealer sales. Those differences include: (1) seasonal factors, (2) coverage (e.g., auto dealer sales include used car sales), and (3) composition (value data can change solely due to shifts in the price of vehicles purchased even if the overall number of units sold is unchanged).

These unit data also are used to compute the *days' supply of unsold vehicles*—which is a widely followed industry inventory-to-sales measure. Normally, the days' supply of unsold cars runs 60 to 65 days—though in some months that figure tends to be higher; for example, in January, it averages about 75 days, while in September, the figure tends to drop to about 55 days with the start of the new model year. But excessive stock relative to demand is likely to result in a paring of production schedules and should be watched.

As of 1996, the Commerce Department began to publish GDP for motor vehicles. Those data are the most comprehensive guide to the industry and, of course, are based on unit production, change in inventories, and vehicle net exports.

Chapter 4

Construction Expenditures

General Description and Analysis of the Data

The official title of this series is "The Value of New Construction Put in Place." Its data are derived from progress reports filed by owners of a sample of construction projects throughout the 50 states and the District of Columbia. The data are valued in nominal and real dollars. The main breakdown in each is divided into private and public construction expenditures, with private construction further broken down into residential building and non-residential building. (See Table 4-1.)

Economic Indicator Information at a Glance

Market Significance	Low
Typical Release Time	10:00 AM Eastern Time First Business Day of the Month
Released By	Commerce Department Census Bureau
Period Covered	Two Months Prior
Web Site	http://www.census.gov/pub/const/ www/c30index

This is a very volatile series, on both the private and the public side. It is also subject to sizable revision. Its market significance is very limited, as financial markets utilize the housing starts statistic as a gauge of the housing market and have little interest in con-

TABLE 4–1   Construction Expenditures: Percentage Breakdown, End of 1996

Private Construction*	75.1%
Residential Buildings	42.2%
Nonresidential Buildings	25.7%
Public Construction	24.9%

* Includes the following categories not shown separately: telecommunications, railroads, electric light and power, gas, petroleum pipelines, and farm nonresidential.

struction spending by business. The release's importance, for analysts, however, is much greater. The data, for both private and public sectors, are direct inputs into GDP calculations, namely, residential investment, business spending on structures, and state and local government spending on structures. This release is also the only source of official data for spending in the latter two economic sectors.

Construction Expenditures over the Business Cycle

Month-to-month changes in construction expenditures follow the business cycle closely. They decline, on average, during re-

FIGURE 4–1   Construction Expenditures

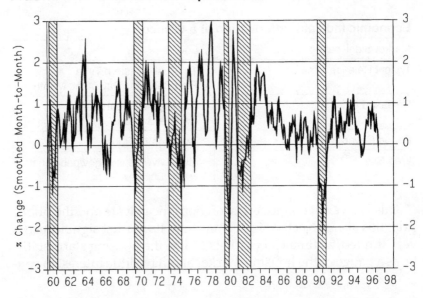

TABLE 4–2 Construction Expenditures, Month-to-Month Percentage Change

February 1958—May 1997, Month-to-Month Percentage Change

| Phase | Historic Low | Normal Bounds | | | Historic High | Series Characteristics | |
		Normal Low	Average	Normal High		Standard Deviation	Share of Total Observations
Recession	−4.8% in Feb 1975	−1.3%	−0.4%	0.5%	4.1% in Jan 1975	1.8 pp.	14.8%
Recovery	−4.8% in Aug 1958	0.2%	1.1%	2.0%	8.6% in Sep 1958	1.8 pp.	22.2%
Expansion	−3.3% in May 1966	−0.2%	0.6%	1.4%	10.6% in Jan 1964	1.6 pp.	62.9%
Slow Phase	−3.3% in May 1966	−0.2%	0.5%	1.2%	4.1% in May 1963	1.4 pp.	29.7%
Rapid Phase	−3.0% in Jan 1994	−0.3%	0.6%	1.5%	10.6% in Jan 1964	1.8 pp.	33.2%
All Phases	−4.8% in Feb 1975	−0.4%	0.5%	1.4%	10.6% in Jan 1964	1.7 pp.	100.0%

cessions, grow strongest during the recovery, and grow more moderately during the expansion. The key is the different timing of the residential and nonresidential construction sectors. Residential construction tends to be a leading indicator of the business cycle, similar to housing starts. Nonresidential investment, however, tends to drop most noticeably only after the recession has begun, and it tends to increase after the recovery has started. These two different patterns create a seemingly average series when construction expenditures are looked at in total. (See Figure 4-1 and Table 4-2.)

Chapter 5

Consumer Confidence Measures

General Description

Three widely followed consumer confidence measures are available from: (1) the University of Michigan, (2) the Conference Board, and (3) ABC News and *Money* magazine. Over the longer run, they all move together; consumer confidence surveys serve as a reflection of national mood about the current business con-

Economic Indicator Information at a Glance

Market Significance	Moderate
Typical Release Time for Conference Board Measure	10:00 AM Eastern Time Last Tuesday of the Month
Period Covered	Current Month
Web Site	http://www.conference-board.org/
Typical Release Time for University of Michigan Measure	10:00 AM Eastern Time Second Friday (1) and Last Day (2) of the Month
Period Covered	First half of Current Month (1) and Full Current Month (2)
Web Site	None
Typical Release Time for ABC News/*Money* Measure	6:30 PM Eastern Time Wednesday
Period Covered	Week Ending Prior Sunday
Web Site	http://www.abcnews.com/

ditions and measure the consumers' degree of optimism or dismay about the future. Sometimes the consumer worries about inflation more than unemployment, and at other times the reverse is true. But in either case, consumer confidence reflects the paramount economic concern facing the nation or the individual. Consumer confidence is far more important to the financial markets during times of national crisis or panic—such as after the 1987 stock market crash, before and after the 1991 Persian Gulf War, after oil shocks, during recessions, and so forth.

Analyzing the Data

The Conference Board survey is done by mail using 5,000 households, while the other two consumer surveys are telephone surveys. The ABC News/*Money* poll, which covers about 1,000 households, is the only weekly poll, though the University of Michigan survey is taken across the month and a preliminary reading for the current survey is released about two weeks into the month (when about half of the total 500-household survey is complete).

All three surveys use different forms for their summary measures: (1) The University of Michigan series is a net difference plus 100; that is, 100 + BETTER − WORSE, where BETTER is the share of the sample reporting better or higher and WORSE is the share reporting worse or lower; (2) the Conference Board measure is calculated as [BETTER/(BETTER + WORSE)] and is the only series that is seasonally adjusted; and (3) the ABC News/*Money* poll data are simply summarized as BETTER − WORSE, and only are reported on a four-week moving average basis.

The Conference Board and University of Michigan surveys include consumer evaluations of both current and future conditions (expectations), while the ABC News/*Money* poll captures only current conditions on a weekly basis. The Conference Board consumer confidence index and the University of Michigan consumer sentiment index are each a weighted average of the current and expectations components of their respective surveys. The Conference Board measure is defined as two-fifths of the present situation index plus three-fifths of the expectations index; hence, it is slightly more weighted to the six-month-ahead expectations. The University of Michigan compiles its composite index based on five questions with a decidedly longer run horizon than that of the Conference Board's measure. The five University of Michigan questions are:

1. We are interested in how people are getting along financially these days. Would you say that you (and your family living there) are better off or worse off financially than you were a year ago?
2. Now looking ahead—do you think that a year from now you (and your family living there) will be better off financially, or worse off, or just about the same as now?
3. Now turning to business conditions in the country as a whole—do you think that during the next 12 months we'll have good times financially, or bad times, or what?
4. Looking ahead, which would you say is more likely—that in the country as a whole we'll have continuous good times during the next five years or so, or that we will have periods of widespread unemployment or depression, or what?
5. About the big things people buy for their homes—such as furniture, a refrigerator, stove, television, and things like that. Generally speaking, do you think now is a good or bad time for people to buy major household items?

Sometimes the current and future expectations can move in the opposite directions, which may be a key theme in understanding the report. For example, if current business is booming and job growth is plentiful, it is possible that consumers are quite upbeat on the present situation but are leery that the boom will continue, and hence expectations for the next six months or longer might decline because consumers think the present is too good to be true for much longer.

Although all three measures basically tell the same story over time, in the short term they can differ. On a monthly average basis—using the end of the month observations, the ABC News/ *Money* poll was the least volatile between the onset of the 1990 recession and mid-1992 (about a year and a half after the end of the recession), while the Michigan survey—which has the smallest sample size—was the most volatile.

The University of Michigan's preliminary month consumer confidence reading can have market impact—if it shows a sharp and unexpected rise or fall. The Conference Board's measure often (though not always) will have a similar theme as the early University of Michigan poll, which makes the Conference Board release less of a surprise for the financial markets—though there have been times when the Conference Board measure posted a dramatic change that impacted the market and the thinking about the consumer. The ABC News/*Money* poll has a following but little or no financial market impact.

The statistical relationship between the University of Michigan consumer sentiment index and the Conference Board consumer confidence index suggests that *every one-point change in the University of Michigan series will result in a two-point change in the Conference Board measure.* Of course, the relationship between these measures, by construction, is not linear, so this result should be viewed only as a rough rule of thumb. Interestingly, the statistical combination of any two of the consumer surveys generally explained the third better than the individual surveys alone, which suggests that each contributes a slightly different and unique perspective on the consumer.

FIGURE 5–1   Conference Board's Consumer Confidence Index

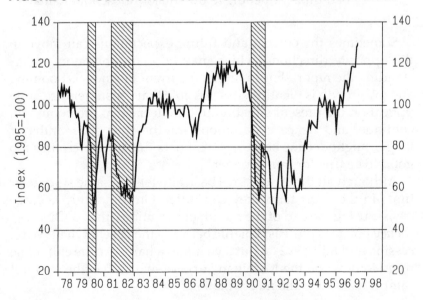

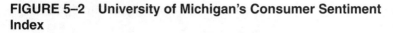

FIGURE 5–2 University of Michigan's Consumer Sentiment Index

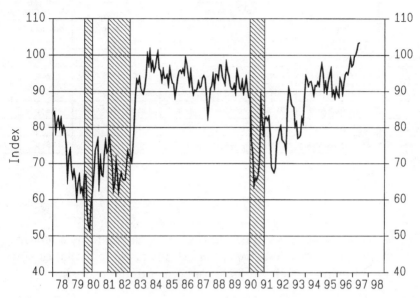

Consumer Confidence over the Business Cycle

As would be expected, consumer confidence is the weakest during recessions, slightly stronger during the recovery phase of the business cycle, and the highest during expansions. (See Figures 5-1 and 5-2 and Tables 5-1 and 5-2.) Consumer expectations

TABLE 5–1 Consumer Confidence Index, Conference Board
February 1969–May 1997, 1985 = 100

Period	Historic Low	Normal Bounds			Historic High	Series Characteristics	
		Normal Low	Average	Normal High		Standard Deviation	Share of Sample
Recession	43.2% in Dec 1974	63.4%	71.7%	80.0%	113.9% in Jan 1970	16.6 pp.	16.8%
Recovery	47.3% in Feb 1992	74.4%	81.3%	88.3%	106.1% in Apr 1984	13.9 pp.	24.7%
Expansion	54.6% in Oct 1992	93.6%	101.3%	109.1%	138.2% in Feb 1969	15.5 pp.	58.5%
Slow Phase	79.4% in Aug 1979	99.1%	105.7%	112.3%	138.2% in Feb 1969	13.2 pp.	29.7%
Rapid Phase	54.6% in Oct 1992	87.5%	95.5%	103.5%	120.2% in May 1988	16.0 pp.	28.8%
All Phases	43.2% in Dec 1974	81.8%	91.4%	101.2%	138.2% in Feb 1969	19.6 pp.	100.0%

TABLE 5–2   Consumer Sentiment Index, University of Michigan

January 1978–June 1997, Index

Period	Historic Low	Normal Bounds			Historic High	Series Characteristics	
		Normal Low	Average	Normal High		Standard Deviation	Share of Sample
Recession	51.7% in May 1980	63.4%	67.0%	70.6%	87.7% in Mar 1991	7.2 pp.	12.8%
Recovery	64.5% in Dec 1980	75.4%	80.5%	85.6%	101.0% in Mar 1984	10.2 pp.	18.4%
Expansion	60.4% in Jul 1979	84.1%	88.7%	93.4%	103.4% in Jun 1997	9.3 pp.	68.8%
Slow Phase	60.4% in Jul 1979	84.2%	89.3%	94.4%	100.9% in Sep 1984	10.2 pp.	34.2%
Rapid Phase	66.1% in Dec 1978	83.0%	86.8%	94.5%	103.4% in Jun 1997	7.7 pp.	34.6%
All Phases	51.7% in May 1980	78.5%	84.4%	90.3%	103.4% in Jun 1997	11.8 pp.	100.0%

have been classified by the Commerce Department as a leading indicator of economic activity based on its timing relationship with the business cycle (at least for conceptual reasons).

Special Factors, Limitations, and Other Data Issues

In the late 1950s and again after the 1987 stock market crash, consumer confidence surveys came under attack by economists. Economists questioned how useful consumer confidence surveys were for predicting consumer spending behavior. Some of the critics pointed out that consumer confidence told us nothing about future consumer spending. But most of the literature—especially the more recent studies—seemed to conclude that consumer confidence had some predictive value when used with other economic indicators. However, one overlooked use for consumer confidence is that it is one of the best predictors of presidential elections (and presidential popularity). In many respects, this should not be surprising. Perception and not the reality about the economy is what influences presidential outcomes. This point is well founded in the political science literature, and it might suggest that a president who is a "great communicator" potentially could shape consumer perceptions and with it enhance one's reelection or the incumbent party's election chance.

References

Friend, Irwin, and F. Gerald Adams, "The Predictive Ability of Consumer Attitudes, Stock Prices, and Non-attitudinal Variables," *Journal of the American Statistical Association*, Vol. 59, No. 308, December 1964, pp. 987–1005.

Fuhrer, Jeffrey C., "On the Information Content of Consumer Survey Expectations," *The Review of Economics and Statistics*, 1988, pp. 140–144.

Garner, C. Alan, "Forecasting Consumer Spending: Should Economists Pay Attention to Consumer Confidence Surveys?" *Economic Review*, Federal Reserve Bank of Kansas City, May/June 1991, pp. 57–71.

Niemira, Michael P., "What's the Relationship among Consumer Confidence Surveys?" *Business Economics*, April 1992, pp. 65–66.

Chapter 6

Consumer Credit

General Description

The Federal Reserve Board's consumer credit release details the amount of installment credit that individuals (consumers) have outstanding. It is a net number, new credit extended minus credit paid down. Such credit is defined as a loan that is scheduled to be repaid in two or more installments. It does not include mortgage debt or any other loan secured by real estate (including home equity loans). Loans secured by other assets are included in consumer installment credit.

Economic Indicator Information at a Glance

Market Significance	Low
Typical Release Time	3:00 PM Eastern Time Fifth Business Day of the Month
Released By	Federal Reserve Board
Period Covered	Two Months Prior
Web Site	http://www.bog.frn.fed.us/releases/g19/

The consumer credit data are broken down into three types of debt and by the institution holding the debt. The three categories are automobile credit, revolving credit, and all other. Included in the latter category (but not restricted to) are vacation loans, education loans and other personal loans, and loans to purchase mo-

TABLE 6–1   Major Holders of Consumer Installment Debt: End of 1996, Percentage

Commercial Banks	44.4%
Securitized Assets	20.6%
Finance Companies	13.4%
Credit Unions	12.0%
Savings Institutions	6.2%
Nonfinancial Institutions	3.4%

bile homes and pools of securitized assets. The proportions of each type of debt at the end of 1996 were automobile, 32 percent; revolving, 39 percent; and other, 29 percent. The types of holders range from commercial banks to retailers to gasoline companies, inter alia. (See Table 6-1.) Debt that has been turned into securitized assets is also included.[1]

Analyzing the Data

What analysis is undertaken is very simple. The market looks at the size of the change in consumer credit relative to where the change has been for the previous three or four months. Even spurious monthly component changes, which can be fairly frequent, or strong evidence that the credit data defy the pattern of sales data in a specific area (automobiles are the obvious example) is typically ignored by the market. Beyond immediate market response, it is difficult justifying much time spent analyzing the information provided.

By the time the consumer credit data are released, the market has already seen actual spending data. Retail sales figures and even more complete consumption expenditure data for the same month come out two to three weeks prior to the consumer credit statistics. Thus the data just provide us with an idea (however inaccurate) of how much of already known spending was financed. In this respect it is of little market significance. As much

---

1   In the 1980s a small industry developed to package credit card or automobile debt and sell the sum total as a single collateralized security. When this was done, the debt was taken off the institution's books, but it still had to be accounted for in some fashion as outstanding consumer debt.

as consumer attitudes toward the use of credit to finance purchases may have conceptual importance, there is no evidence that this percentage changes before actual spending habits change. In fact, the growth in spending leads the growth in installment credit (see Figure 6-1). The consumer credit data merely validate spending trends; they do not reveal new ones. Furthermore there are some technical reasons why consumer credit is of dubious value.

Two developing trends in the 1980s caused consumer installment debt to miss key elements of consumer spending power. One is the growing move toward leasing motor vehicles instead of purchasing them. In 1996 about a third of vehicle "sales" were leases. This is part of the reason that the auto component of consumer credit has had such a poor relationship with actual sales on a month-to-month basis.

The second problem with the consumer installment credit data is their exclusion of credit secured by real estate, specifically home equity loans. Not only are individuals using home equity loans to fuel new purchases normally financed by auto or personal loans, but they are using it to pay down outstanding debt.

It is somewhat difficult to detail a typical market response to the consumer credit report. Superficially strong (weak) credit

FIGURE 6–1 Nominal Consumer Spending and Consumer Installment Credit 1981–1995: Quarterly, Year-over-Year Growth

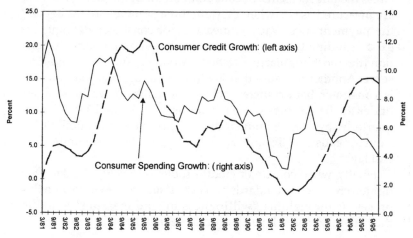

growth would be negative (positive) for fixed-income markets and positive (negative) for equities and the dollar. But all is not as it seems. One could also say that the greater the credit growth, the closer the consumer is to being overextended, with the next step being a slowing of consumption and economic activity. Under such an interpretation a spurt in consumer credit would

---

BOX 6–1 Measuring Consumer Debt Stress

One of the recently popular measures of consumer debt problems is a calculated measure produced by the Federal Reserve Board following work done at the New York Federal Reserve Bank. That measure is the **consumer debt-service burden** ratio, which is a quarterly measure of consumer and mortgage debt-service payments as a ratio to disposable income. These data take into account payment streams (past levels of extensions, debt, and average maturities) and interest rates at which loans were made. The ratio is a conceptually superior measure of aggregate consumer debt stress compared with the alternative, the ratio of the stock of installment debt to disposable income, and it is available for both mortgage and installment credit. However, to the extent that people charge purchases to gain special credit card bonus points, that still will inflate the recorded credit balances calculated as a ratio of either debt to income or the consumer debt-service burden.

Other indicators that provide a window on consumer debt stress include measures of **consumer credit delinquency**—which are measured as late when they are three or more months beyond the payment date. Various measures of consumer delinquency exist including those reported by the American Bankers Association (the most popularly watched), Moody's, and the Federal Reserve. Another measure that is followed in the financial markets is **consumer bankruptcies,** which are tallies of various filings under the Bankruptcy Code (Chapters 7, 11, 12, and 13), released quarterly by the Administrative Office of the United States Courts, Statistics Division. All bankruptcy filings are under federal law.

Finally, when consumer credit problems develop, banks often tighten credit loan standards and card issuance. A window on this process is through the **"willingness-to-lend measure"** found in the Federal Reserve Board's *Survey of Senior Loan Officers.*

FIGURE 6–2   Change in Consumer Credit Outstanding

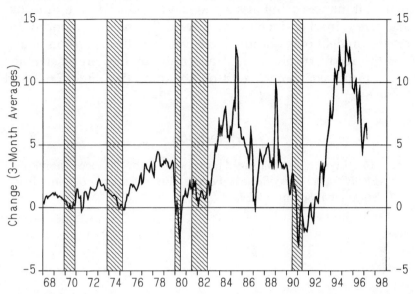

be positive for fixed-income markets and negative for equities and the dollar. Although the first interpretive reaction is typical, one can never be sure when the markets will choose the latter. It is just one more reason to approach the consumer credit data with a little bit of apprehension. (See Box 6-1.)

Consumer Credit over the Business Cycle

Net consumer credit outstanding shows a pronounced, and expected, business cycle pattern. During recessions net credit

TABLE 6–2   Consumer Installment Credit (Net Change)
January 1978–April 1997, Dollars

| | | Normal Bounds | | | | Series Characteristics | |
Phase	Historic Low	Normal Low	Average	Normal High	Historic High	Standard Deviation	Share of Total Observations
Recession	−4299 mn. in Dec 1990	−612 mn.	289.3 mn.	1191 mn.	4046 mn. in Sep 1981	1804 mn.	12.9%
Recovery	−2512 mn. in Apr 1992	248 mn.	1692.9 mn.	3138 mn.	7988 mn. in Feb 1984	2890 mn.	18.5%
Expansion	−1554 mn. in Dec 1979	3647 mn.	5592.0 mn.	7537 mn.	24826 mn. in Jun 1985	3890 mn.	68.5%
Slow Phase	−1554 mn. in Dec 1979	3936 mn.	6092.9 mn.	8250 mn.	24826 mn. in Jun 1985	4314 mn.	34.5%
Rapid Phase	−1255 mn. in Jan 1987	3269 mn.	4977.8 mn.	6686 mn.	13714 mn. in Aug 1994	3417 mn.	34.0%
All Phases	−4299 mn. in Dec 1990	2136 mn.	4183.6 mn.	6231 mn.	24826 mn. in Jun 1985	4095 mn.	100.0%

outstanding behaves similarly to nominal consumer spending; that is, it increases, but at a significantly reduced pace. A recovery sees a marked increase in size of the average monthly increases in debt outstanding. However, it is the expansion phase, not the recovery phase, that accounts for the largest average gains in net consumer credit outstanding. (See Figure 6-2 and Table 6-2.)

Reference

Paquette, Lynn, "Estimating Household Debt Service Payments," *FRBNY Quarterly Review,* Federal Reserve Bank of New York, Summer 1986, pp. 12–23.

Chapter 7

Consumer Price Index

General Description

The Consumer Price Index (CPI) measures the average change in prices of a fixed basket of goods and services. There are two measures of the rate of inflation at the consumer level. The first is the CPI-U, and it is the focal point of financial markets. It measures price changes for all urban consumers and encompasses approximately 80 percent of the population. The second price measure is the CPI-W. It measures price changes for all urban wage earners and covers 35 percent of the population. (See Box 7-1.)

Economic Indicator Information at a Glance

Market Significance	High
Typical Release Time	8:30 AM Eastern Time. Around the 10th Business Day of the Month
Released By	Labor Department Bureau of Labor Statistics
Period Covered	Prior Month
Web Site	http://stats.bls.gov/news.release/cpi.toc.htm

The reason for two similar price measures is grounded in politics, not economics. In the late 1970s (the CPI-W was officially

---

BOX 7–1   Measuring the Cost of Living

In 1930, John Maynard Keynes wrote that the appropriate way to measure changes in the value of money was to develop an index number that would measure the changing cost of aggregates of goods and services yielding the same level of "utility" or consumer satisfaction. That view remains the objective of price measurement today and was brought back into the limelight by the Senate Finance Committee's December 1996 Boskin Commission report entitled *Toward a More Accurate Measure of the Cost of Living,* which was crafted under the chairmanship of Michael Boskin, a Stanford University professor and former economic adviser to President Bush.

What's an Ideal Index?

Three years before that observation by Keynes, Irving Fisher published an exhaustive study on index formulae. Fisher framed the index measurement problem, and to his credit, his framework is still used today. In a nutshell, Fisher set forth two tests to judge the thousands of formulae he looked at. The first benchmark that Fisher used was known as the *time reversal test,* and the second was the *factor reversal test.* In essence, the first criterion for a superior price or quantity index was that if today's prices were interchanged with yesterday's base-period prices in the index formula, then the result would be the reciprocal of the original index, which essentially said that the price (quantity) change going forward was identical to the price (quantity) change moving backward. The second test was to interchange the price and quantity factors in the index formula and if the product of the two measures yielded the current period's aggregate expenditure divided by the base year's aggregate expenditure, then the index was "reversible" and not biased. Only a few index formulae passed these two statistical tests, and Irving Fisher dubbed those that passed both tests as "ideal" indexes. That is the theory behind an *ideal index,* which is a phrase that has been brought back into the economic lingo by the Boskin Commission, which was charged with a mission to prove that the Consumer Price Index overstated inflation. Unfortunately, for practical reasons the CPI and the PPI are not "ideal" index formulae, which leads to one recommendation of the commission to change the formula for the

CPI. But that still would not eliminate other biases that exist in pricing goods.

Pricing Problem

Three major sources of bias are typically associated with index formulation: (1) outlet substitution bias, (2) quality adjustment bias, and (3) new goods bias. However, it has been argued that the distinction between the quality adjustment and new goods bias is not always distinguishable. In a nutshell, if consumers shift where they shop, that could result in outlet substitution bias; if there is a substantial change in technology or the degree of service embedded into a product or service, that could result in a quality bias; and depending on the stage of its own product cycle, when a new good or service is added into the market basket, that can impart a bias. None of these issues are new; the Boskin report just summarized them and suggested a magnitude for them, as shown in the table below.

Boskin Commission's CPI Bias Estimates Relative to an Assumed True Cost-of-Living Index
(Percentage Points per Year)

Source of Bias Estimate of Its Magnitude	
Substitution	0.40 pp.
New Products/Quality Change	0.60
New Outlet	0.10
Total	**1.10 pp.**
Plausible Range	**(0.80–1.60 pp.)**

Source: *Toward a More Accurate Measure of the Cost of Living*, Dec. 4, 1996, p. 68.

Are Biases Additive?

Although the Boskin Commission alluded to the problem that it may be incorrect to sum the bias estimates, this point was passed over as an aside, and the commission added them up anyway for the larger impact. In a survey of CPI biases by Wynne and Sigalla (1996), the two researchers questioned whether summing various biases could be done because they were not necessarily mutually exclusive, which raises an *additivity bias* in the Boskin conclusion.

Biases due to the Inflation Rate

It is widely accepted that the percentage share of the CPI change due to biases, that is, the **relative bias,** is larger when the CPI pace is lower. Of course, the literature is clear in suggesting that it is not the inflation rate per se that determines the degree of substitution within the consumer market basket but the amount of relative price change (substitution elasticities). The corollary of this is that the degree of **absolute bias** is affected by the inflation rate environment. That is, during high inflationary times, such as in the 1970s, the estimate of the **absolute bias** would be larger than in lower inflationary times, such as the 1990s. If this is correct, then the calculations of absolute bias based on studies between 1967 and 1996 (as reported by the commission) are an overstatement of the current bias and, possibly, future bias. Support for this comes from the work by Bryan and Cecchetti (1993), which found that CPI substitution bias over the 1967–1992 period was 0.6 percentage point (pp.) per year, but was 0.88 pp. per year between 1967 and 1982 and *understated* inflation by 0.07 pp. per year between 1983 and 1992. This leads to a *period selectivity bias* in the Boskin report—that is, select the period that best makes your case.

Much Ado about Nothing?

One of the most comprehensive surveys of index bias was done by Jack Triplett in 1975 and updated in 1988. Neither of those two surveys was touched upon in the Boskin report. Why? Triplett (1975, p. 66) concluded that "estimates of substitution bias that have so far been made indicate that it is extremely small, so small that substitution bias cannot be viewed as an important empirical defect of fixed-weight consumption price indexes." Old survey aside, Boskin and company decided to consciously ignore that survey.

The Boskin Commission—which was the latest high-level commission to recommend changes to the CPI—reviewed many of the same issues that committees before have examined, including the Stigler Commission in 1961 and the Mitchell Committee in 1944. Moreover, the Bureau of Labor Statistics is keenly aware of all these problems and has in place several changes to correct some of these problems.

But like Cervantes's Don Quixote, the BLS is chasing an impossible goal to have an ideal price measure. The problems that the BLS faces in the construction of the CPI always will remain to some degree. More timely changes to expenditures weights will alleviate one problem, as Stigler's group noted years ago, but at the same time, the BLS would commit another statistical problem—it will no longer have a fixed-weight price index. Moreover, the alternative to **specification pricing** (narrowly defined commodities and services) is for the BLS to return to **unit value pricing**—which it abandoned in 1934. Unit value pricing of broad classes of goods and services, such as shirts or cars, would allow "both changes in prices of comparable items and the shifting composition of lower and higher quality items." Chain-weighted indexes ("rolling weights") may solve some problems but would create new ones. The Stigler Committee observed that "the danger in the use of a chain link index is that errors of measurement are locked into the index and carried in subsequent periods."

introduced in January 1978) when inflation was rampant, labor leaders were convinced that inflation faced by workers was greater than that portrayed by the CPI-U. As a concession to labor, the CPI-W was created and cost-of-living increases in union contracts were generated from it. At best, there is only a marginal difference between the inflation rates of the two series since only the component weightings differ by relatively small amounts. (See Box 7-2.)

Prices are collected in 91 urban areas around the country, with more than 19,000 retail establishments and 57,000 housing units included (the housing units are for pricing housing costs). (See Box 7-3.) All taxes included in the final purchase price are part of the calculations. Price changes for items covered in the CPI are calculated for each area and then averaged together to form a national average.

**BOX 7–2   Alternative Measures of Consumer Inflation:
A Geometric Mean and a Median**

Some measures of consumer inflation are currently available
monthly. They provide an alternative to the official CPI. One is
the experimental geometric mean CPI, which is produced by the
BLS with the intent that parts of it will be incorporated within the
official CPI over time. The second measure is the median CPI,
which is calculated by the Cleveland Federal Reserve Bank as a
conceptual alternative measure of underlying inflation.

The BLS's experimental geometric mean CPI was introduced
on April 10, 1997. In introducing those data, the BLS announced
that "the experimental CPI using geometric means, or CPI-U-XG,
is a supplement to the price information available from the BLS
and does not replace the published CPI-U or CPI-W indexes. The
BLS currently is evaluating the full or partial adoption of the geometric mean formula in the CPI-U and CPI-W." For further information on the merits of this alternative, see the BLS's Internet
page located at **http://stats.bls.gov/cpigmexp.htm.**

The median CPI is calculated from the major components of
the official CPI release. However, instead of reporting the data as
a sum of the pieces, this "expenditure-weighted median" CPI
takes the middle observation. It is argued by the Cleveland Federal Research Bank that this measure is superior for monetary
policy objectives. For further information on the median CPI, see
the Cleveland Fed's Internet page located at **http://www.clev.frb
.org/research/mcpi.htm.**

There are no revisions to prior months' data with each CPI release and it is only the seasonally adjusted data that are revised
once a year, generally in February. The reason for this is the numerous cost-of-living clauses in labor contracts and government
programs tied to the CPI. If there were to be revisions to prior
years, it would create havoc regarding past payments.

The most basic division of the CPI is between goods and services. The former accounts for just fewer than 43 percent of the
index and services the remaining 57 percent. There are some general rules concerning the inflation trends of the two sectors. One
is that goods sector inflation is more volatile than service sector
inflation. The chief reason is that the goods, or commodity, sector

---

BOX 7–3   Housing Costs and the CPI

In the late 1970s and early 1980s mortgage rates and home prices were skyrocketing. This had a very strong effect on the CPI since both were among the factors upon which the Bureau of Labor Statistics calculated home ownership costs. It was a realistic method, and there was no issue about the veracity of the rise in these costs. But this was a time when rising, double-digit inflation was a very sensitive political issue. Much was made of the fact that not everyone bought a house; most families rented. Therefore, the CPI was considered to be overstating the rate of inflation faced by the majority of consumers.

As a result of this criticism, in January 1983, the BLS formally switched to what is called "owners' equivalent rent." This measure of housing costs excludes actual interest costs and housing prices and determines home ownership costs by estimating what it would cost owners to rent their house. The change had the desired effect—then. Interestingly enough, though, this method came under criticism in the early 1990s. Then the method was said to overstate inflation—because it did not pick up the weakness in housing prices or declining mortgage rates.

---

is heavily influenced by food and energy prices. These two areas account for approximately one-half of the commodity component. Energy services, however, account for only about 3.5 percent of service sector prices. As will be discussed, price changes in the food and energy sectors are especially volatile. (See Box 7-4.) A second rule is that service sector inflation lags commodity inflation. Its peaks and troughs (on average) are about six to nine months behind those in the goods sector.

Another decomposition—and the one that markets focus on the most—is the breakdown of the CPI into the food, energy, and all other categories. The latter is referred to (somewhat obviously) as the CPI ex-food and energy, or more colloquially as the "core" rate of inflation. The reasons for "ex-ing" out the food and energy components are to strip out the most volatile components of inflation and to be able to focus on demand-driven inflationary pressures.

One final categorization is by major purchase group (see Table 7-1). There can be specific lower levels of detail that are of inter-

---

BOX 7–4   The 1998 Consumer Price Index Revision

Effective with the February 1998 release of January 1998 data, 1993–1995 consumer spending patterns will replace 1982–1984 spending patterns as the basis for weighting the approximately 200-item strata in the CPI. The BLS observed that this change, for example, was likely to lower the weight for food and beverages. At the same time, the BLS will introduce a revised CPI item structure. The major component breakdown will be: (1) food and beverages, (2) housing, (3) apparel, (4) transportation, (5) medical care, (6) recreation, (7) education and communication, and (8) other goods and services. The BLS will introduce new geographic sampling from the 1990 Census, new sample rotation procedures, and "technological improvements" in survey taking. The last category includes a revised housing sample for rental units, implementing an improved "price relative computation system" for rent and rental equivalency and a new data processing system for data review and imputation, which will be incorporated into the index with the release of January 1999 data. For more information, see the *Monthly Labor Review,* December 1996, which devoted seven articles to the revision.

---

est to the markets, such as car prices and airline fares, because they can have an unusually strong effect on a given monthly CPI. However, in general the major purchase groups are the lowest levels at which market-relevant analysis is conducted.

Analyzing the Data

The immediate focus of the markets when the CPI is released is on the month-to-month change for the overall CPI and the core rate of inflation. The latter usually carries more weight than the overall inflation reading, as the market is most sensitive to demand-type pressure (or lack thereof). Little interest is paid to the annual rate of inflation for a given month. Readings that are two-tenths or more from expectations (above or below, of course) are large enough to significantly affect the markets and potentially hold a new inflation story.

Once the market has absorbed the inflation readings in the core, energy, and food sectors, attention is turned quickly to the

TABLE 7–1   CPI: Relative Importance of Major Components: December 1996*

By Key Market Grouping	
Ex-food and energy	77.04
Energy	7.05
Food	15.90
By Major Purchase Category[†]	
Food and Beverage	17.48
Housing	41.20
Apparel and Upkeep	5.33
Transportation	17.14
Medical Care	7.35
Entertainment	4.35
Other Goods and Services	7.15

* Total may not add to 100 since these are relative importances, not weights.
† Energy prices do not have a separate billing in this breakdown. They are distributed
  through other categories, particularly the housing and transportation components.

source of any surprises. The typical breakdown is into the six previously mentioned major purchase categories, such as housing, apparel, and medical care. The greater the number of components that contributed to the surprising change, the greater the likelihood the result will more sharply affect the subsequent behavior of financial markets.

It is difficult finding a consistent level of dissection beyond these six categories. Most times they will serve the very useful and necessary function of determining any price change. However, analysts and the markets also develop a sense of which sectors, over particular spans of time, are most likely to be the source of spurious price shocks. Car prices are the best example of a sector that can be responsible for such shocks. Apparel also has had its moments when it was solely responsible for a surprising one-month move in the CPI. When these surprises come in the components known to be unusually volatile, the markets are more likely to dismiss the resulting inflationary shock. It is the surprising change that has no attributable component but is fueled by numerous small changes in numerous components that will send the markets to their largest moves.

FIGURE 7–1   Consumer Price Index

Month-to-Month Percentage Change, 3-Month Averages.

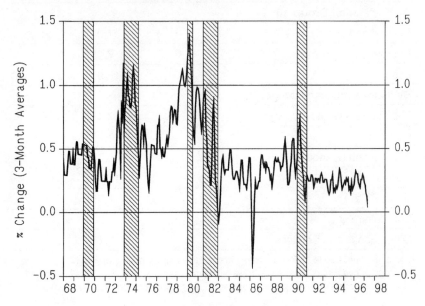

FIGURE 7–2   Consumer Price Index Less Food and Energy

Month-to-Month Percentage Change, 3-Month Averages.

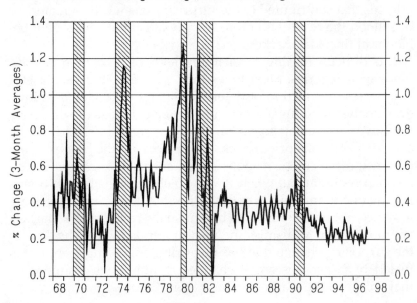

TABLE 7–2   Consumer Price Index
January 1948–May 1997, Month-to-Month Percentage Change

| Phase | Historic Low | Normal Bounds | | | Historic High | Series Characteristics | |
		Normal Low	Average	Normal High		Standard Deviation	Share of Total Observations
Recession	−0.8% in Jul 1949	0.2%	0.4%	0.6%	1.4% in Sep 1974	0.4 pp.	16.2%
Recovery	−0.4% in Jan 1950	0.2%	0.3%	0.5%	1.1% in Nov 1980	0.3 pp.	20.9%
Expansion	−0.5% in Mar 1986	0.2%	0.3%	0.5%	1.8% in Aug 1973	0.3 pp.	61.0%
Slow Phase	−0.5% in Mar 1986	0.2%	0.3%	0.5%	1.8% in Aug 1973	0.3 pp.	29.5%
Rapid Phase	−0.4% in Jan 1953	0.2%	0.3%	0.5%	1.6% in Dec 1950	0.3 pp.	31.5%
All Phases	−0.8% in Mar 1948	0.1%	0.3%	0.5%	1.8% in Aug 1973	0.4 pp.	100.0%

More so for inflation data than for other economic data, financial markets (especially fixed-income markets) are willing to assume surprises as just one-time occurrences if they are comfortable with the underlying inflation trend. Thus a strong (weak) CPI reading that is fueled by a burst (drop) in energy prices will be dismissed in an environment in which there is no reason to believe that oil prices are poised for a sustained rise (fall). In fact even if there is breadth to a particular month's change, if it contrasts with the markets' views of the underlying inflation trend, there often is no lasting trading response to the number.

Consumer Prices over the Business Cycle

The first thing to note is that inflation has its own cycle, one that lags the growth cycle. For this reason, looking at average

TABLE 7–3   Consumer Price Index Less Food and Energy
February 1957–May 1997, Month-to-Month Percentage Change

| Phase | Historic Low | Normal Bounds | | | Historic High | Series Characteristics | |
		Normal Low	Average	Normal High		Standard Deviation	Share of Total Observations
Recession	−0.3% in Jul 1960	0.3%	0.5%	0.7%	1.4% in Mar 1980	0.4 pp.	15.5%
Recovery	−0.1% in Dec 1982	0.3%	0.4%	0.5%	1.2% in Dec 1980	0.2 pp.	21.7%
Expansion	−0.3% in Jan 1963	0.2%	0.3%	0.5%	1.4% in Jul 1981	0.2 pp.	62.8%
Slow Phase	−0.3% in Jan 1963	0.2%	0.4%	0.5%	1.3% in Jan 1980	0.2 pp.	30.4%
Rapid Phase	0.0% in Jan 1973	0.2%	0.3%	0.4%	1.4% in Jul 1981	0.2 pp.	32.4%
All Phases	−0.3% in Jul 1960	0.2%	0.4%	0.5%	1.4% in Mar 1980	0.3 pp.	100.0%

month-to-month changes for the CPI can be misleading, as they are pretty much identical during each phase of the business cycle. This pertains to the core CPI rate as well. In fact, the core rate shows a more stable pattern throughout the cycle than does the overall CPI. Historic highs and lows for the core CPI are matched in the recession and expansion phases and are only two-tenths different than during the recovery. (See Figures 7-1 and 7-2 and Tables 7-2 and 7-3.)

References

Bryan, M. F., and Cecchetti, S. G. (1993), "The Consumer Price Index as a Measure of Inflation," *Economic Review*, Vol. 29, No. 4, Federal Reserve Bank of Cleveland, pp. 15–24.

Price Statistics Review Committee (1961), *The Price Statistics of the Federal Government*, National Bureau of Economic Research, New York.

Triplett, J. E. (1975), "The Measurement of Inflation: A Survey of Research on the Accuracy of Price Indexes," in Paul Earl, ed., *Analysis of Inflation*, Lexington Books, Lexington, MA, pp. 19–82.

Triplett, J. E. (1988), *Price Index Research and Its Influence on the Data: A Historical Review*, paper presented at the Conference on Research on Incomes and Wealth, Washington, DC.

Wynne, M., and F. D. Sigalla (1996), "A Survey of Measurement Biases in Price Indexes," *Journal of Economic Surveys*, Vol. 10, No. 1 (March), pp. 55–89.

Chapter 8

Cyclical Indicators

General Description

The composite cyclical indicators got a new lease on life after the U.S. Department of Commerce decided to request "competitive bids" from the private sector to continue and improve these time-honored data. In December 1995, the Conference Board became the official source for these widely publicized composite indexes of leading, lagging, and coincident indicators. The composite cyclical indicators are compiled based on their timing characteristics with business cycle turning points and grouped into three indexes that tend to lead, lag, or be coincident with the business cycle. The classification of these indicators was based on extensive research since the 1920s by the National Bureau of Economic Research and the Commerce Department. Since the composite data contain little new information, they tend to have less

Economic Indicator Information at a Glance

Market Significance	Low
Typical Release Time	10:00 AM Eastern Time One Business Day After the Release of Personal Income
Released By	The Conference Board Business Cycle Indicators Project
Period Covered	Prior Month
Web Site	http://www.conference-board.org/

market impact than a primary indicator (such as employment, orders, etc.). However, for the general public and for the general perception of the state of the economy, these summary statistics
provide a clear picture of the stage of the business cycle. At most,
the market focus is on the leading indicator composite only.

Analyzing the Data

The **composite index of leading indicators** currently is made
up of 10 components: (1) average weekly hours for manufacturing, (2) average weekly initial claims for unemployment insurance, (3) new orders for consumer goods and materials, (4) vendor
delivery time—percent of purchasing managers reporting slower
deliveries, (5) new orders for nondefense capital goods, (6) building permits for private housing, (7) stock prices, S&P 500 stock
price index, (8) real M2 money supply, (9) interest rate spread,
10-year Treasury bond yield less federal funds rate, and (10) index
of consumer expectations from the University of Michigan. The
leading indicator composite led the 1990 recession by six months
and over the last five recessions led by an average of 8.2 months.
The leading indicator turned up two months prior to the 1991 expansion and over the last five recessions led by an average of 4.2
months. (See Figure 8-1 and Table 8-1.)

The **composite index of coincident indicators** is made up of
four series: (1) employees on nonagricultural payrolls, (2) personal income (inflation adjusted) less transfer payments (inflation adjusted), (3) industrial production, and (4) manufacturing
and trade sales (inflation adjusted). (See Table 8-2.)

The **composite index of lagging indicators** includes: (1) the
average duration of unemployment (in weeks), (2) the manufacturing and trade inventories-to-sales ratio (1992 dollars), (3) the
change in the index of labor cost per unit of output for manufacturing (six-month span), (4) the average prime rate charged by
banks, (5) commercial and industrial loans outstanding (millions
of 1992 dollars), (6) the ratio of consumer installment credit
outstanding to personal income, and (7) the change in CPI for
services (six-month annual percentage change). The lagging indicator composite led the 1990 business cycle peak by nine
months and over the last five recessions lagged by 2.4 months.
The lagging indicator bottomed 21 months after the 1991 busi-

FIGURE 8–1 Composite Leading Index

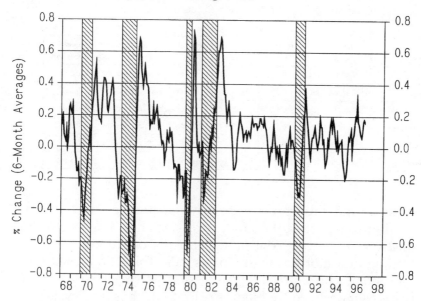

ness trough—which was historically long—and lagged, on average, 12.6 months after the expansion began over the last five cycles. (See Table 8-3.)

The **ratio of the coincident-to-lagging indicator composites** provides yet another companion measure for cyclical analysis. This measure is developed from a statistical basis, whereby the ratio of any measure in the numerator (top of the ratio), which

TABLE 8–1 Leading Indicator Composite
February 1959–April 1997, Month-to-Month Percentage Change

Phase	Historic Low	Normal Bounds			Historic High	Series Characteristics	
		Normal Low	Average	Normal High		Standard Deviation	Share of Total Observations
Recession	−2.1% in Mar 1980	−0.4%	−0.1%	0.1%	1.3% in Jun 1980	0.5 pp.	14.6%
Recovery	−0.8% in Dec 1980	0.1%	0.3%	0.5%	1.4% in Apr 1975	0.4 pp.	20.9%
Expansion	−0.9% in Oct 1979	−0.1%	0.1%	0.2%	1.1% in Dec 1959	0.3 pp.	64.5%
Slow Phase	−0.9% in Oct 1979	−0.1%	0.0%	0.2%	1.1% in Dec 1959	0.3 pp.	30.5%
Rapid Phase	−0.7% in Jun 1981	−0.1%	0.1%	0.2%	0.8% in Aug 1972	0.3 pp.	34.0%
All Phases	−2.1% in Mar 1980	−0.1%	0.1%	0.3%	1.4% in Apr 1975	0.4 pp.	100.0%

TABLE 8–2 Coincident Indicator Composite
February 1959–April 1997, Month-to-Month Percentage Change

Phase	Historic Low	Normal Bounds			Historic High	Series Characteristics	
		Normal Low	Average	Normal High		Standard Deviation	Share of Total Observations
Recession	−1.5% in Dec 1974	−0.5%	−0.3%	−0.1%	0.5% in Feb 1982	0.3 pp.	14.6%
Recovery	−0.8% in Aug 1992	0.2%	0.4%	0.5%	1.4% in Sep 1983	0.3 pp.	20.9%
Expansion	−1.2% in Aug 1959	0.1%	0.3%	0.4%	1.9% in Dec 1959	0.3 pp.	64.5%
Slow Phase	−0.8% in Apr 1979	0.1%	0.2%	0.4%	1.9% in Dec 1959	0.3 pp.	30.5%
Rapid Phase	−1.2% in Aug 1959	0.2%	0.4%	0.5%	1.3% in Apr 1978	0.3 pp.	34.0%
All Phases	−1.5% in Dec 1974	0.0%	0.2%	0.4%	1.9% in Dec 1959	0.4 pp.	100.0%

turns up and down prior to the denominator measure (bottom of the ratio), will lead the numerator. Technical lingo aside, this measure provides a confirming measure or cross-check on the leading indicator turning-point signals. The ratio turned down four months prior to the 1990 recession, and over the last five recessions it declined 8.6 months prior to the business cycle peak. Its record on calling troughs is similar to that of the leading indicator itself. The ratio turned up two months prior to the 1991 expansion and turned up 4.4 months, on average, prior to the last five business cycle troughs.

The keys to interpreting the cyclical indicator report include:

- Look at the leading indicator change—ask yourself how strong is the increase? Between 1959 and 1997, the average monthly increase was 0.1 percent, with a normal band of

TABLE 8–3 Lagging Indicator Composite
February 1959–April 1997, Month-to-Month Percentage Change

Phase	Historic Low	Normal Bounds			Historic High	Series Characteristics	
		Normal Low	Average	Normal High		Standard Deviation	Share of Total Observations
Recession	−1.7% in Jul 1980	−0.3%	−0.1%	0.2%	1.0% in Mar 1980	0.5 pp.	14.6%
Recovery	−1.9% in Jun 1975	−0.4%	−0.2%	0.0%	0.8% in Feb 1984	0.4 pp.	20.9%
Expansion	−0.7% in Sep 1986	0.0%	0.2%	0.3%	1.1% in Apr 1979	0.3 pp.	64.5%
Slow Phase	−0.7% in Sep 1986	−0.0%	0.1%	0.3%	1.1% in Apr 1979	0.3 pp.	30.5%
Rapid Phase	−0.6% in Feb 1987	0.0%	0.2%	0.3%	1.0% in Aug 1959	0.3 pp.	34.0%
All Phases	−1.9% in Jun 1975	−0.1%	0.1%	0.2%	1.1% in Apr 1979	0.4 pp.	100.0%

–0.1 percent to +0.3 percent. During periods of slow growth, the leading indicator has averaged 0.0 percent per month, while it has averaged 0.1 percent per month during rapid-growth phases of the expansion. The leading indicator tends to be the strongest in the return-to-previous-peak phase of the cycle, with an average monthly rise of 0.3 percent. Due to the narrow band over the cycle, it is often better to look at year-over-year growth rates and levels of the leading indicator to get a more cyclical perspective.

- Be less concerned with which components are contributing to the monthly change than with the magnitude of the total index, unless there is a known special factor biasing a component. Our research has shown that there is more cyclical information in the total indicator than in the individual components. It has been widely recognized that a basket of indicators is more reliable than any individual indicator (the "diversification" concept).
- Keep an eye on the lagging indicators—these indicators are generally overlooked, but reflect cost pressures in the economy.

Special Factors, Limitations, and Other Data Issues

The main goal of the cyclical indicators—and the leading indicator composite, in particular—is as a precursor of business cycle turning points. As such, cyclical indicators tend to have limited appeal at other times when the economy is recording solid growth—whether it is slow, moderate, or strong. But since the leading indicator is a sensitive measure of economic activity, it tends to dip ahead of growth cycle slowdowns as well. It is at those times that the indicator itself can be difficult to read. Moreover, studies showed that a three-month decline rule for interpreting the leading indicator change is not reliable in calling a turning point. Hence, more elaborate frameworks have been devised to distinguish growth cycle and business cycle turning-point signals. Some of the more popular techniques used today to screen the leading indicators for relevant turning-point information include Neftci's sequential probability method, Hamilton's Markov turning-point model, and the Zarnowitz and Moore sequential signals.

References

Neftci, Salih, "Optimal Prediction of Cyclical Downturns," *Journal of Economic Dynamics and Control,* 1982, pp. 225–241.

Niemira, Michael P., and Giela T. Fredman, "An Evaluation of the Composite Index of Leading Indicators for Signaling Turning Points in Business and Growth Cycles," *Business Economics,* October 1991, pp. 49–55.

Niemira, Michael P., and Philip A. Klein, *Forecasting Financial and Economic Cycles,* John Wiley & Sons, New York, 1994.

Zarnowitz, Victor, *Business Cycles: Theory, History, Indicators, and Forecasting,* University of Chicago Press, Chicago, 1992.

Chapter 9

Durable Goods Orders and Shipments

General Description

The report on durable goods orders is one part of a series of manufacturing and trade reports that continually gets built into other more comprehensive reports on the manufacturing and trade sectors. The market focus of this report is new orders, though the report contains data on shipments and unfilled orders and the new orders data can be quite volatile.

Economic Indicator Information at a Glance

Market Significance	Moderate to High
Typical Release Time	8:30 AM Eastern Time About the 10th Business Day of the Month
Released By	Labor Department Bureau of Labor Statistics
Period Covered	Prior Month
Web Site	http://www.census.gov/ftp/pub/ indicator/www/m3/index.htm

The underlying survey used to collect data on shipments, new and unfilled orders, and inventories for durable goods, as well as the more encompassing manufacturing report, is completed by most manufacturing firms with 1,000 or more employees and representative smaller ones. Generally companies with fewer than

**TABLE 9–1   Selected Component Shares of New Orders
for Durable Goods**

	End of 1996 Shares*
Consumer Goods and Materials	69%
Nondefense Capital Goods	26%
Defense Capital Goods	5%
Transportation Equipment	25%
Nondefense Capital Goods Ex-Aircraft	22%

* The first three shares comprise all of durable orders. The second two are important
subsets of capital goods.

100 employees are not sampled; instead data are estimated from industry averages.

New orders are defined as the intent to buy for immediate or future delivery. A new order must be supported by binding legal documents (i.e., signed purchase agreements, letters of intent). The orders series is a net number, measuring the current month's orders less cancellations of previous orders.

To insure consistency within the shipments and orders data, *new orders are derived* from backlogs and shipments using the following identity:

New Orders = Change in Unfilled Orders + Shipments

Several components of the new orders detail are equal to shipments, by definition, since those industries do not maintain backlogs. The most notable example is motor vehicles. Motor vehicles are assumed to be the same as the value of car and truck assemblies. Hence, watching auto and truck production schedules is one way to anticipate a portion of durable goods orders. Other categories that match shipments and orders are lumber, farm machinery, metal cans, glass containers, and other transportation equipment. (See Table 9-1.)

Analyzing the Data

Certain "high-value" sectors can dominate the change in these data, so it is appropriate to view durable goods orders excluding some extremely volatile sectors such as defense and transportation. Defense orders account for about 5 percent of total orders but contribute about 50 percent of the variability in the month-to-month change in total orders. Similarly, transportation orders, which account for about 25 percent of total orders, can be dominated by large swings in aircraft orders; and although their percentage swings are not as large as those for defense orders, they too can dominate total orders by their sheer size. Hence, *total durable orders less defense orders* and *total orders less transportation orders* are two key measures to watch to understand the underlying trend. However, it is not possible to isolate defense orders from transportation orders or from the three other categories into which the durable orders report is initially broken (the four categories are primary metals, electrical machinery, industrial machinery, and transportation). That means a sharp move in defense orders also will show up in the major industry detail, making it difficult to use that detail to better understand the data. As such, *impressions* of the strength or weakness of this report still can be dominated by a narrowly based increase in defense or transportation.

Another important component to watch is nondefense capital goods orders, especially without aircraft and parts, the latter for the same reason we look at total orders ex transportation. Nondefense capital goods orders less aircraft account for about 20 percent of total orders and exclude most of the volatile categories. Nondefense capital goods orders less aircraft include: (1) nondefense portions of ordnance, (2) turbines, (3) internal combustion engines, (4) construction, mining, and material handling equipment, (5) metalworking machinery, (6) special industry machinery, (7) electrical transmission and distribution equipment, (8) electrical industrial apparatus, (9) communications equipment, (10) railroad equipment, and (11) search and navigation equipment.

Finally, another useful measure is consumer goods orders. Although not explicitly shown, by definition consumer goods orders are total durable orders minus capital goods orders. This component can be dominated by its transportation subset—car production/orders—also; but to the extent that consumer spending on durables accounts for large swings in overall economic activity, it's a component worth watching (consumer goods orders in a different variation are part of the leading indicators).

Durable Goods Orders over the Business Cycle

Durable goods new orders have a typical-cycle pattern, with the strongest gains in the recovery phase of the cycle. On average, durable orders increase by 1.7 percent per month during the recovery and then moderate to about a third that pace during the expansion. There is a good deal of variability in these data, as reflected by the large standard deviation around the mean of about four percentage points. (See Table 9-2 and Figure 9-1.) Unfilled orders, on the other hand, tend to expand the most during the expansion phase (as expected) when demand catches up with and then exceeds supply. Unfilled orders should not be the focus of the market's attention until capacity utilization notches over 83 percent, since backlogs will be drawn down even in a recovery due to the slack in capacity utilization. (See Table 9-3 and Figure 9-2.)

Durable Goods Orders' Relationships with Other Series

There are two series that may tell us something about durable goods orders. The first is machine tool orders as compiled by the Association for Manufacturing Technology. This series is generally reported on the last Monday of every month and may be reported before the durable orders report. Although machine tool orders are conceptually covered in the durable goods report, they represent less than 0.5 percent of total durable orders. Moreover on a year-over-year basis, machine tool orders are more than five times as volatile as durable goods orders. Their

TABLE 9–2 New Orders for Durable Goods
March 1958–May 1997, Month-to-Month Percentage Change

| Phase | Historic Low | Normal Bounds | | | Historic High | Series Characteristics | |
		Normal Low	Average	Normal High		Standard Deviation	Share of Total Observations
Recession	−9.3% in Nov 1990	−2.9%	−1.0%	1.0%	8.3% in Jul 1980	3.9 pp.	14.6%
Recovery	−7.5% in Apr 1984	−0.2%	1.7%	3.6%	13.9% in Jul 1991	3.8 pp.	28.7%
Expansion	−8.1% in Aug 1964	−0.9%	0.6%	2.2%	11.1% in Jan 1964	3.1 pp.	63.1%
Slow Phase	−7.7% in Jan 1990	−1.3%	0.4%	2.0%	9.8% in Dec 1988	3.3 pp.	29.7%
Rapid Phase	−8.1% in Aug 1964	−0.6%	0.9%	2.3%	11.1% in Jan 1964	2.9 pp.	33.4%
All Phases	−9.3% in Nov 1990	−1.1%	0.6%	2.4%	13.9% in Jul 1991	3.5 pp.	100.0%

FIGURE 9–1 Durable Goods Orders

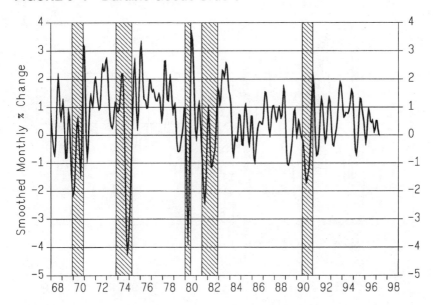

usefulness for forecasting durable goods orders, therefore, is very limited.

A second source of potential information about the durable goods report is aircraft orders announced by major producers such as Boeing. These announced orders are often considered a harbinger of the comparable component in the durable orders series. However, as little as 10 percent of the announced orders actually are booked in the month that they were announced. In some cases airlines have requested that their aircraft order announce-

TABLE 9–3 Unfilled Orders for Durable Goods
February 1958–May 1997, Month-to-Month Percentage Change

| Phase | Historic Low | Normal Bounds | | | Historic High | Series Characteristics | |
		Normal Low	Average	Normal High		Standard Deviation	Share of Total Observations
Recession	−2.9% in Feb 1958	−0.8%	−0.1%	0.5%	3.3% in Aug 1974	1.3 pp.	14.8%
Recovery	−1.5% in Jun 1975	−0.2%	0.3%	0.8%	2.8% in Mar 1984	0.9 pp.	22.2%
Expansion	−2.8% in Jan 1960	0.2%	0.7%	1.2%	3.4% in Mar 1973	1.0 pp.	62.9%
Slow Phase	−2.8% in Jan 1960	0.1%	0.6%	1.1%	3.3% in Dec 1962	1.0 pp.	29.7%
Rapid Phase	−1.2% in Mar 1993	0.3%	0.9%	1.4%	3.4% in Mar 1973	1.1 pp.	33.2%
All Phases	−2.9% in Feb 1958	−0.0%	0.5%	1.1%	3.4% in Mar 1973	1.1 pp.	100.0%

FIGURE 9–2   Unfilled Goods Orders

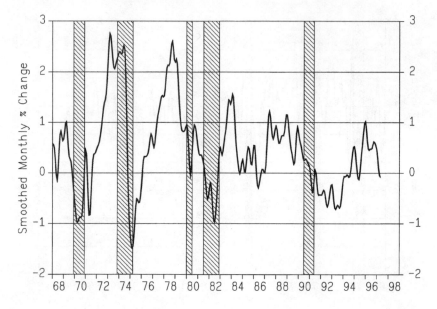

ment be delayed for internal company reasons. In other instances federal government approval is required prior to a sale being consummated. Finally cancellations can depress any month's aircraft orders, as orders are a net number.

As far as using information from the durable goods report, there are two important ways to do so. One is as input for the leading indicators index. Two components of this index are drawn from the report: new orders for nondefense capital goods (as already mentioned) and new orders for consumer goods. These components are the final input into leading indicator forecasts. The second way is to view data on shipments of nondefense capital goods less aircraft and parts as a source for GDP estimates of business spending on durable equipment. In fact, along with motor vehicle purchases and imports of capital goods, these data constitute a key element in analysts' forecasts of this GDP component.

Chapter 10

Employment

General Description

Employment is the single most important economic data series for the financial markets because it is an extremely timely and comprehensive measure of business activity. As such, this report is always a major focus of politicians and monetary policy officials and, in turn, commands the full attention of the financial markets around the world. Employment generally is viewed as one of the best concurrent measures of business activity, although some studies have shown that employment lags output changes.

Economic Indicator Information at a Glance

Market Significance	Very High
Typical Release Time	8:30 AM Eastern Time First Friday of the Month
Released By	Labor Department Bureau of Labor Statistics
Period Covered	Prior Month
Web Site	http://stats.bls.gov:80/newsrels.htm

On the day that the employment report is released, the commissioner of the Bureau of Labor Statistics has a monthly briefing on the employment situation for members of the Joint Economic Committee of Congress. At that hearing, the commissioner reviews, amplifies, and qualifies the employment data and discusses any known anomalies in or forthcoming changes to the data. When Congress is not in session, the commissioner holds a press conference to discuss the report.

Because the employment report has so many complex dimensions, at times financial market participants tend to dissect this report more than most economic reports. Moreover, in recent years, the financial markets tend to be more susceptible to mundane technical issues associated with the employment report methodology. Consequently, the level of technical detail included in the following discussion is intentionally far greater than in other chapters.

Understanding the Data

The U.S. Labor Department's Bureau of Labor Statistics (BLS) produces two independently derived measures of employment on a monthly basis. The *establishment* or *payroll* measure is based on payroll records and measures employment in nonagricultural industries. The second measure, *household* employment, is based on a survey and measures civilian noninstitutional employment of persons aged 16 years and older and includes agricultural workers and the self-employed.

The payroll series is derived from the Current Employment Survey (CES) and measures the **number of jobs** (which includes double-counting from multiple jobholders). On the other hand, the household measure is derived from the Current Population Survey (CPS) and counts the **number of people** that are working. Over the long run, the household and payroll measures of employment have similar fluctuations and can be used as cross-checks on each other. However, for any given month it is not uncommon that these two measures move in opposite directions. Generally, the payroll series, which is the smoother measure, is given more weight by the financial markets. The unemployment rate is computed based on the household survey measure of employment and the labor force.

The monthly employment report covers an array of detail that fills in the employment picture by age, race, sex, and type of occupation and by state. However, rarely do those details move the financial markets, even though they may be useful for the analyst to look at, so as to understand the full story. As of 1996, the regional employment data for the largest 10 states, which had been part of the standard employment release, were dropped from this early month employment report due to budget and statistical coverage concerns and are now released later in the month in a separate report. The employment report also covers hours and earnings, which from time to time are crucial to the financial markets when potential wage inflation is the pressing interest.

In a nutshell, some of the major keys for understanding the employment report should include:

- Use a **business cycle framework** for perspective on the significance and meaning of the monthly change in household and payroll employment. Additionally, in this business cycle context, look at the manufacturing payroll employment change as a sensitive cyclical measure of business conditions.
- Do not lose sight of **longer-term themes** such as the contraction in the defense-related industries, restructuring in an industry, the growth of business services, and so forth. These themes are likely to drive future employment.
- Be aware of any **strike activity** that may have occurred during the month, which could weaken a given month's payroll employment change, or the return of strikers, which could boost payroll employment. One week before the employment report is issued, the BLS releases a summary of strike activity during the reference survey week for payroll employment. These data reflect workers directly involved in work stoppages affecting 1,000 workers or more. This strike report is found at the Internet site http://stats.bls.gov/cesstrk.htm.
- Keep in mind that employment will be impacted by **special events** such as hiring for the decennial population count (which is mandated by the Constitution). In 1990, for example, hiring for census enumerators escalated by 340,000 people, from 17,000 jobs in January to a high for the year of 361,000 in June. This reversed rapidly in July—dropping off by 173,000 in that month, by another 127,000 jobs in August, and by 40,000 in September. The Census Bureau plan for the decennial census in the year 2000 anticipates over

a quarter of a million temporary employees will be hired within a few months to accomplish the follow-up for failing to return the census questionnaire, assuming that the Census Bureau supplements the current direct collection of information with sampling estimates for nonresponse. However, without the sampling, the Census Bureau estimates that they would have to hire an additional 59,000 temporary employees for that same operation. The Census Bureau's use of statistical sampling is a hotly debated political issue before the Congress.

- Understand that **weather anomalies** affect monthly employment tallies, as well. Adverse or unseasonable weather often impacts construction employment and some weather-dependent service businesses (such as at ski slopes in the winter). Aside from specific industry employment categories, unusual weather can affect *hours worked*, and if the problem lasts at least a week—as in January 1996—it can impact the household employment measure "employed but not at work due to bad weather."

- Observe that the strength or weakness in a reported employment change is influenced—strongly at times—by the **seasons.** There are three main seasonal effects on employment: (1) *seasonal hiring patterns,* such as in the retail industry during the Christmas season and summer hiring of school-aged workers, (2) *seasonal plant shutdowns,* particularly in the automotive industry during the summer and often at the turn of the year, and (3) *seasonal layoffs of workers,* such as with teachers and support services that are associated with educational systems. January is the largest month for seasonal layoffs during the year, and the seasonal adjustment factors attempt to counter that typical seasonal layoff. However, with nearly 2 million fewer jobs in January than in December—purely for seasonal reasons—any slight change in *layoff timing* gets amplified in the January seasonally adjusted employment tally. Moreover, if there is less-than-normal seasonal hiring, then expect fewer layoffs once the season is over, which also may distort months that are dependent on those interyear layoff patterns (such as January in the post-Christmas period and September in the post-summer hiring season).

- Recognize that the **unemployment rate** (inverted) is a leading indicator at business cycle peaks but a lagging indicator at business cycle troughs.
- Watch the length of the **workweek** since businesses adjust hours before employment and those short-term adjustments more readily reflect private sector demand changes.
- Be careful not to overinterpret month-to-month changes in **average hourly earnings** (a wage measure); this measure is volatile and conceptually flawed because it does not hold employment shares constant. Consequently, change in average hourly earnings can occur simply due to changes in employment shares without any change in the wages paid by industry. Year-to-year growth in average hourly earnings provides a better, though still incomplete, picture of wage trends.
- Look at the **employment diffusion index,** which is calculated over one-month spans, to determine how widespread the employment gains are. Two measures are provided within the employment report: one measure for total payroll employment (which currently accounts for 356 industries) and a second measure for manufacturing employment (which currently covers 139 industries). A diffusion index is bounded by zero and 100 percent, with the midpoint of 50 percent indicating an equal number of industries increasing employment and decreasing employment. During recessions, the total diffusion index, measured over one-month spans, has averaged 42.0 percent compared with a reading of 32.8 percent for the manufacturing component. During the recovery phase of the cycle, the total diffusion index was 57.3 percent, while the manufacturing index was 55.0 percent. During expansions, the total employment diffusion index has averaged 58.7 percent, with a 61.6 percent average for the rapid-expansion phase of the cycle and a 55.9 percent average during the slow-expansion phase. The manufacturing employment diffusion index has averaged 51.8 percent during expansions, with a 56.9 percent reading during rapid expansions and 46.7 percent average during slow-expansion phases. Hence, the manufacturing index shows more industries tend to contract employment than expand their workforce during slowdown phases of the expansion.

These averages provide some benchmarks to evaluate the data.

- Be aware that the growth in the **aggregate hours index,** which is derived from weekly hours multiplied by employment, is often viewed as a "loose" proxy for real GDP growth. The concept is based on the relationship that the growth rate in real output can be approximated by adding the growth rates of aggregate hours worked plus productivity. A simple statistical relationship using the growth in the hours index to estimate real GDP growth explained about 50 percent of the quarterly fluctuation between 1989 and 1996, with a standard error of 1.2 percentage points. That means that there is a wide 1.2 percentage point band around the current quarter's forecast. Hence, one should not rely too heavily on this "top-down" projection for real GDP, though it does provide some guidance.

- Keep in mind that the **BLS currently updates seasonal factors for the establishment data every six months.** Once a year, usually in late May, those seasonal factors are revised historically with the annual benchmark revision, and provisional seasonal factors are derived for the March-through-October period. In late November, the BLS issues new seasonal factors for the next six months. The November update generally is a nonevent for the financial markets (and for analysis purposes), but the June update of the seasonal factors (which is released prior to the June payroll employment report) could be significant at times.

Box 10-1 provides a handy reference guide and summary of standard terminology used in the employment report or associated with employment.

Background on Payroll Data

Payroll employment, hours, and earnings statistics are collected for the payroll period that includes the 12th day of the month. The one exception to this rule is for federal government employment, which is an end of month tally, and those data are provided to the Labor Department by the federal government's Office of Personnel Management (OPM) and also are separately published in an OPM

BOX 10–1   Workforce Terms

Establishment: This term is defined by the BLS as, "A single physical location where business is conducted or where services or industrial operations are performed."

Establishment Employment: Paid nonfarm employment consists of full- and part-time employees, including salaried workers and executives of corporations, who were on the payroll in the pay period including the 12th of the month. Included are employees on sick leave, holidays, and vacations. Those not included are proprietors and partners of unincorporated businesses.

BLS-790 Form: This is the title of the monthly survey form, which is sent to establishments by the states and jurisdictions, to collect employment information. The form, also referred as the "shuttle form," is customized to specific broad industries (such as manufacturing, construction, public education, etc.).

ES-202 Report: The payroll employment data produced by the BLS are adjusted to the more comprehensive count of employment derived from the so-called ES-202 program. The ES-202 program is named after the form that employers file with their state unemployment insurance offices. On that form, the company reports the number of employees.

Employment Diffusion Index: This index measures the percentage of industries in which employment was growing. The index is defined as the percentage of the group of industries (total and manufacturing) that showed an increase over the stated period (one-, three-, six-, or 12-month spans) plus one-half of the percentage of those industries that showed no change. Hence, a reading of 50 percent means no change. A reading above 50 percent implies more industries increased employment than cut back and vice versa for an index reading of less than 50 percent. Julius Shiskin, a former commissioner of the BLS, once suggested that the employment diffusion index was a key measure to determine whether the economy was in a recession. It tends to be a very sensitive measure and tends to turn up or down before a business cycle peak or trough.

Unemployment Rate: The unemployment rate is defined as the difference between the labor force (LF) and the employed workforce (E) divided by the labor force times 100; that is, rate = $100 \times (LF - E) / LF$. In addition to the national unemployment rate, the BLS calculates state and selected industry and occupational unemployment rates. Alternative measures are routinely published by the BLS and are designated as U-1 to U-6, which are more or less inclusive compared with the standard unemployment rate (which is designated as U-3).

Labor Force Participation Rate: This measure is the share of the civilian noninstitutional population that is aged 16 years and over that is in the labor force.

Discouraged Workers: The number of people who say they want a job but are not actively seeking employment because they believe that their search would be in vain.

Full Employment: The term *full employment* cannot be found as the title of any official economic statistic. Full employment is a theoretical concept, which has been defined over the years in many different ways. One of the classic definitions was from U.K. economist William Beveridge, who defined it as the point where the number of unemployed persons equals the number of unfilled vacancies. Unfortunately, there are no unfilled vacancy employment statistics for the United States—the only measures that come close are the Conference Board's help-wanted advertising index and the Manpower Hiring Intention survey. In the theoretical economics literature, "full employment" has been replaced by the phrase (which was due to Milton Friedman) "non-accelerating inflation rate of unemployment" (NAIRU), which itself is subject to considerable uncertainty in its measurement.

Household: This is a primary sampling unit (PSU) used for the Current Population Survey. It is made up of one or more individuals living together in the same household.

Okun's Law: The late Arthur Okun—a former member of the Council of Economic Advisers—formulated a rule of thumb that describes the relationship between real growth and its impact on the unemployment rate. Although Okun later "rescinded" what has become known as "Okun's law," most economists still use the concept. It provides a ballpark estimate of the real GDP growth needed to budge the unemployment rate. Our recent update of that rule, using a variant suggested by the Federal Reserve Bank of Atlanta some years ago, implies that real GDP growth of 2.4 percent is the threshold that needs to be exceeded for an impact on the unemployment rate. But the results are quite dependent on the period of estimation.

publication on federal civilian workforce statistics, entitled *Employment and Trends*. All other nonfederal government information is collected from a representative sample of 390,000 establishments covering 500 industries from across the nation, which mirrors the population or universe of about 6.5 million establishments (that is, the sample size is 0.06 percent of the establishment population, but because it is weighted more heavily toward large employers, that sample accounts for about one-third of the employment universe). The survey, which is the largest of its kind in the world, is collected by four major methods: (1) by mail using the BLS-790 shuttle survey form, (2) by a data collector, who calls the respondent to obtain the data using computer-assisted telephone interviews, (3) from a dial-in phone system, where the respondent calls a computer and punches in the information on a touchtone phone (this is referred to as "Touch-Tone data entry"), and (4) by electronic data interchange (EDI), where the respondent sends in data electronically or by tape, diskette, etc. Currently, about half of the survey information is collected electronically. These data are collected by state employment security agencies and sent back to the BLS, which in turn compiles and adjusts the data to produce the monthly report.

Because the data are collected from a small sample, statistical adjustments are made to the data to gross them up to the population (using a technique known as **link relative,** which means the current month's estimate equals the previous month's estimate multiplied by the change in the matched sample), and once a year those data are readjusted to the underlying population (which is referred to as the "benchmark"). An ongoing statistical correction to the sample is known as the **bias adjustment,** which is included in the estimate of payroll employment to capture hiring by new businesses that are not yet accounted for in the BLS's sample. The bias adjustment factor, which currently boosts the level of payroll employment by around 150,000, is often misunderstood by the financial markets. The monthly change in the bias factor is small—for the most part, less than 5,000; yet it is that impact which incrementally will boost the payroll employment *change* and not the overall level of the adjustment. The bias factor currently is derived by the BLS using three pieces of ongoing information: (1) the required actual amount of revision over the preceding three benchmarked years, (2) the recent change in employment growth, and (3) accounting for the quarterly employment census or universe measure, which is available with a lag of about six months. These quarterly nonagricultural employment data come from administrative records of the state unemployment insurance (UI) program, which covers approximately 99 percent of all nonagricultural employment. Four times a year, all employers covered by unemployment insurance are required to file their employment and wages with the state employment agencies. BLS tracks these UI data for the bias factor adjustment and also uses them as the primary data source for the annual benchmark revision to the payroll data. The remaining 1 percent of the employment universe not covered by UI is derived mainly from Interstate Commerce Commission and Social Security Administration records.

The state unemployment insurance data program, which is called the ES-202 data, provides the universe data to which the monthly industry payroll tallies are calibrated. Although the UI data are more comprehensive than the current employment survey, there are known coverage differences between the payroll employment tally and the E2-202 measure. Some industries tend to be only partially covered by unemployment insurance, which requires the BLS to augment the ES-202 employment counts. The main employment categories that are in the CES measure but not in the ES-202 tally are railroad employees, state and local government elected officials, student workers at school, and some workers at small nonprofit organizations.

The annual **benchmark** revision to payroll employment usually is released in June for the preceding three years ending in March of the preceding year. Table 10-1 shows how significant those revisions have been in recent years. In some years the revisions have been large—such as for 1994—and in other years the impact has been small—such as for 1996. In the inter-benchmark period, between March of two successive years, the BLS distributes the difference between the updated employment level and the prior estimate evenly across the prior year. This technique is referred to as the **wedge back** procedure. In the post-benchmark period— that is, the most recent year beginning in the preceding March— the effect of the benchmark adjustment is simply through the link-relative updating with a new level and updated bias adjustment factors. As a result, when a benchmark adjustment is released, the prior year's monthly changes tend to be negligible.

TABLE 10–1   Percent Differences between Nonfarm Employment Benchmarks and Estimates by Industry Division, March 1989–March 1996

Industry	1989	1990	1991	1992	1993	1994	1995	1996
Total	(2)	−0.2	−0.6	−0.1	0.2	0.7	0.5	(2)
Mining	−3.7	−3.3	−0.6	−0.8	2.2	−0.7	0.2	0.5
Construction	−1.5	−0.8	−0.2	−2.6	1.6	1.9	−1.6	0.2
Manufacturing	−1.0	0.3	0.1	−0.8	1.1	1.3	0.3	1.0
Transportation and public utilities	−1.7	−0.3	−1.0	−0.6	1.0	2.2	−0.7	−1.2
Wholesale trade	0.8	−2.6	−0.2	0.7	−2.6	1.2	1.2	−1.7
Retail trade	0.5	−0.3	−0.3	0.9	−0.2	1.3	1.6	0.5
Finance, insurance, and real estate	−1.1	−1.4	−0.4	−1.5	1.5	2.1	−1.8	−1.1
Services	0.8	0.3	−1.6	0.2	0.1	−0.8	0.9	0.1
Government	0.3	0.2	−0.3	0.4	−0.1	0.4	0.2	−0.1

Source: Bureau of Labor Statistics.
(1) Differences are based on comparisons of final, published March estimates and benchmark levels, as originally published.
(2) Less than 0.005 percent.

Hours and earnings data are also part of the payroll employment database. The CES data provide information on hourly earnings for production and nonsupervisory employees, while the ES-202 wage data are an imperfect universe for the BLS's purpose. The ES-202 wage data measure total quarterly wages without accounting for the number of hours paid. From a business cycle standpoint, hours tend to increase before employment does. Moreover, since the late 1980s, employers have pushed the workweek to record lengths in an effort to hold employment levels and costs, which has lengthened the lead time between hours and new hiring.

Because of the methodology employed by the BLS, the CES data at the national, state, and regional levels are independent estimates. The regional data will not sum to state totals, and the state data will not sum to the national totals. Although there is some BLS research to change the methodology to force a concordance between the three data sets, it still is only a future goal. In recent years, some analysts have attempted to exploit the difference between the sum-of-the-states total and the national total employment tally as a sign of future revisions to the national data. This is incorrect; the BLS attributes the differences in the data sets to methodology and not raw information.

Adjusting the Data

Seasonal Adjustment: Beginning in mid-1996, the BLS applied the **X-12 seasonal-adjustment** methodology to the payroll employment data (and the BLS is expected to apply it to the household data in the future). For the first time, the X-12 seasonal-adjustment computer program accounted for the span of weeks between survey periods. In some months, the span is five weeks, and in other months the span between the reference points in the adjacent months is four weeks. In the past, economists were fond of exploiting that fact to argue for the likelihood of a higher-than-trend change or lower-than-trend change in a given month. For example, it was argued that if the seasonal hiring pattern was strong for a given month and the length was five weeks since the last employment snapshot was taken (compared with four-week spans in prior years for that month), the extra week could inflate the jobs by some amount. Although this survey-span argument was never strong for most months (as the BLS has since found out), it did matter at times. However, with this new adjustment for the survey span, this argument has been eliminated. But, still, this new adjustment method is not devoid of problems, and BLS analysts still review the seasonal factors derived from the program. Currently, the BLS does not adjust the following industries to control for the effects of a four- versus five-week interval between surveys: (1) motor vehicles and equipment, (2) local and interurban passenger transit, (3) educational services, and (4) membership organizations. All seasonal factors derived by the BLS are multiplicative (as opposed to additive factors).

Holiday Adjustment: If the reference week falls during the week including Good Friday/Easter or Labor Day, the BLS explicitly will adjust the hours data for those holidays; otherwise there could be a spurious drop at that time.

Benchmark Adjustment Announcements: Over the last 10 years, it has become customary for the BLS's commissioner to notify the Joint Economic Committee of Congress—and the public—of the expected size of the benchmark revision to the payroll employment data at the November hearing on the employment report. By the fall of each year, the unemployment insurance records from the previous March's aggregate employment count are available, and the BLS has a good idea of the magnitude of the upcoming benchmark revision, which will not be officially unveiled until June of the subsequent year.

Future of Payroll Employment Collection Methods

The BLS has an internal mandate to move its nonsample payroll survey to a survey-based measure, because in part the current data collection method does not directly measure new business "births" (it is indirectly derived and imposed on the final set of data using the bias adjustment, as noted above) and in part the current "quota sample" contains potentially significant statistical biases.

As of June 1995, the BLS launched a two-year research effort to develop the new sample design, which was followed by a production test of these redesigned survey methods and procedures beginning in July 1997 with phased-in implementation (by industry). The BLS has stated that:

> If results of the production test are satisfactory, the Bureau will proceed as scheduled with a phased-in implementation of the new CES sample design beginning in June 1999, coincident with the publication of March 1998 CES national benchmark revisions. The wholesale trade industry series for CES national estimates will be converted to the new probability-based procedures at that time. Probability-based estimates for state and area wholesale trade series are targeted for introduction in March 2000 with the next state benchmark revision. After the initial conversion of wholesale trade, BLS will continue a phase-in of the new design by major industry division. Implementation of the new sample and estimators for major divisions will be scheduled to coincide with the publication of benchmark revisions, in order not to disrupt published over-the-month changes for current month estimates with a continually changing sample composition. Thus, implementation of the redesign for the second group of industries tentatively is scheduled to coincide with the publication of March 1999 benchmark revisions in June 2000. Conversion of all industries is expected to be completed approximately 4 years from the start of implementation.

These new methods of data compilation will change the look and volatility of the data reported in the future. At the extreme, a purely survey-based estimate of the level of employment might be more choppy than the current payroll jobs measure—much as the household measure of employment is. However, we expect that during the transition from a nonsample-based estimate to a sample-based estimate of employment, a modified link-relative adjustment will be used initially, which will continue the "smooth nature" of payroll employment. In the future, statistical confidence bands around a payroll estimate will be included in the monthly report, as well.

However, as these changes occur, the financial markets are likely to continue their laser-like focus on these data and scrutinize them as to their implication for where the economy is and will be headed and how policy makers will respond to the message from these data. They will continue to be one of the handful of economic data that will surely move the markets. But in a transition period, the seasonal-adjustment factors used with the old data may no longer apply, which initially could make for even more volatility in these data.

Payroll Employment Behavior over the Business Cycle

Payroll employment—adjusted for the current level of employment—tends to decline by nearly 290K jobs per month during recessions, rebound by about 310K jobs per month during the recovery phase, and averages nearly 300K jobs per month during expansions, with nearly 370K jobs added per month during the rapid-growth expansion and about 225K jobs added per month during the slow-growth phase of the business cycle. (See Figure 10-1 and Table 10-2.)

Employment Insights from the CES Tally

Payroll employment is divided into its major industries based on the current Standard Industrial Classification (SIC) codes, which will be updated and superseded by the North American Industrial Classification System (NAICS). The first major distinction in the payroll employment tally is between goods-producing and service-producing industries employment. Employment

FIGURE 10–1   Payroll Employment Change

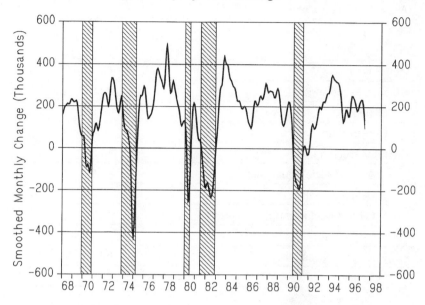

within the service-producing industries is approaching four times as large as good-producing industries employment and is generally where most of the job gains have occurred. The other major industry shares are shown in Table 10-3.

The BLS also calculates some analytical measures of payroll employment, which are unpublished but available upon request and are occasionally discussed at the BLS commissioner's

TABLE 10–2   Payroll Employment Change*
(January 1948–May 1997)

Phase	Historic Low	Normal Bounds			Historic High	Series Characteristics	
		Normal Low	Average	Normal High		Standard Deviation	Share of Total Observations
Recession	–894K in Oct 1949	–493K	–292K	–91K	224K in Feb 1974	402K	16.2%
Recovery	–340K in Aug 1983	140K	317K	493K	1115K in Sep 1983	353K	20.9%
Expansion	–687K in Jul 1956	152K	305K	457K	745K in Apr 1978	305K	62.9%
Slow Phase	–687K in Jul 1956	79K	231K	384K	687K in Aug 1952	305K	32.7%
Rapid Phase	–443K in Aug 1959	238K	378K	518K	745K in Apr 1978	280K	30.2%
All Phases	–894K in Oct 1949	6K	207K	408K	1,115K in Sep 1983	402K	100.0%

Normal bands and averages adjusted for current level of employment; historic high and low actual change.

TABLE 10–3   Payroll Employment Shares

(Average Shares, 1992–June 1997)

Category	Share
Total Payroll	100.0
Total Private	83.3
Goods Producing	20.8
Mining	0.5
Construction	4.4
Manufacturing	16.0
Motor Vehicle Equipment	0.8
Defense-related	0.9
Other Manufacturing	14.3
Service Producing	79.2
Private Services	62.5
Retail	18.0
Wholesale	5.5
Services	27.8
Business Services	5.5
Health Services	7.9
Other Services	14.4
Other Private Services	11.2
Government	16.7
Federal Government	2.5
State and Local Government	14.2

Source: Bureau of Labor Statistics.

monthly testimony to the Joint Economic Committee of the U.S. Congress. Following from the research effort of the Small Business Administration in which the SBA derived a measure of "small-business related employment" using input-output tables, which are percentages of an industry's product accounted for by the demand from another industry (such as the motor vehicle industry—a motor vehicle is an *output* product that uses *inputs* from the steel, glass, rubber, and other industries), the BLS compiles **analytical employment** categories of defense-dependent industries, construction-related industries, auto-related industries, and export-sensitive industries. These series are useful measures for understanding employment dynamics. For example, the export-sensitive industries data are an echo of export growth. Although there are many caveats in the construction and use of these data, they do offer analysts some insight not available otherwise.

Background on Household Data

The Current Population Survey is used to collect information on the labor markets from individuals for a single week (Sunday through Saturday), which generally includes the 12th day of the month (which is referred to as the **reference week**), as is the case for the establishment survey. The one exception to the rule is for December when the CPS survey week rule currently is that the reference week cannot extend beyond December 13, since anything after that date would make it difficult to compile the data due to the holiday period. Hence, for example, in 1996, the survey period was for December 1–7, but between 1997 and 1999 it should revert to the normal timing. Consequently, in December, the reference week for the CPS can differ from the CES reference week.

The CPS is a rotating panel survey of about 60,000 households. About three-fourth of the sample is the same for any two months in which households are in the sample for four months, out for eight months, and then back in the survey for another four months before leaving the sample altogether. Respondents are asked about the employment status of all members of their households who are 16 years old and over.

The CPS uses an **activity-based definition** of employment and unemployment to classify individuals into one of three categories: (1) employed, (2) unemployed, or (3) not in the workforce. An employed person must be 16 years of age or older (14 years or older before 1967) to be included in the survey count. By definition, an employed person for the reference week was: (1) a civilian wage and salary worker who was paid for any work performed (this includes domestics and other private household workers) or was self-employed (in a business, professional practice, or farm) during the reference week, (2) an unpaid person who worked 15 or more hours, or (3) a person who temporarily did not work due to illness, bad weather, vacation, labor-management disputes, or personal reasons—whether paid or unpaid—but has a job or a business.

At the beginning of 1994, the Bureau of Labor Statistics—which is the sponsoring agency for the household survey, whereas the survey itself is conducted by the U.S. Census Bureau—introduced a new survey questionnaire and collection methods for labor force data. This was the most substantial change in the survey since 1967 and resulted in some breaks in the data series. The unemployment rates (the total and by demographic and occupational characteristics) as well as participation rates and employment-to-population ratios were all affected by this new methodology. Based on an overlap or parallel survey of 12,000 households using the new methods, compared with the 60,000-household sample using the existing survey and collection methods, the overlap survey showed a dramatic increase in adult women labor force participation with a substantially higher unemployment rate, a lower participation rate of adult men, and a considerably higher teenager participation rate and unemployment rate, all compared with the existing measures at the time. Overall, it showed that the unemployment rate was higher by about 0.5 percentage point (pp.), the labor force participation rate was higher by about 0.5 pp. as well, and the employment-to-population rate was higher by 0.2 pp. But despite this spike in the data due to new methods, the testing showed that the use of new technology and redesign of the survey produced more accurate survey responses. The new survey also implemented dependent interviewing, which means that the interviewer had access to data from the previous month's responses of households that already were participating, which helped provide more consistency and continuity from month to month. The use of computer-assisted data collection—either computer-assisted telephone interviewing (CATI) or computer-assisted personal interviewing (CAPI)—made this change possible. This radical change also caused the seasonal factors of the household data to be called into question. Unfortunately, it will take 3 to 5 years after the introduction of these new data in 1994 to build up enough data to provide any conclusive evidence of whether the survey redesign and new collection methods have resulted in a shift in the seasonal profile of the unemployment rate and related measures.

Household Employment Behavior over the Business Cycle

In any stylized description of the labor markets over the business cycle, it is typical to suggest that employment tends to lead changes in the labor force—either in the upswing of the business cycle or during the downswing. As a result of the timing differences, the resulting unemployment rate tends to turn down simultaneously when the economy begins to strengthen but tends to move higher after a business cycle peak. Typically, once employment weakens shortly after a business cycle peak, more people tend to flock into the labor force—with the memory of good times for jobs and a high expectation of finding a job. But, by then, the job markets are not growing as rapidly and the unemployment rate begins to rise. With this in mind, the initial analysis of the household measures over the business cycle should be determined based on separate assessments of employment, the labor force, and the unemployment rate.

1. *Evaluating Employment Changes:* Probably the first question that must be asked in determining the significance of an employment changes is: What was the household employment change, and how does it compare with the last three-month average monthly change? Can the current month's change be viewed as a correction for the prior month's change? After accounting for the volatility of the series and its possible correction for the prior month's changes (a surge or a plunge), ask yourself if the theme of the household employment change (stronger, weaker, about the same) is consistent with the picture painted by the payroll employment measure? How does the change in household employment compare with its average cycle pattern? Table 10-4 shows the average change in household employment, adjusted to the current level of employment by monthly percentage changes, over the course of the business cycle. (See also Figure 10-2.) Several observations are worth noting: (1) household employment tends to grow the fastest during the recovery phase of the cycle—about 260K per month, (2) household employment growth is about 100K stronger during the rapid-growth phase of the expansion than during the

TABLE 10–4 Household Employment Change*

(January 1948–May 1997)

Phase	Historic Low	Normal Bounds			Historic High	Series Characteristics	
		Normal Low	Average	Normal High		Standard Deviation	Share of Total Observation
Recession	−761K in Dec 1953	−415K	−169K	78K	639K in Feb 1954	493K	16.2%
Recovery	−669K in May 1991	45K	285K	525K	991K in Jun 1983	480K	20.9%
Expansion	−947K in Mar 1960	−13K	233K	480K	1286K in Apr 1960	493K	62.9%
Slow Phase	−947K in Mar 1960	−65K	181K	428K	1,286K in Apr 1960	493K	32.7%
Rapid Phase	−773K in Jan 1968	32K	272K	512K	857K in May 1984	480K	30.2%
All Phases	−947K in Mar 1960	−78K	181K	441K	1,286K in Apr 1960	519K	100.0%

* Normal bands and averages adjusted for current level of employment; historic high and low actual change.

slow-growth phase of the expansion, and (3) the slow-growth phase for household employment is indistinguishable from the overall average pace of employment growth.

2. *Evaluating the Labor Force:* Longer-run dynamics control the trend pace of labor force growth, including the growth of the female labor market participation (the big surge occurred already) and the growth in the population

FIGURE 10–2 Household Employment Change

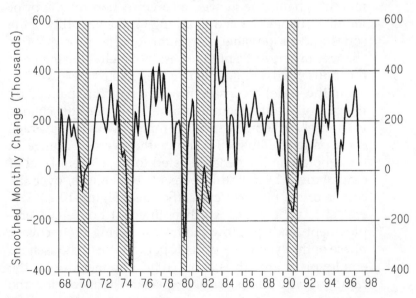

aged less than 16. Superimposed upon those trends is the cyclical dynamic alluded to above.

3. *Assessing whether the Unemployment Rate Change Is Significant:* The unemployment rate must change by more than 0.2 pp. in order to be viewed as a statistically significant move. Moreover, the unemployment rate is a result of how fast the labor force grows relative to the employment. Typically, the unemployment rate enters the market thinking through two channels: (1) the political channel—if the unemployment rate is very high, there is political pressure for the Federal Reserve to ease rates, other things being equal—and (2) the inflation channel— a low unemployment rate is viewed as a trigger for higher inflation. Two common inflation theories that exist are the Phillips curve hypothesis of inflation, which suggests that there is a tradeoff between wage inflation and the unemployment rate, and the accelerationist hypothesis of inflation, which typically is couched in terms of what rate of unemployment is consistent with nonaccelerating inflation. Although both theories have empirical shortcomings, they are dredged up by the financial markets from time to time when the markets worry about the inflationary consequences of some low level of the unemployment rate.

Table 10-5 shows the unfolding of the unemployment rate over the business cycle. It is obvious from that table that the unemployment rate is a lagging indicator. For example, the average

TABLE 10–5   Unemployment Rate
(January 1948–May 1997)

Phase	Historic Low	Normal Bounds			Historic High	Series Characteristics	
		Normal Low	Average	Normal High		Standard Deviation	Share of Total Observations
Recession	2.7% in Aug 1953	5.5%	6.3%	7.2%	10.8% in Nov 1982	1.7%	16.2%
Recovery	4.3% in May 1955	6.6%	7.2%	7.9%	10.8% in Dec 1982	1.3%	20.9%
Expansion	2.5% in Jun 1953	4.6%	5.2%	5.9%	7.5% in Aug 1984	1.3%	62.9%
Slow Phase	2.9% in Apr 1952	4.4%	5.0%	5.7%	7.4% in Jul 1985	1.3%	32.7%
Rapid Phase	2.5% in Jun 1953	4.7%	5.3%	6.0%	7.5% in Aug 1984	1.3%	30.2%
All Phases	2.5% in Jun 1953	4.9%	5.7%	6.5%	10.8% in Dec 1982	1.6%	100.0%

unemployment rate during the recovery phase of the business cycle is 0.9 pp. higher than during the recession. Similarly, the unemployment rate tends to be higher during the rapid phase of the business cycle expansion than during the slow-expansion phase of the cycle. (See Figure 10-3.)

Employment Insights from the CPS Tally

The CPS collects information on the labor force, which from time to time may shed light on a particular issue. For example, one must look to the household data to answer questions such as: What percentage of the workforce holds more than one job? What percentage of the workforce consists of blue-collar workers? What percentage of the workforce is made up of teenagers? What percentage of the workforce is black? How many part-time workers are there? What is the average duration of unemployment?

Clearly, this degree of detail does not play any role in the financial markets' initial reaction to the data, but it can play a role in the background or theme issue. For example, it was widely and incorrectly noted in the business press that the 1990 reces-

FIGURE 10–3   Unemployment Rate

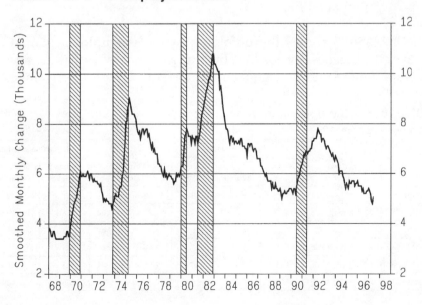

sion was a "white-collar recession." The fact was that more blue-collar workers lost jobs than white-collar workers during that recession; what only was true was that *relative to its own history,* there were more white-collar jobs lost during that recession than in prior periods. That too was misleading given the fact that: (1) the workforce is growing, and (2) a larger percentage of the labor force held white-collar jobs during the 1990 recession than in prior recessions, which has been a secular development. This is just one illustration of how and when the detail might be useful to understand or refute a prevailing theme.

Bridging the Gap between the Household and Establishment Measures

Similarly-titled series exist from the CPS and CES, but the concepts covered are generally different, and so care must be taken in interpreting the data or evaluating someone's comment on the data that may be found in the press. In some cases, the counterpart series is buried in the detailed report and consequently not generally obvious to financial market participants. For example, there are two measures of "average weekly hours." The more common average weekly hours series is found on the payroll side, and that series measures **average weekly hours paid.** Hence, it would include, for example, hours not at work but on paid vacation or leave as well as other nonworking hours paid for at nonfarm establishments. However, there is a second, more comprehensive measure of **average weekly hours worked** from the CPS, which, as the words imply, measures only hours actually worked—it excludes vacation hours, doctor visits during a workday, etc., and covers self-employment (about 9 mn. people) as well as agricultural workers. Moreover, the CPS hours worked series has been more steady over the last 20 or 30 years than the CES hours paid series, which has a more pronounced downward drift. In 1975, hours worked averaged 38.4 hours while hours paid averaged 36.1 hours—a gap of just over two hours. By 1995, hours worked averaged 39.2 hours while hours paid averaged 34.4 hours—a gap of almost five hours.

Another example of similarly titled series that exist between the two surveys is **manufacturing employment.** Again, the more common definition is from the payroll report, but a second measure is tabulated from the CPS, which is larger than the payroll concept. The reason why the household manufacturing measure is larger than the payroll manufacturing measure may not be obvious. With multiple job-holdings inflating the payroll measure, one might expect that the household measure would be smaller since it counts people and not jobs. But the answer lies in the fact that the CPS survey asks workers to classify themselves by industry. If an individual works for a factory but is placed there by a temporary-help firm, the payroll employment counts the individual as a service worker but the household report may count the individual as a manufacturing worker, if that is what the individual tells the enumerator. This distinction should be kept in mind if one cites a manufacturing unemployment rate, for example, and compares it with the payroll manufacturing change—that would be incorrect and possibly misleading.

The examples could go on—such as the number of female (male) workers and the number of jobs held by females (males). But from a financial market perspective, similar concepts found in the household and establishment tallies, either for the totals or in the details, should be used as "story cross-checks"—just so long as one recognizes what the similarities and differences are between the two measures.

Special Factors, Limitations, and Other Data Issues

Payroll employment data are affected by strikes, weather disruptions, holidays, and temporary hiring such as government hiring associated with the decade Census, summer jobs programs funded by the federal government, workers hired to work on election day at the polls, and workers involved in military reserve call-ups. So these factors must be taken into account in interpreting the data, since many of these impacts are temporary and not associated with an improvement or worsening in the labor market.

The rapid rise of temporary help companies (such as Manpower, Kelly Services, etc.) during the 1980s has changed the character of the payroll employment data. Historically, if a manufacturing firm hired a part-time worker, that person would be classified as a manufacturing worker. However, if that same manufacturer contracted with a temporary help company to provide a worker to do that same function, then the worker would be classified as a business service employee. This obviously changes the interpretation of the industry detail. Moreover, if the same temporary help firm employee works for two firms on a part-time basis, that worker would be counted only once in the payroll employment report because that individual is working for only one temporary help company. This tends to eliminate some of the inevitable double-counting of workers who traditionally held multiple part-time jobs and has resulted in a downward bias in payroll employment growth.

Household employment by definition is not impacted by labor strikes or other temporary work disruptions. However, household employment changes tend to be more volatile from month to month than the payroll series. For example, between 1990 and 1995, the standard deviation of the payroll employment change was 174K, while the household employment change was 298K— or about 1.7 times as volatile.

Monthly Revisions

Payroll employment is revised twice after its initial monthly release, which is referred to as the **first-closing estimate,** and the subsequent revisions are referred to as the **second** and **third** closings. One key source of revision is due to nonresponses or late responses among the approximately 390,000 establishments. The nonresponse rate for establishments is currently just under 40 percent for the first-closing estimate, which is considerably below the 50 percent rate that existed during the mid-1980s. Moreover, between 1991 and 1995, the BLS figured that the average size of the payroll revision from the first-closing to the second-closing estimate was reduced by 29 percent due to better outlier handling and a lower nonresponse rate of participants. Although about 60 percent of the sample establishments report employment for the month by the first-closing date, those establishments account for substantially more than 60 percent of employment based on total sample size. In addition, another source of revision is due to the federal government's own employment records, which are not available in time for the first estimate. Although the Office of Personnel Management (OPM) makes a preliminary estimate of federal government employment for the BLS using an assumption of no employment change

TABLE 10–6   Average Payroll Employment Changes per Month and Revisions between First Release and Subsequent Estimates (Thousands of Jobs), 1988–1995

Month	1st Release	2nd Release	3rd Release	1st–2nd	2nd–3rd
January	96	95	117	−1	22
February	259	235	247	−24	12
March	115	125	122	10	−3
April	92	125	140	33	15
May	113	177	186	64	9
June	126	188	216	62	28
July	107	108	123	1	15
August	74	74	84	0	10
September	106	111	149	5	38
October	125	71	75	−54	4
November	124	129	159	5	30
December	129	103	116	−26	13
Average	**122**	**128**	**144**	**6**	**16**

where records are not available, the BLS uses that estimate only as a check on its estimate of the number of federal government employments found on state employment records.

Although the degree of revision is getting smaller, it is helpful to look at the average revisions over the last few years to infer when revisions tend to occur and by how much. This is only a guide and does not necessarily help one to forecast revisions. But several interesting tidbits are discernible between 1988 and 1995, as shown in Table 10-6. February payroll employment showed the largest monthly gain of any month during the year, while August tended to have the smallest average gain. It was found, based on the standard deviation of the individual months, that November was the most volatile month for payroll employment changes, while May tended to be the least volatile compared with the same month of prior years. Between 1988 and 1995, the May revision to the payroll count had the largest upward change of any month of the year between the first closing and the second closing. Over the subsequent two monthly revisions to the payroll tally, data for the month of June had the largest cumulative upward change.

TABLE 10–7 Payroll Employment Changes (Initially Reported Change) and Market Reaction, January 1996–January 1997

Release Date	Market Consensus	Actual	Bond	Stocks	Dollar
Jan. 19, 1996*	+120K for Dec.	+151K	−0.01 pp.	+60.33 pt.	+0.2%
Feb. 2, 1996	+75K for Jan.	−201K	+0.07	−31.07	−0.2
Mar. 8, 1996	+300K for Feb.	+705K	+0.24	−171.24	+0.3
Apr. 5, 1996	+75K for Mar.	+140K	+0.17	Closed	+0.2
May 3, 1996	+123K for Apr.	+2K	+0.07	−20.24	−0.1
June 7, 1996	+165K for May	+348K	+0.14	+29.92	+0.1
July 5, 1996	+150K for June	+239K	−0.05	−30.29	+0.2
Aug. 2, 1996	+200K for July	+193K	−0.10	+85.08	+0.3
Sept. 6, 1996	+230K for Aug.	+250K	−0.04	+52.90	+0.2
Oct. 4, 1996	+160K for Sept.	−40K	−0.10	+60.01	0.0
Nov. 1, 1996	+190K for Oct.	+210K	+0.02	−7.45	−0.3
Dec. 6, 1996	+180K for Nov.	+118K	+0.03	−55.16	0.0
Jan. 10, 1997	+190K for Dec.	+262K	+0.10	+78.12	0.0

* Release delayed because of federal government shutdown.

Household employment figures—including the unemployment rate—do not get revised on a monthly basis.

Market Reaction

In evaluating the financial market reaction to the employment report, there are few absolutes. However, it can be said that the market response tends to be more intense for employment than many of the less comprehensive and important data—though sometimes the impact is immediate and can be reversed later in the trading day. Moreover, even if there are simultaneously released economic data from other government statistical agencies or private groups, the employment report tends to be the dominant financial market mover. As a reflection of the type of market response in the recent past, the Table 10-7 shows the day's changes in the government bond yield, stocks, and the dollar for days when the employment report was released. The bond-yield effect is proxied by the 30-year government bond yield at the close of the day's trading; the closing change in the Dow Jones

Industrial Average stock price index is used to assess the stock market impact; the percentage change in the Morgan Guaranty trade-weighted dollar exchange rate index is shown for the day's foreign exchange.

Relationship to Other Data

Jobless Claims: There are numerous measures that the market look to for some gauge of current or future employment trends. Some measures have been around awhile, and some are new on the scene. The weekly jobless claims data (see Chapter 24) provide one timely measure of the performance of the labor markets. Although the quality and coverage of the unemployment insurance data have diminished, those data still are viewed as a precursor of the upcoming employment report. A simple illustrative statistical relationship between the change in payroll jobs and the initial jobless claims, which was estimated between 1990 and mid-1996, is shown below:

Change in Payroll Employment
$$= -2.93 \times \text{Level of Initial Unemployment Claims}$$
$$-1.33 \times \text{Change in Unemployment Claims} + 1,245$$

This relationship explained 59 percent of the monthly change in payroll employment and worked reasonably well in mirroring trends. However, there can be big monthly differences between the two series due to coverage and other special factors. One such example occurred for January 1996. This relationship predicted a payroll job gain of 135K for January, but the actual change was down by 66K jobs. One source of that difference was that jobless claim filings were held down by heavy snowstorms but the payroll tally reflected the snowstorm impact. Although the average change from the equation was 193K jobs between 1995 and mid-1996, which compared quite favorably with the actual average change of 202K jobs, the volatility tells an important story. The actual standard deviation was 128K jobs over that 1½-year period, while the standard deviation in the estimated change was 58K jobs. Although the jobless claims data will continue to be watched by the financial markets as a guide to the strength in the labor markets, it is an imperfect guide on a monthly basis and appears unlikely to pick up the big "surprises" on a monthly basis. Additionally, some analysts prefer to use the jobless benefits data instead of initial jobless claims for the reference survey week as a conceptually better proxy for employment growth. But, still, this is only an imperfect proxy for the strength or weakness in the labor market.

Jobs Hard to Find: The Conference Board's "jobs hard to find" survey question from the monthly consumer confidence report has mirrored the pattern of the unemployment rate exceedingly well over time and is routinely shown that way within the Conference Board's report. This report is released prior to the monthly employment tally and hence can be a useful barometer to watch.

Announced Layoffs: Helping to bring to prominence the visibility of "announced layoffs" was the Worker Adjustment and Retraining Notification Act (WARN), which was enacted into law on August 4, 1988, and became effective on February 4, 1989. Generally, an employer is subject to the WARN law if it employs 100 or more people (excluding people on payroll less than six months and people working less than 20 hours per week). Under this federal legislation, an employer generally must give at least 60 days notice if there is to be a plant closing that affects 50 or more employees, or if there is to be a mass layoff—a layoff that affects either 500 or more employees or 50–499 employees if they make up at least 33 percent of the employer's workforce. Tallies of announced layoffs began in earnest with Dan Lacey's *Workplace Trends* in which quarterly corporate staff cuts by number of positions and by companies were recorded since 1990. After *Workplace Trends* ceased publication, the mantle was picked up by Challenger, Gray & Christmas, Inc., an outplacement consulting firm, which continued the announced layoff count but on a monthly basis in its *Challenger Employment Report.* But announced layoffs may be rescinded, in part or in total, and may be over a very extended period, so it is unclear as to its significance for the monthly Labor Department employment report.

Help-Wanted Advertising: The help-wanted advertising index was first constructed in 1964 by the Conference Board based on 52 cities, with historical data going back to 1951 for 45 cities. These data measure the ad lineage and not the number of jobs, which makes this series an imperfect measure of job vacancy. Nonetheless, prior to her tenure as BLS commissioner, Katherine

G. Abraham wrote a paper, when she was at the Brookings Institution, in which she looked at help-wanted advertising as a
proxy for job vacancy. She compared two states' employment vacancy rates (Minnesota and Wisconsin), which existed for a time,
against state help-wanted advertising data. Although Abraham
argued that the national help-wanted data needed to be "nor-
malized" to account for a drift in the series, she concluded that
"the help-wanted index, after adjustment for some identifiable
sources of drift, is a useful indicator of job vacancies." Moreover,
Abraham argued that the vacancy-unemployment relationship
may have shifted. As time goes on, it is likely that an "Internet
Job Advertising" index will be more useful for tracking employment vacancies than the printed word. Already, job openings are
listed on the Internet. Although the concept of a national employment vacancy rate, similar to what Australia or Japan publishes, has been recommended over the years by various
presidential commissions reviewing U.S. labor force data, that
measure has never been developed.

Manpower Employment Outlook Survey: Manpower, Inc.—the
largest temporary-help firm in the world—conducts a quarterly
telephone survey of hiring intentions among more than 16,000
public and private employers in 484 U.S. cities. The survey began
in the third quarter of 1976 and covers 10 industry categories:
mining; construction; manufacturing–durable goods; manufacturing–nondurable goods; transportation and public utilities;
wholesale and retail trade; finance, insurance, and real estate; education (public and private); services; and public administration.
Our research suggests that although the concept of the survey is
to assess hiring intentions, the reality is that intentions appear to
be formed based on the recent performance of actual hiring. As a
result, the hiring intention survey tends to be coincident with or
lag slightly behind actual employment growth. Still, it is a confirming indicator of the employment picture even though its
forecasting importance is negligible.

Chapter 11

Employment Cost Index

General Description

The employment cost index (ECI) is one of the most comprehensive measures of labor costs. It includes both wages and benefits for state and local government and the private sector employees. Wages and salaries account for about 72 percent of total labor costs, while the remaining 28 percent is benefits. The importance of the ECI has varied over time for the financial markets, given the overall concern with labor costs and inflation.

Economic Indicator Information at a Glance

Market Significance	Moderate
Typical Release Time	8:30 AM Eastern Time Last Thursday of the First Month of the New Quarter
Released By	Labor Department Bureau of Labor Statistics
Period Covered	Prior Quarter
Web Site	http://stats.bls.gov/news.release/ eci.toc.htm/

Analyzing the Data

The ECI measures compensation per employee hour worked during the pay period including the 12th day of the last month of each quarter (March, June, September, and December) using fixed-weight shares of labor. Self-employed, owner-managers, and unpaid family workers are excluded from the survey coverage. The wage and salary component of the ECI measures the average straight-time hourly earnings, where straight-time earnings are total earnings before deductions and excluding premium pay for overtime, weekend, or late-shift work. Earnings include production bonuses, commissions, and cost-of-living adjustments but exclude nonproduction bonuses such as payments in kind, room and board, and tips. On the benefit side, the ECI measures 23 distinct benefit categories:

Hours-Related Benefits:

1. Premium pay for overtime and work on holidays and weekends
2. Vacations
3. Holidays
4. Sick leave
5. Other paid leave

Supplemental Pay:

6. Shift differentials
7. Nonproduction bonus
8. Severance pay
9. Supplemental unemployment benefit funds

Insurance:

10. Life insurance
11. Health benefits
12. Sickness and accident insurance

Pension and Savings Plans:

13. Pension and retirement benefits
14. Savings and thrift plans

Legally Required Benefits:

15. Social security
16. Railroad retirement
17. Railroad supplemental retirement
18. Railroad unemployment insurance
19. Federal Unemployment Tax Act
20. State unemployment insurance

21. Workers' compensation
22. Other legally required benefits

Merchandise Discounts:

23. Merchandise discounts (for retail trade employees only)

The ECI sample consists of about 4,440 private nonfarm establishments and 1,000 state and local government establishments. Federal government employees are not included in these data. Overtime pay is included in the benefits category with its appropriate fixed-weight share. Hence, an increase in the use of overtime by employers would not have any impact on the ECI, although it would increase the per worker labor costs actually paid by the employer.

In addition to the split in compensation between wage and salaries and benefits, the ECI also is compiled by: (1) occupational classes (professional, specialty, and technical; executive, administrative, and managerial; administration support; and blue-collar occupations), (2) type of industry (goods producing and service producing), (3) bargaining status (union and nonunion), (4) region (Northeast, South, Midwest, and West), and (5) area size (metropolitan areas and nonmetropolitan areas).

The BLS seasonally adjusts some of the major components and presents those on a quarter-to-quarter seasonally adjusted basis, while other non-seasonally adjusted components are presented on a year-over-year basis.

Key questions to interpreting the ECI report include:

- In looking at the composition of the change, how much of the change in labor costs was due to wages and how much of it was due to benefits?
- Do these data reflect any regional pressure points for tight labor markets? Often with relatively low unemployment rates in parts of the country, those are the regions that tend to reflect the wage and benefit pressure first as the demand for labor is outstripping supply. Similarly, are there signs of regional labor costs unwinding due to slack in the labor markets?
- Is there any sign of bargaining power pushing up wages? Look at the nonunion versus union labor costs differences.

- Are there any long-term changes in the labor markets that are holding costs down or causing costs to rise? For example, during the early 1990s, the secular shift toward health maintenance organizations (HMOs) and other forms of managed care resulted in compression of benefit costs. Ask yourself, are there any remaining benefits from secular shifts?

Over the Business Cycle

The short history of the ECI data, which began in 1979, makes cyclical analysis very tricky—especially given that there was a secular unwinding of inflation during the 1980s which impacted these data, as did the rise of HMOs. As a result, the ECI shows very little cyclical sensitivity from the 1980s forward. Between 1982 and 1997, the average quarterly increase in the ECI was 1.2 percent (+/–0.3 pp.), with essentially no statistical difference in the recession (+1.4 percent per quarter), the recovery (+1.4 percent), and the expansion (+1.1 percent). (See Figure 11-1 and Table 11-1.)

FIGURE 11–1   Employment Cost Index

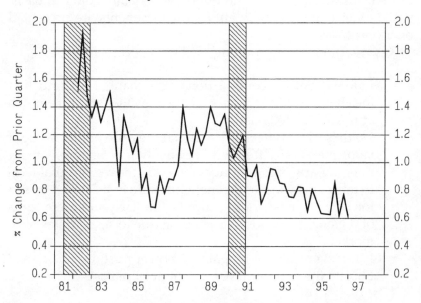

TABLE 11–1   Employment Cost Index
1982 Q2–1996 Q4, Quarter-to-Quarter Percentage Change

Phase	Historic Low	Normal Bounds			Historic High	Series Characteristics	
		Normal Low	Average	Normal High		Standard Deviation	Share of Total Observations
Recession	1.0% in 1990Q4	1.2%	1.4%	1.5%	1.9% in 1982Q3	0.3 pp.	10.2%
Recovery	0.7% in 1992Q2	1.0%	1.2%	1.3%	1.5% in 1984Q1	0.3 pp.	22.0%
Expansion	0.6% in 1996Q3	0.8%	1.0%	1.1%	1.4% in 1989Q3	0.2 pp.	67.8%
Slow Phase	0.6% in 1995Q4	0.9%	1.0%	1.1%	1.4% in 1989Q3	0.3 pp.	39.0%
Rapid Phase	0.6% in 1996Q3	0.8%	0.9%	1.0%	1.4% in 1988Q1	0.2 pp.	28.8%
All Phases	0.6% in 1996Q3	0.9%	1.0%	1.2%	1.9% in 1982Q3	0.3 pp.	100.0%

Relationship with Other Series

The ECI is conceptually superior to the more timely average hourly earnings data, which are contained in the employment report. Average hourly earnings provide an imperfect monthly window of wage costs alone. Yet financial market participants are increasingly recognizing the technical limitation of those monthly data (especially since public officials are downplaying the data). For example, the average hourly earnings data are affected by changing employment shares from month to month, but the ECI is not. The average hourly earnings data do not account for irregular bonuses or excluded retroactive pay, nor do they account for employer-paid benefits or Social Security taxes, while the ECI accounts for those factors.

Chapter 12

Federal Budget

General Description

The federal budget release tallies the federal government's receipts and outlays. It is a rolling snapshot of the government's budget deficit, and its importance to the financial markets, on a release basis, is usually very limited.

Economic Indicator Information at a Glance

Market Significance	Low
Typical Release Time	2:00 PM Eastern Time Around the 15th Business Day of the Month
Released By	Treasury Department
Period Covered	Prior Month
Web Site	http://www.fms.treas.gov/mts

The U.S. government's fiscal year runs from October to September. Within a fiscal year, each month's result should be considered distinctly different from other months' results since there is a strong seasonality to monthly budget numbers. Thus, April's results should be compared with the results of previous Aprils, not with deficits in March or May. The main reason for making these kinds of comparisons is tax receipts, which flow into the Treasury at prescribed times. April is the most obvious month since it is when individual tax payments are made. But June, September, and December are months in which corporate tax payments are made, and surpluses are also possible.

There also can be variations on the expenditure side, but generally speaking it is receipts that create volatility in the monthly budget numbers. Monthly receipts can fluctuate as much as 100 percent. In fiscal 1996 the average absolute month-to-month change in receipts was 42 percent, while expenditures had an average absolute change of only 9 percent.

One final aspect of the federal budget is the usage of *on-budget* and *off-budget* totals. Off-budget items are receipts and outlays that are excluded from budget totals by law. The key components are the two Social Security trust funds and the Postal Ser-

---

BOX 12–1   Commonly Used Budget Terms

Baseline Budget: The budget based on extant legislation remaining in place. It is then used as the standard against which one measures the effect that changes in revenue and expenditure legislation would have on the budget.

Budget Resolution: A resolution, or a set of guidelines, of the House and Senate that outlines Congress's budget plans for the next five years. It is not law. The resolution is put into effect via specific revenue and expenditure legislation.

Discretionary Spending: Programs for which Congress annually appropriates funds. These functions bear the brunt of budget cuts.

Entitlements: Any person or entity that meets the established legal requirements for entitlement programs can receive payments. Appropriations are set by Congress only to the extent that Congress changes the legal requirements for receiving benefits. Social Security and Medicare are entitlement programs.

Off-Budget: Spending or revenues not part of the budget totals as legally defined, especially regarding the Budget Enforcement Act of 1990. Two off-budget programs are Social Security trust funds and the Postal Service.

vice fund. The published federal budget numbers, and those cited in most analyses, combine both on- and off-budget results. In fiscal 1996 the total year's deficit was $107.36 bn., comprised of a $174.3 bn. on budget deficit and a $67 bn. off-budget surplus.

Analyzing the Data

An individual month's deficit usually carries little market significance. Even the fixed-income markets, whose literal existence or center of gravity (for non-Treasury issuance) is based on U.S. Treasury debt, find minimal trading value in the government's monthly fiscal tally.

This is not to say that financial markets lack a deep concern about the size of the central government's deficit. Any news that would significantly alter the outlook for the deficit would have a dramatic effect on all financial markets. The passage of what is commonly called the Gramm-Rudman Act in late 1985, an act that purportedly set fixed deficit targets that culminated in a balanced budget, is a good example of how important deficit news can be to financial markets. Although a fall in oil prices contributed to the constructive tone of the markets, long-term interest rates fell about 100 basis points between October 1985, when the Gramm-Rudman Act was passed, and the end of 1985. Stock prices also responded positively, rising a sharp 11.3 percent (S&P 500) in the final two months of the year.

The markets' ambivalence to the monthly deficit numbers is because there is little value added in each month's tally. Fiscal-year estimates of the deficit are made by the Office of Management and Budget and the Congressional Budget Office, and they are well known by market participants. The Treasury also provides a quarterly estimate of its new cash needs, an estimate that incorporates the Treasury's latest estimate of the deficit. Certainly these estimates of the deficit change as the fiscal year progresses, but it is a gradual process in which one month's deficit does not significantly affect the full year's tally. If there is one technical point to be aware of when the budget is released, it is the effect the calendar can have on the expenditure side. Specifically, significant monthly payments are made by the government on the first and third days of each month. Chief among them are Social Security payments, retirement benefits, and payroll expenditures. If these days fall on a weekend or a holiday, the payments are moved up to the prior business day. The most frequent occurrence is when the first of the month falls on a weekend. Then the payments would be made on the final business day of the prior month, bloating that month's deficit and reducing the subsequent month's expenditure tally. The effect is around $7 bn. The largest payments are Social Security payments, on the third of each month. Although not as common, it can happen that the first three days of a month fall on a combined weekend and holiday. In those instances the effect on each month's deficit can be as large as $30 bn.

For a discussion of the federal budget and the CPI, see Box 12-2.

BOX 12–2   The Federal Budget and the CPI

Much has been written about the upward bias in the Consumer Price Index. Although estimates of this overstatement of inflation vary widely, the effect on the budget outlook could be significant. The Congressional Budget Office has estimated the effect a reduction of 1 percent in the CPI would have on the federal budget. The biggest effect is from a reduction in payments that are adjusted annually by the change in the CPI. Social Security payments are the largest program that is adjusted this way, and reduced payments here account for three-quarters of the expenditure effect. After 10 years smaller payments are about $45 bn. lower than they would have been without the lower CPI. The final year's effect for all other benefit programs would be about $19 bn.

There would also be an effect on the revenue side since personal income tax brackets, the personal exemption, and the standard deduction are indexed to inflation. By the 10th year, the CBO estimates that revenues would be about $44 bn. higher with the lower CPI. In the final year of the 10-year period, the deficit would be about $140 bn. lower (assumed lower debt-service payments account for the remaining difference) than it otherwise would have been.

TABLE 12–1 Federal Government Receipts
January 1968–July 1997, Year-over-Year Percentage Change

Phase	Historic Low	Normal Bounds			Historic High	Series Characteristics	
		Normal Low	Average	Normal High		Standard Deviation	Share of Total Observations
Recession	−10.2% in Oct 1982	1.4%	5.4%	9.5%	19.7% in Mar 1975	8.1 pp.	16.1%
Recovery	−33.5% in May 1975	−0.1%	6.2%	12.5%	77.3% in May 1976	12.6 pp.	23.7%
Expansion	−28.0% in Mar 1968	5.1%	11.2%	17.4%	83.0% in Jul 1968	12.3 pp.	60.2%
Slow Phase	−5.0% in Mar 1990	5.9%	9.4%	13.0%	30.1% in Jan 1969	7.1 pp.	30.6%
Rapid Phase	−28.0% in Mar 1968	5.3%	13.2%	21.1%	83.0% in Jul 1968	15.8 pp.	29.6%
All Phases	−33.5% in May 1975	3.1%	9.1%	15.2%	83.0% in Jul 1968	12.1 pp.	100.0%

TABLE 12–2 Federal Government Expenditures
January 1968–July 1997, Year-over-Year Percentage Change

Phase	Historic Low	Normal Bounds			Historic High	Series Characteristics	
		Normal Low	Average	Normal High		Standard Deviation	Share of Total Observations
Recession	−22.3% in Jan 1982	5.1%	11.1%	17.1%	39.4% in Dec 1974	12.0 pp.	16.1%
Recovery	−14.3% in Aug 1992	4.0%	10.1%	16.2%	59.6% in Sep 1980	12.2 pp.	23.7%
Expansion	−30.8% in Jan 1993	2.6%	8.8%	15.0%	62.9% in Apr 1968	12.4 pp.	60.2%
Slow Phase	−23.9% in Sep 1979	2.4%	7.5%	12.6%	45.6% in Sep 1985	10.2 pp.	30.6%
Rapid Phase	−30.8% in Jan 1993	3.5%	10.6%	17.8%	62.9% in Apr 1968	14.3 pp.	29.6%
All Phases	−30.8% in Jan 1993	3.4%	9.5%	15.7%	62.9% in Apr 1968	12.3 pp.	100.0%

Government Finances over the Business Cycle

The cyclicality of the federal budget deficit is very strong, and it is especially noticeable during recessions. Then the deficit increases sharply. This pronounced change is most evident on the receipt side. The average year-to-year increase in federal government receipts is only 5.4 percent in recessions, compared with 6.2 percent during recoveries and 11.2 percent during expansions. The large jump in the growth of receipts during expansions, historically, has been due as much to higher inflation rates as to a greater number of individuals being on payrolls. Expenditures show much less of a cyclical pattern. In fact, the average growth of expenditures is greater during recessions, +11.1%, than during expansions (+8.8%), a fact accounted for by the countercyclically nature of fiscal policy.

Chapter 13

Gross Domestic Product

General Description

The National Income and Product Accounts (NIPA) is the formal name for the gross domestic product (GDP) report. NIPA is the hallmark of the Commerce Department's effort to provide a comprehensive accounting of product demand and of the factors of production. Built as a system of interlocking sector accounts, the GDP report provides the most comprehensive reading of the nation's economic health. There are three basic sets of quarterly data, which are revised on a monthly basis, contained within the NIPA report: current-dollar estimates of GDP and its components, constant or inflation-adjusted estimates of GDP and its components, and, finally, output and price indexes for the same con-

Economic Indicator Information at a Glance

Market Significance	Very High for Initial Estimate of Quarter but Progressively Less Important for Revisions
Typical Release Time	8:30 AM Eastern Time About the 20th Business Day of the Month
Released By	Commerce Department Bureau of Economic Analysis
Period Covered	Prior Quarter
Web Site	http://www.doc.gov/

cepts. The market's focus of attention is the percentage change of the inflation-adjusted data, which is expressed in annualized growth rate terms (see Box 13-1), with the sole exception of the corporate profits data, which are presented on a quarter-to-quarter basis because of their volatility. Given that these are the most comprehensive data on the economy, they naturally command a high degree of interest in the financial markets.

Analyzing the Data

The GDP report contains two estimates for real GDP, which are constrained to be equal. The first estimate is built from the

---

BOX 13–1   Calculating an Annualized Growth Rate

The convention used to express growth rates for GDP and its components is to annualize the quarterly growth rate, which is calculated as

$$\text{Rate} = ((\text{GDP[current period]}/\text{GDP[prior period]})^4 - 1) \times 100$$

where the current- and prior-period data are in level terms (billions of dollars). For example, if the first-quarter level of real GDP was \$7,094.4 billion and the fourth-quarter level was \$6,993.3 billion, the annualized change would be computed as

$$((7{,}094.4/6{,}993.3)^4 - 1) \times 100 = (1.014^4 - 1) \times 100$$
$$= (1.059 - 1) \times 100 = 5.9\%$$

Economists generally express the annual growth rate as the current year's fourth quarter over the prior year's fourth quarter (denoted by Q4 over Q4 or Q4/Q4) as a way of measuring change within the year. An alternative and superior presentation would be to average growth rates (using a geometric mean) during the year—which is generally not done because of the added effort.

Sometimes the Q4/Q4 growth rates can be substantially different from the calendar-year annual growth rates. It is even possible to have a very different impression viewing growth on a Q4/Q4 basis versus on a calendar-year growth rate basis. For example, the 1990 calendar-year real GDP growth was 1.2 percent while the 1990 Q4/Q4 growth rate was −0.2 percent.

final demand categories, such as consumption (*C*), investment (*I*), government spending (*G*), and net exports (*NE*). The second estimate is derived from the income side of the accounting ledger, which includes personal income (*PI*) and corporate profits (*PR*). In its most basic form, GDP = *C* + *I* + *G* + *NE* = *PI* + *PR*. Although that is the basic national income accounts identity, there are numerous refinements to it in practice, and a statistical discrepancy is added to the income side to force equality between the two measurement approaches. In 1996, for example, personal consumption expenditures accounted for 68.0 percent of nominal or current-dollar GDP, which was the largest single component, while compensation of employees accounted for 58.7 percent of nominal GDP, which was the largest component of the income ledger.

There are three sequential estimates of GDP—which is the output of goods and services produced by labor and property located in the United States, along with its components for any given quarter and annual benchmark revisions to account for more comprehensive and late available data. The first estimate of real GDP for the quarter is released about 20 business days after the completion of the given quarter. Subsequent to that initial or "advance" estimate, those quarterly data are revised twice over the next two months based on increasingly more complete underlying or source data, which yield the "preliminary" and "final" estimates of GDP. Following the second or "final" revision, the Commerce Department does not revise the GDP data for that quarter, even if there are known historical revisions to the underlying data used to estimate them, until an annual benchmark update is done, which is generally in July of each year. With the benchmark revision, the Commerce Department updates historical data for a period of three years, implements methodology improvements, if any, and computes new seasonal factors. More comprehensive methodology revisions to GDP occur less frequently, and those revisions could extend back to 1929, when the annual data start.

The entire set of NIPA tables is composed of 138 annual, quarterly, and monthly tables, which are grouped into nine categories: (1) National Product and Income, (2) Personal Income and Outlays, (3) Government Receipts and Expenditures, (4) Foreign Transactions, (5) Saving and Investment, (6) Income, Employment, and Product by Industry, (7) Quantity and Price Indexes, (8) Supplemental Tables—which include reconciliation tables between various sets of data—and (9) Not Seasonally Adjusted Tables. Only once a year does the Commerce Department release unadjusted data, and those data tend to be released with a lag.

For definitions of frequently used national income terms, see Box 13-2. The keys to interpreting the national income report include:

- Keep in mind that, currently, about **every \$18 bn. change in real GDP is equivalent to a 1 percentage point change in real GDP** on a quarter-to-quarter annualized basis. This rule of thumb is particularly useful to quickly assess the

---

BOX 13–2   Glossary of Key National Income Terms

Output and Price Measures

Gross National Product: GNP measures the value of goods and services produced by the labor and property supplied by U.S. residents.

Gross Domestic Product: In 1991, the Commerce Department shifted its focus from real GNP to real GDP. GDP measures the value of goods and services produced within the borders of the United States.

Gross Domestic Purchases: This is a measure of domestic demand—regardless of whether demand is met from a foreign source; it is defined as gross domestic product less net exports and is simply described as "purchases by U.S. residents of goods and services wherever produced."

Command-Basis GNP: Command-basis real GNP arose out of a conceptual problem in deflating imports and exports separately. For example, if the foreign exchange value of the dollar declined and import prices rose faster than export prices, then that could boost reported output. To counter this problem, the Commerce Department began to publish a measure of real GDP, which deflated exports and imports by the same implicit price deflator for imports.

Chain-Weighted Price Index: A chain-weighted price index is a geometric growth rate formulation that incorporates quantity weights from two adjacent years. The chain-weight concept is a cross between the implicit price index—whose quantity weights vary from quarter to quarter—and a fixed-weight price index— whose quantity weights are fixed at some point in time. Today, the Commerce Department no longer publishes the fixed-weight price indexes since the chain-weighted index is essentially an "evolving fixed-weight index," and the department downplays the implicit price indexes for conceptual reasons. For comparison, in 1996, the GDP chain-weighted price index rose by 2.1 percent, while the GDP implicit price index rose by 2.0 percent.

Through the Profit Maze

Overview: Which measure of profitability is most important? According to our analysis, it all depends on your purpose. But the simple answer is that pretax corporate profits are the best national income measure of shareholder earnings growth, while the operating profits measure is the best indicator of stock price growth. (See the table below.) Here are some terms to put the various measures into perspective.

Profits from Current Production: This measure, also known as corporate profits with inventory valuation adjustment (IVA) and capital consumption adjustment (CCAdj), or sometimes referred to as *pretax economic profits* or *operating profits,* is corporate profits before taxes and generally is net of company receipts and expenses as defined by federal tax law. The main differences between the National Income Account (NIA) concept and the treatment under federal tax laws are: (1) NIA receipts exclude capital gains and dividends received, (2) NIA receipts exclude depletion and capital loss, (3) NIA inventories are valued at replacement cost, and (4) NIA depreciation is adjusted for consistent accounting practices and valued at current replacement cost. By definition, profits from current production equal pretax profits plus IVA and CCAdj.

Corporate Profits with IVA: This measure is similar to profits from current production except it reflects depreciation account methods used for federal tax returns. Industry profits are shown this way because industry capital consumption adjustments are not available.

Evaluating National Income Measures of Corporate Profitability

Profit Measure	Economic Significance	Relationship with Stockholder Earnings	Relative Score	Rank	Relationship with Stock Prices	Relative Score	Rank
1. "Operating" Profit	Best gauge of profits from current production	Ranked as third lowest	58	4	Best gauge of stock prices	100	1
2. Pretax Profit	Measures income from current production but includes "paper" inventory profits	Best gauge of stockholder earnings of the six measures evaluated	100	1	Relationship weakens sharply, in third place	27	3
3. Aftertax Profits	Same as pretax profits but excludes tax payments	Close runner-up for best performance, with second highest score	97	2	Extremely weak relationship with stock prices	7	6
4. Economic Profits	Same as operating profits but excludes tax payments	Ranked as second lowest	30	5	Second best measure to watch	84	2
5. Net Cashflow	Conceptually, the best indicator of future capital spending	Lowest relationship with stockholder earnings	21	6	Ranked in fourth place	20	4
6. Real Aftertax Profits	Same as aftertax profits but adjusted for inflation	In third place, but still quite high	94	3	A low fifth-place reading	16	5

Note: Scoring system based on best correlation between National Income and Product Accounts (NIPA) profit measures and shareholder earnings and stock prices based on the S&P 500 and calculated on a year-over-year percentage change basis from 1960 to 1992. The series with the highest explanatory power was set equal to 100 (an arbitrary scale); all other series are ranked by their relative performance to the highest one.

Pretax Profits: This measure also is known as *book profits* and represents profits used in federal income tax returns. It equals the sum of taxes, dividends, and retained earnings.

Profits Tax Liability: This is the tax liability paid to all governmental units (federal, state, and local) on corporate income. These taxes are calculated on an accrual basis.

Profits Aftertax: This measure is pretax profits minus profit tax liabilities.

Dividends: These are payments in cash or other assets, excluding the corporation's own stock, made to U.S. residents from domestic and foreign companies. These payments exclude dividends received by U.S. corporations.

Undistributed Corporate Profits: This measure is more commonly known as *retained earnings* and is pretax profits minus taxes and dividends.

Inventory Valuation Adjustment (IVA): This is the difference between the cost of inventories as recorded in federal tax returns and inventories valued at current replacement cost.

Capital Consumption Adjustment (CCAdj): This adjustment converts depreciation as recorded for tax purposes to a consistent accounting basis valued at current replacement cost.

Shareholder Profits: Composites of corporate earnings, such as those aggregate measures reported by Standard & Poor's or Dow Jones are operating profits minus depreciation, taxes, and nonoperating expenses as recorded in company income statements.

Economic Profits: This measure is after-tax profits plus the IVA and the CCAdj.

Net Cashflow with Adjustments: This measure equals depreciation plus retained earnings with IVA and CCAdj and represents an internally generated source of funds for business, which would be supplemented by external financing (mainly from funds raised in the credit markets). A large increase (or decrease) in internal funds will tend to create less (or more) borrowings by business, assuming business faces a steady demand for funds to purchase capital expenditures or inventories.

impact on real GDP growth of the change in the real trade balance or the change in business inventory investment, which is expressed in dollar terms in the report.

- Separately view the real GDP growth rate as **final sales** and the **inventory change.** If the change in inventories was large, then ask yourself whether it was more likely involuntary or voluntary accumulation or decumulation. The answer to that question could have significant implications for future growth prospects.

- Focus upon the **GDP chain-weighted price index** as the most comprehensive measure of prices in the economy. It is a more comprehensive price indicator than the CPI or PPI since it covers the consumer, business, government, and net exports. Additionally, the chain-weighted price index for gross domestic purchases less food and energy is an all-inclusive "core" inflation measure, which is compiled by the Commerce Department, but it currently commands little financial market attention.

- Look at the pace of **exports** and **imports.** Has the pace strengthened or weakened? Is the nominal trade deficit dramatically different from the real deficit? If so, this might suggest two things: (1) the foreign exchange impact on trade is substantial (which is referred to as the *J-curve effect*—when a change in the dollar's value inflates/deflates the nominal deficit through higher/lower prices before it impacts the volume of imports/exports), and/or (2) the price of an imported good, such as oil, inflates the nominal deficit but does not change the volume imports.

- Evaluate the strength of real **capital spending.** Look at producers' durable equipment—which includes computers, vehicles, and other equipment—and nonresidential structures. Often the two major components, producers' durable equipment and structures, are moving differently. Also take a look at nominal producers' durable equipment versus real producers' durable equipment since rapidly declining computer prices have a big impact on pushing up the real value of spending.

- Keep an eye on the **savings rate.** Recognize, however, that the savings rate is conceptually flawed, since it assumes that the entire purchase price of a car, for example, is offset against disposable income in the current period instead of

• what might be a fraction of the purchase price as a monthly payment on a loan or lease for that vehicle. Still, it provides a benchmark for determining how strong or weak future consumption might be.

- Do not overlook **net cashflow**—which is calculated from the corporate profits data. A strong increase or a sharp decline in the net cashflow has implications for the credit borrowing needs of companies.

- Be aware that, generally, **real GDP revisions** become increasingly unimportant to the financial markets. The average revision from the advanced report to the final was 0.6 percentage point between 1981 and 1992, with two-thirds of the revisions between –0.6 percentage point lower to +0.9 percentage point higher.

Real GDP through Time and over the Business Cycle

One of the most striking secular changes to real GDP growth occurred in the early 1980s. The volatility of real GDP showed a marked narrowing. The significance of that change should not be overlooked since less volatility suggests that forecasting the future path of growth is likely to be less fraught with error. Reduced economic volatility also means that business planning is easier, which further dampens future volatility through the capital spending channel. Superimposed on that secular pattern is the business cycle. Over the course of the business cycle between 1951 and 1996, real GDP has contracted by an average of 0.8 percent during recessions, increased by an average of 3.8 percent per quarter during the return-to-previous-peak phase, and grew by a 4.3 percent during the expansion. There also is a marked difference in growth rates during the slow- and fast-growth phases of the expansion. During the slow-growth phase of the expansion, real GDP grew by an average of 3.2 percent, while it has risen by 5.5 percent per quarter during the fast-growth phase. (See Figure 13-1 and Tables 13-1 to 13-4.)

Chain-Weighted Price and Quantity Indexes

In late 1995, the Bureau of Economic Analysis of the U.S. Department of Commerce introduced new measures of output and prices, which are calculated as "chain-weighted" indexes. Al-

FIGURE 13–1   Real GDP and Inventories

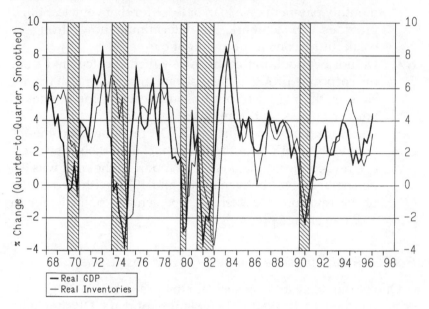

though those indexes were ultimately supposed to replace the inflation-adjusted dollar figures for real GDP and its components, the Commerce Department decided to continue reporting the real-dollar figures in addition to the chain-weighted indexes due to some of the criticism of those indexes.

The chain-weighted index idea is simple and even appealing on the surface, although the formulation is not without some limitation. One benefit of the chain-weighted quantity index is

TABLE 13–1   Aftertax Corporate Profits
1951 Q2–1996 Q4, Quarter-to-Quarter Percentage Change

Phase	Historic Low	Normal Bounds			Historic High	Series Characteristics	
		Normal Low	Average	Normal High		Standard Deviation	Share of Total Observations
Recession	–21.6% in 1953Q4	–6.7%	–2.9%	1.0%	14.9% in 1954Q1	7.8 pp.	18.6%
Recovery	–12.7% in 1992Q3	1.9%	5.0%	8.1%	20.7% in 1975Q3	6.2 pp.	24.6%
Expansion	–18.7% in 1986Q1	–1.1%	1.8%	4.6%	17.4% in 1987Q1	5.7 pp.	56.8%
Slow Phase	–18.7% in 1986Q1	–2.9%	–0.3%	2.2%	9.9% in 1960Q1	5.1 pp.	34.4%
Rapid Phase	–14.9% in 1951Q2	0.3%	3.2%	6.2%	17.4% in 1987Q1	5.9 pp.	22.4%
All Phases	–21.6% in 1953Q4	–1.7%	1.8%	5.2%	20.7% in 1975Q3	6.8 pp.	100.0%

TABLE 13–2　Real GDP
1951 Q2–1996 Q4, Quarter-to-Quarter Annualized Percentage Change

Phase	Historic Low	Normal Bounds			Historic High	Series Characteristics	
		Normal Low	Average	Normal High		Standard Deviation	Share of Total Observations
Recession	−10.8% in 1958Q1	−3.6%	−1.7%	0.3%	4.9% in 1981Q3	3.8 pp.	18.6%
Recovery	−3.9% in 1970Q4	3.5%	5.4%	7.2%	11.8% in 1955Q1	3.7 pp.	24.6%
Expansion	−3.5% in 1981Q2	2.1%	3.8%	5.4%	16.1% in 1978Q2	3.4 pp.	56.8%
Slow Phase	−2.4% in 1960Q2	1.3%	2.5%	3.8%	8.9% in 1960Q1	2.5 pp.	34.4%
Rapid Phase	−3.5% in 1981Q2	2.9%	4.7%	6.5%	16.1% in 1978Q2	3.6 pp.	22.4%
All Phases	−10.8% in 1958Q1	1.1%	3.2%	5.3%	16.1% in 1978Q2	4.2 pp.	100.0%

that it allows the quantity-of-purchase weights to vary over time. Hence, real output is based on more contemporaneous spending patterns. Another benefit of the chain-weighted index approach is that cyclical fluctuations in real output will be unaffected by future shifts in base periods. Historically, these revisions have tended to diminish the depth of earlier recessions and have caused a rewriting of economic history.

On the other hand, several problems with these data are likely to creep into the analysis over time. First, **real output is likely to be more volatile.** Consider the example contained in Table 13-5. A fixed-weighted quantity index is compared with a chain-weighted quantity index. Over those periods for this example, the fixed-weighted quantity index had a standard deviation of 38 percentage points while the chain-weighted measure varied by 86 percentage points. The Commerce Department, of course, is aware of this problem. Between 1959 and 1995, the average

TABLE 13–3　Chain-Weighted GDP Price Index
1951 Q2–1996 Q4, Quarter-to-Quarter Annualized Percentage Change

Phase	Historic Low	Normal Bounds			Historic High	Series Characteristics	
		Normal Low	Average	Normal High		Standard Deviation	Share of Total Observations
Recession	0.7% in 1961Q1	3.7%	5.4%	7.0%	13.0% in 1974Q4	3.4 pp.	18.6%
Recovery	−0.2% in 1954Q3	2.5%	3.9%	5.3%	11.2% in 1980Q4	2.8 pp.	24.6%
Expansion	0.2% in 1953Q1	2.5%	3.5%	4.6%	9.7% in 1980Q1	2.2 pp.	56.8%
Slow Phase	0.2% in 1952Q1	2.7%	3.8%	4.9%	9.7% in 1980Q1	2.2 pp.	34.4%
Rapid Phase	0.2% in 1953Q1	2.3%	3.4%	4.4%	8.7% in 1978Q2	2.1 pp.	22.4%
All Phases	−0.2% in 1954Q3	2.6%	3.9%	5.2%	13.0% in 1974Q4	2.6 pp.	100.0%

TABLE 13–4   Real Nonfarm Inventory
1951 Q2–1996 Q4, Quarter-to-Quarter Annualized Percentage Change

		Normal Bounds				Series Characteristics	
Phase	Historic Low	Normal Low	Average	Normal High	Historic High	Standard Deviation	Share of Total Observations
Recession	–6.2% in 1958Q1	–2.2%	–0.1%	2.0%	9.6% in 1973Q4	4.2 pp.	18.6%
Recovery	–6.1% in 1982Q4	–0.1%	2.0%	4.1%	11.4% in 1984Q1	4.2 pp.	24.6%
Expansion	–3.5% in 1952Q2	3.2%	4.8%	6.4%	18.7% in 1951Q2	3.2 pp.	56.8%
Slow Phase	–3.5% in 1952Q2	3.0%	4.8%	6.6%	18.7% in 1951Q2	3.7 pp.	34.4%
Rapid Phase	–1.8% in 1986Q4	3.5%	5.1%	6.7%	18.7% in 1951Q2	3.2 pp.	22.4%
All Phases	–6.2% in 1958Q1	1.5%	3.5%	5.5%	18.7% in 1951Q2	3.9 pp.	100.0%

growth rate gap between the two measures—real GDP and the chain-weighted GDP index—was 0.2 percentage point, with a smaller gap during recessions and a larger gap during expansions. So over extended periods the story line should be the same, but over shorter periods there can be more of a gap. For example, in the second quarter real GDP rose 0.5 percent while the chain-weighted measure fell 0.2 percent.

One problem with the chain-weighted quantity indexes is **lack of additivity.** To circumvent this problem and for the convenience of data users, the Commerce Department separately computes real-dollar value statistics derived from the chain-weighted indexes. Unfortunately, computing real-dollar value statistics sepa-

TABLE 13–5   Comparison of Chain-Weighted and Fixed-Weighted Indexes

Months→		1	2	3	4	5
Item 1	Quantity	12	12	12	12	12
	Price	$ 6	$ 3	$ 2	$ 2	$20
Item 2	Quantity	4	2	3	1	10
	Price	$ 7	$10	$15	$30	$ 7
Differences in Quantity Index Forms						
Fixed-Weighted Index		100.0	86.0	93.0	79.0	142.0
% Change			–0.1%	0.0%	–0.1%	0.8%
Chain-Weighted Index		100.0	79.6	97.7	50.5	138.7
% Change			–0.2%	0.2%	–0.4%	1.7%

rately from the indexes for the totals and individually for the components yields "residuals"—the dollar difference between the total and the sum of the most detailed components per NIPA table. Each NIPA table has its own unique "residual" line, and the Commerce Department warns that "the residual tends to become larger as one moves further from the base period." Some of those residuals already are especially large, for example, the 1996 residual for real private fixed investment (NIPA Table 5.5) was about $22 bn., or 2 percent of real private fixed investment.

Computing and Understanding Quantity and Price Indexes

The Commerce Department's formal primer for using and understanding the quantity and price indexes says:

> To compute the quantity indexes, changes in the quantities of individual goods and services are weighted by their prices. (Quantity changes for GDP are often referred to as changes in "real GDP.") For the price indexes, changes in the prices for individual goods and services are weighted by quantities produced. (In practice, the current-dollar value and price indexes for most GDP components are determined largely using data from federal government surveys, and the real values of these components are calculated by deflation at the most detailed level for which all the required data are available.)

In reality, however, financial market participants do not care whether real GDP is calculated based on an index or a dollar figure. However, it is important to keep in mind some of the other caveats in using these data.

As the Commerce Department explained:

> BEA prepares measures of real GDP and its components in a dollar-denominated form, designated "chained (1992) dollar estimates." These estimates . . . are computed by multiplying the 1992 current-dollar value of GDP, or of a GDP component, by the corresponding quantity index number. For example, if a current-dollar GDP component equaled $100 in 1992 and if real output for this component increased by 10 percent in 1993, then the "chained (1992) dollar" value of this component in 1993 would be $110 ($100 × 1.10). Note

that percentage changes in the chained (1992) dollar estimates and the percentage changes calculated from the quantity indexes are identical, except for small differences due to rounding.

Standard View of Real GDP

The standard view of real GDP is through the final demand side, as shown in Table 13-6. The various final demand components—consumption, investment, government spending, and foreign trade—are discussed, monitored, and forecasted. Moreover, monthly data are available to build up to the quarterly averages of the final demand—such as monthly consumer spending data, monthly capital spending indicators, and so forth.

Nonstandard Views of Real GDP

There are various alternative ways to view the components of real GDP (see Table 13-7.) In addition to the typical final demand categories that dominate the news reporting and the way the market participants react to the data, the Commerce Department provides several "other" frameworks. Real GDP could be viewed as the sum of goods plus services plus structures (that is, by major type of product as found in NIPA Table 1.4). Or real GDP could be viewed as the sum of major sectors—business, households and institutions, and general government (NIPA Table 1.8). It is possible to view real GDP as the sum of some of its major components, such as motor vehicles, computers, and all other (with a bit of calculation). On that basis, for example, it is possible to see the impact of the computer boom on real GDP growth. Computer output accounted for 4.4 percent of real GDP in 1996 but contributed, nearly 40 percent of the overall 1996 real GDP growth.

Key Source Data: Tracking Changes and Estimating Current Quarter Growth

Since the National Income Accounts are derived from a host of data sources, market participants tend to follow the unfolding of the current quarter through the "key source" data that are used to calculate GDP. These key source data include all or part of

TABLE 13-6 Real GDP and Its Components, 1981-1996

	1981	1982	1983	1984	1985	1986	1987	1988	1989	1990	1991	1992	1993	1994	1995	1996
	Percent change from preceding year															
Real gross domestic product	2.3	-2.1	4.0	7.0	3.6	3.1	2.9	3.8	3.4	1.2	-.9	2.7	2.3	3.5	2.0	2.4
Personal consumption expenditures	1.2	1.2	5.2	5.2	4.7	4.0	3.1	3.9	2.3	1.7	-.6	2.8	2.8	3.1	2.3	2.5
Durable goods	1.2	-.1	14.7	14.5	9.7	9.0	1.5	6.3	2.6	-.6	-6.4	5.8	7.3	7.2	3.2	5.4
Nondurable goods	.9	.6	2.9	3.5	2.3	3.2	1.9	2.8	2.3	1.0	-1.0	1.5	2.0	3.1	2.3	1.4
Services	1.5	1.9	4.7	4.1	5.0	3.2	4.2	4.0	2.3	2.6	.8	2.9	2.4	2.2	2.2	2.4
Gross private domestic fixed investment	1.9	-7.6	7.2	16.5	4.8	.7	-.7	2.4	1.7	-3.1	-8.0	5.7	6.8	10.1	6.0	6.8
Nonresidential	5.3	-4.4	-1.7	17.3	6.2	-3.5	-1.1	4.4	4.0	-.6	-6.4	1.9	6.4	9.8	9.5	7.4
Structures	7.9	-1.5	-10.4	14.3	7.3	-10.8	-3.6	.5	2.2	1.1	-10.7	-6.8	-1.7	1.5	7.3	4.9
Producers' durable equipment	3.7	-6.4	4.6	19.2	5.5	1.0	.3	6.4	5.0	-1.5	-4.1	6.2	10.0	13.2	10.4	8.3
Residential	-8.0	-18.2	41.1	14.6	1.4	12.0	11.0	-2.0	-3.7	-9.3	-12.3	16.6	7.6	10.8	-2.3	5.3
Exports of goods and services	1.2	-7.1	-2.6	8.3	2.7	7.4	11.0	15.9	11.7	8.5	6.3	6.6	2.9	8.2	8.9	6.5
Imports of goods and services	2.6	-1.3	12.6	24.3	6.5	8.4	6.1	3.9	3.9	3.9	-.7	7.5	9.2	12.0	8.0	6.4
Government consumption expenditures and gross investment	.7	1.3	2.8	3.1	6.1	5.1	2.7	1.3	2.8	3.0	.6	.5	-.2	-.1	.0	.8
Federal	4.2	3.2	5.4	2.4	6.9	4.6	3.1	-1.8	1.3	2.0	-.5	-2.1	-3.6	-3.8	-3.6	-1.1
National defense	5.4	6.9	5.7	4.0	7.5	5.2	4.0	-.9	-1.0	.0	-1.0	-5.5	-5.4	-5.2	-5.2	-1.8
Nondefense	1.1	-5.9	4.6	-2.2	5.1	2.8	.1	-4.9	9.2	8.0	1.1	7.2	1.0	-.7	-.2	.3
State and local	-2.0	-.3	.7	3.8	5.3	5.5	2.4	3.9	4.0	3.8	1.4	2.4	2.2	2.5	2.4	2.0
Addenda:																
Final sales of domestic product	1.1	-.9	3.7	5.0	4.6	3.5	2.6	4.1	3.0	1.6	-.7	2.5	2.1	2.9	2.4	2.7
Gross domestic purchases price index	9.2	5.9	3.8	3.5	3.2	2.6	3.4	3.6	4.2	4.5	3.7	2.8	2.5	2.2	2.4	2.1

TABLE 13–7   An Alternative View of Real GDP (Calendar-Year % Change)

Year	Real GDP	Real Computer Output*	Real Motor Vehicle Output	Real GDP Less Vehicles and Computers*
1989	3.4	9.5	0.8	3.3
1990	1.3	1.2	−8.4	1.7
1991	−1.0	3.6	−11.0	−0.7
1992	2.7	15.2	12.9	2.1
1993	2.3	13.0	6.6	1.9
1994	3.5	18.6	11.9	2.7
1995	2.0	21.4	−4.1	1.7
1996	2.4	27.0	−2.6	1.7
1996 Share	*100.0%*	*4.4%*	*3.3%*	*92.3%*

* Calculated by authors.

reularly published data, such as nonautomotive, nonbuilding retail sales, unit vehicle sales, business inventories, nondefense capital goods shipments, construction spending, foreign trade balances, and so on. Each new piece of information is assembled by the Commerce Department and private sector economists into the GDP package. For the initial release of the real GDP data, the Commerce Department must make some assumptions about missing monthly data, such as the latest month's export and import data.

Once the quarter's real GDP is initially estimated and released by the Commerce Department, those same key source data provide a glimpse into likely revisions to the current quarter's GDP tally as new information is released and replaces the Commerce Department's assumptions or as data are revised by the source agency. Hence, one often hears comments such as the Commerce Department assumed a trade gap of some number and it turned out to be something else, which means real GDP is likely to be revised higher/lower.

Creating Quarterly Estimates When No Data Exist

Often data for NIPA simply do not exist on a quarterly basis or are not available with sufficient currency on an annual or quarterly basis (such as the Internal Revenue Service data from the *Statistics of Income*). Under those circumstances, the Bureau of Economic Analysis will estimate the data for the current GDP report. The bureau uses four types of estimation methods[1] within the accounts: (1) "commodity flow," (2) "retail control," (3) "perpetual inventory," and (4) "fiscal year analysis." However, from a market perspective it is not necessary to know this. The main point to keep in mind is that GDP is not nearly as precise a number as many financial market people assume. The second point is that although there are numerous extrapolations, interpolations, and missing source data contained within every release of the GDP report, the Commerce Department tries to apply, over time,

---

1   For the record, the Commerce Department describes when it uses each of these estimation methods as follows:

> The "commodity-flow method" is used to obtain the value of final users' purchases of goods and services (that is, commodities) for BEA's benchmark input-output accounts. These values serve as the benchmark for the NIPA estimates of personal consumption expenditures (PCE), of producers' durable equipment (PDE), and of the commodity detail for State and local government consumption expenditures and gross investment. The method is also used for PDE in nonbenchmark years, but it is implemented in an abbreviated form. An even more abbreviated commodity-flow method is used for current quarterly estimates of PDE. The "retail-control method" is used to estimate over one-third of the value of PCE for periods other than benchmark years. The method provides the indicator series used in extrapolating and interpolating the total of "most goods" and the "control" total to which the PCE categories and residential PDE included in this group must sum. The PCE categories covered by the "retail-control group" consist of all goods except autos and trucks, food furnished to employees, food and fuel produced and consumed on farms, standard clothing issued to military personnel, school lunches, and net foreign remittances. The "perpetual-inventory" method is used to derive estimates of fixed capital stock, which in turn form the basis for the estimates of consumption of fixed capital. The perpetual-inventory method is based on investment flows and a geometric depreciation formula; it is used instead of direct measurement of the capital stock because direct measurement is seldom statistically feasible on a comprehensive basis. The "fiscal year analysis" method provides the framework for the annual and quarterly estimates of Federal Government consumption expenditures and gross investment. The estimates of expenditures are prepared by program—that is, by activity for a group of line items or for an individual line item in the Budget of the U.S. Government. For most programs, the fiscal year analysis begins by adjusting budget outlays for coverage and for netting and grossing differences between these outlays and NIPA expenditures. The expenditures total (as adjusted) for a program is then classified by type of NIPA expenditure—for example, transfer payments and interest paid—with nondefense consumption expenditures and gross investment determined residually. When a fiscal year analysis is completed, the detailed array of NIPA expenditures by program and by type of expenditure serves as a set of control totals for the quarterly estimates.

a standard and reasonable methodology for pulling together various pieces and sources of data of varying quality and frequency into a relatively consistent "package."

The NIPA data are not perfect, but nothing could be under the circumstances. It is more important to view these data as a rough approximation of reality—which means that it may not be so important whether real GDP grew by 3.2 percent or 3.5 percent—we really do not know the figure that finely. On the other hand, major threshold differences do matter—say, 2.0 percent growth versus 3.5 percent, which might imply the difference between "high growth" versus "low growth."

References

Carson, Carol S., and George Jaszi, *The Use of National Income and Product Accounts for Public Policy: Our Successes and Failures,* Staff Paper 43, U.S. Department of Commerce, Washington, D.C., January 1986.

Corporate Profits: Profits before Taxes, Profits Tax Liability, and Dividends, U.S. Department of Commerce, Washington, D.C., 1985.

Foreign Transactions, U.S. Department of Commerce, Washington, D.C., 1987.

GNP: Overview of Source Data and Estimating Methods, U.S. Department of Commerce, Washington, D.C., 1987.

Landefeld, J. Steven, and Robert P. Parker, "Preview of the Comprehensive Revision of the National Income and Product Accounts: BEA's New Featured Measures of Output and Prices," *Survey of Current Business,* July 1995, pp. 31–38.

Chapter 14

Home Sales: New One-Family and Existing

New One-Family Sales: General Description

The new one-family home sales series is derived directly from the housing starts data. It is presented in a seasonally adjusted, annualized format. Commerce Department field representatives continuously follow up on the individual starts information, from the time a permit is taken out to the house's completion. Then, it is catalogued as being for sale (a separate series within the home sales release), having been sold, or having been built by the landowner. A sale is defined as the signing of the initial contract to purchase. The new home sales data also include an estimate of presold homes, that is, homes sold even before a permit is taken out. This estimate is historically based, and actual sales in this category versus the estimate can be the source of major revisions to the new home sales data. Finally, a home built by and for the owner is not classified as a sale.

Economic Indicator Information at a Glance

Market Significance	Moderate
Typical Release Time	10:00 AM EST Near the End of the Month
Released By	Commerce Department/HUD
Period Covered	One Month Prior
Web Site: New Home Sales	http://www.census.gov/pub/const/ www/c25index.html

New one-family home sales account for about 15 percent of the home sales market. Along with the existing home sales data provided by the National Association of Realtors (NAR), they fill out the buy side of the housing market. Conceptually, builders will not build unless they see demand, and they will keep building if demand holds up, so home sales should be considered the initial step in the housing market's response to a change in interest rates (or any other factor that affects the housing sector). Home sales, in total, also are a very good leading indicator of consumption, particularly durable goods purchases.

A casual glance at the housing starts and new home sales series reveals an obvious discrepancy between the levels of each. At a time when single-family starts may be running between 700,000 and 900,000 units, single-family sales may register only in the 400,000-to-600,000 range. Clearly, some starts wind up in the for-sale category, while the remaining difference is homes that are for rental purposes and those built by and for the landowner, as previous mentioned.

The new home sales data are broken down only one way, by region. There are four: the Northeast, South, Midwest, and West. Also provided is the aforementioned months' supply of houses for sale, a statistic used to forecast housing starts (albeit with limited effect).

Existing Home Sales: General Description

The existing home sales series is compiled by the National Association of Realtors from a national sampling of 125 multiple listing realtors. The monthly data are broken down into the same four regions as the housing starts and new home sales series. A more comprehensive quarterly survey samples 600 realtors and offers a state-by-state view of existing home sales.

Existing home sales account for about 85 percent of the home sales market, making them a key economic variable if not a key fixed-income or equity market variable. New home sales always were considered the more important of the two statistics because they had a direct impact on housing starts. However, existing home sales are a better indicator of consumption trends than are new home sales given their huge share of the home sales market.

Economic Indicator Information at a Glance

Market Significance	Moderate
Typical Release Time	10:00 AM EST The 25th of Each Month or the First Business Day Thereafter
Released By	National Association of Realtors
Period Covered	One Month Prior
Web Site: Existing Home Sales	http://www.realtor.com

TABLE 14-1 New Home Sales
January 1963–May 1997, Units

Phase	Historic Low	Normal Bounds			Historic High	Series Characteristics	
		Normal Low	Average	Normal High		Standard Deviation	Share of Total Observations
Recession	338K in Sep 1981	430K	466K	502K	636K in Jul 1980	72.6K	13.8%
Recovery	487K in Sep 1991	584K	626K	668K	872K in Mar 1977	84.1K	20.3%
Expansion	358K in Sep 1966	578K	636K	693K	880K in Mar 1986	115.6K	65.9%
Slow Phase	358K in Sep 1966	553K	612K	671K	880K in Mar 1986	118.5K	31.0%
Rapid Phase	415K in Jun 1981	595K	648K	701K	872K in Oct 1978	106.4K	34.9%
All Phases	338K in Sep 1981	551K	610K	670K	880K in Mar 1986	119.5K	100.0%

Analyzing the Data

The key difference between the new home sales and existing home sales data is the definition of a sale. The existing home sales data include two definitions of a sale. One is the signing of the initial contract. The second is the final closing of the sale. Fully 60 percent of the existing home sales data are based on closings. For new home sales, only the initial signing of a contract is considered a sale. The result is that the existing home sales series lags the new home sales series, making it a bit less timely as an indicator of cyclical peaks and troughs (see Figure 14-1).

As far as analyzing each series, the general guidelines are the same. The more widespread the overall change across the four regions, the more credibility the result has with analysts and financial markets. One can also compare the behavior of the two series to see whether they are generating a consistent picture of

FIGURE 14–1   Home Sales: New and Existing Single-Family Sales

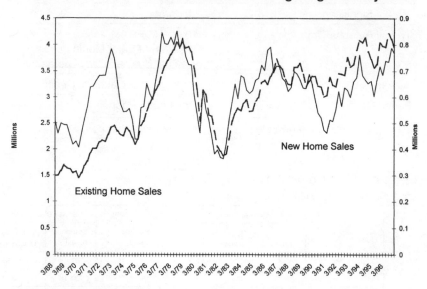

FIGURE 14–2   New Home Sales

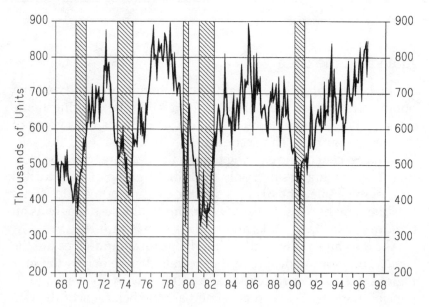

the home sales market. As is often the case with series of this nature, comparing the latest result with a trailing average is of prime importance.

Home Sales over the Business Cycle

The cyclical behavior of total home sales is rather strong, as one would expect from such an interest-sensitive sector. In each cycle since the 1960s both new home sales and existing home sales have led the business cycle. However, the consistency of the lead time is greater for the trough than the peak of the cycle. New home sales have peaked anywhere from eight to four quarters before the top of the business cycle. (See Figure 14-2 and Table 14-1.) Existing home sales have a slightly narrower range of four to six quarters. (See Figure 14-3 and Table 14-2.) The cyclical peaks of each series typically do not align, having done so only once in the last 35 years. Their troughs, however, have aligned four out of five times, with both having a lead time of only one to three quarters versus the cyclical troughs.

FIGURE 14–3 Existing Home Sales

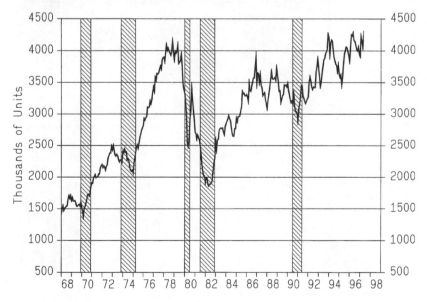

TABLE 14–2   Existing Home Sales
January 1968–May 1997, Units

		Normal Bounds				Series Characteristics	
Phase	Historic Low	Normal Low	Average	Normal High	Historic High	Standard Deviation	Share of Total Observations
Recession	1,370K in Mar 1970	1,981K	2,232K	2,484K	3,320K in Aug 1990	502.9K	16.1%
Recovery	1,850K in Dec 1970	2,604K	2,853K	3,103K	3,640K in May 1977	498.5K	23.8%
Expansion	1,420K in Jan 1968	2,836K	3,236K	3,636K	4,280K in May 1996	800.5K	60.1%
Slow Phase	1,540K in Nov 1969	2,812K	3,193K	3,573K	4,280K in May 1996	760.5K	28.0%
Rapid Phase	1,420K in Jan 1968	2,796K	3,213K	3,631K	4,260K in Dec 1993	835.1K	32.1%
All Phases	1,370K in Mar 1970	2,590K	2,983K	3,376K	4,280K in May 1996	785.4K	100.0%

As far as their cyclical growth behavior, the series again retain distinct personalities. New home sales tend to follow the interest rate cycle. They are their weakest and their strongest during recessions, the latter occurring as the housing sector leads the economy out of recessions. The average growth pace picks up only marginally during the recovery stage. By the expansion phase the good times are over for the new home sector, with the average month-to-month change actually declining. Existing home sales growth follows the business cycle more closely. On average, they decline during recessions, grow strongest during recoveries, and show only marginal gains during the expansion phase.

Chapter 15

Housing Starts and Building Permits

General Description

The housing starts release is one of the most important looks at the residential housing sector. It is the key release from the "supply" side. Although this release is usually of moderate interest to financial markets, its importance rises around turning points in the business cycle.

Given the housing sector's interest sensitivity, starts should be one of the first sectors to suffer the ill effects of rising interest rates or benefit from the positive effects of falling interest rates. Significant reactions of starts and permits to changing interest rates are likely to be one of the first signals that the interest rate cycle is nearing a peak or trough. For this reason, building permits are one of the components of the leading indicators index.

Economic Indicator Information at a Glance

Market Significance	Moderate to High
Typical Release Time	8:30 AM Eastern Time About the 15th Business Day of the Month
Released By	Commerce Department Census Bureau
Period Covered	Prior Month
Web Site	http://www.census.gov/pub/const/ www/c20index.html

Housing starts are released as a seasonally adjusted, annualized rate of the number of residential housing units started in a given month. Commerce Department field representatives, after first receiving permit information, survey building sites to determine actual starts. The sample survey consists of 844 permit sites (local, county, and state building permit offices) out of 17,000 potential sites. *Building permits* are a separate survey. Without the need to survey building sites, it is possible for all 17,000 source information sites to be included in the permit survey.

Both starts and permits are broken down two ways: by the number of housing units per foundation and by the regions in which they exist. The unit categories are one (single-family residence), two to four, and five or more. The latter two categories are analytically grouped together and called the *multi-family sector*. The regional breakdown is Northeast, South, Midwest, and West. The single-family sector represents the bulk of starts and permits data on a level basis. The single-family portion, accounting for about 85 percent of starts and about 82 percent of permits. However, the multi-family sector typically contributes much of the volatility to the release. For example, in 1996 (a typical year) single-family permits and starts averaged month-to-month absolute changes of 2.0 percent and 4.7 percent, respectively, while multi-family permits and starts came in at an average of 6.6 percent and 12.2 percent, respectively.

Two final points about the housing data. First, single-family starts are one of the inputs into the calculation of the residential housing component of GDP, although not the primary one. That honor goes to the appropriate component in the construction expenditure data. Second, although financial market participants insist upon viewing building permits as a leading indicator of housing activity, it is worth noting that this relationship is meaningful only for the multi-family sector. In the single-family sector, at least two-thirds of the necessary permits are taken out in the same month as the actual starts (for a related analysis of the relationship between permits and starts, see the section on starts and permits over the business cycle).

Analyzing the Data

Given the limited detail of the release, interpretation of the data is rather straightforward, albeit in the context of series that are normally fairly volatile. The financial markets focus on the over-all percentage change in the level of housing starts and building permits from the previous month. From there focus turns quickly to the breakdown between single- and multi-family starts and permits. Since the single-family sector dominates the residential housing market in terms of economic activity, the change in this sector is of more importance to analysts and market participants. This is the sector that reveals the extent to which interest rates and other fundamentals are affecting buyers and builders. Multi-family starts and permits are a less reliable guide. Such things as tax issues and zoning ordinances can play a relatively large role in any given month in determining this sector's movement. In this sense, a strong (weak) starts and permits release that is heavily concentrated in the single-family sector is considered a cleaner view of the residential housing sector than is one that derives its strength (weakness) from the multi-family sector. It is also impor-tant to see if starts and building permits at each level are moving in the same direction, an occurrence that is typical but not to be taken for granted.

A second level of analysis is the regional breakdown. In par-ticular, the breadth of the change is critical to interpretation. An increase (decrease) that is spread across all four regions should be considered a more meaningful change than one that is con-centrated in one or even two regions. Housing starts and permits are also series that are subject to rather large revisions, a fact that could affect one's interpretation of the current month's data.

Housing starts and permits data are unusually susceptible to weather influences. Awareness of precipitation levels around the country (a data publication is offered by the National Weather Service) can be an invaluable tool in analyzing (and forecasting) this release. Each series is also extremely volatile. Analysis of one month's outcome must always be done in the context of what each series has done in the previous month and the most recent three-month average.

Housing Starts and Building Permits over the Business Cycle

Both starts and permits show a clear, strong cyclical bias; their interest sensitivity is apparent. However, the timing of their peaks and troughs relative to the business cycle is less than uni-form, especially once a recession has begun.

FIGURE 15–1   Housing Starts

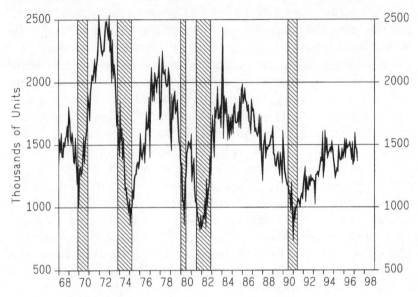

FIGURE 15–2   Residential Building Permits

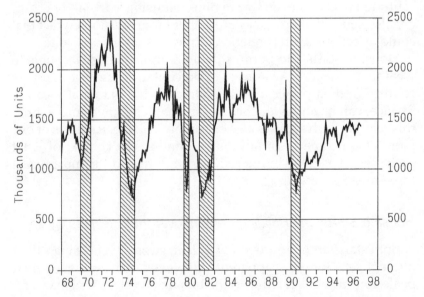

TABLE 15–1   Housing Starts

January 1959–May 1997, Units

Phase	Historic Low	Normal Bounds			Historic High	Series Characteristics	
		Normal Low	Average	Normal High		Standard Deviation	Share of Total Observations
Recession	798K in Jan 1991	1,059K	1,173K	1,288K	1,752K in Feb 1974	229.6K	14.5%
Recovery	996K in May 1991	1,363K	1,537K	1,711K	2,494K in Jan 1972	348.0K	21.0%
Expansion	843K in Oct 1966	1,417K	1,566K	1,715K	2,485K in Oct 1972	298.2K	64.4%
Slow Phase	843K in Oct 1966	1,387K	1,513K	1,640K	2,266K in May 1973	253.2K	30.4%
Rapid Phase	1041K in Jul 1981	1,457K	1,623K	1,789K	2,485K in Oct 1972	332.5K	34.0%
All Phases	798K in Jan 1991	1,338K	1,503K	1,668K	2,494K in Jan 1972	329.7K	100.0%

Generally speaking, starts and permits peak anywhere from six months to a year before a recession begins, with a lead time of 10 to 12 months the most common. Their relationship to the trough of the cycle is a bit more ambiguous. The two series bottomed at the very beginning of both the 1970 and the 1981–1982 recessions, two months and four months after the onset of each respective recession. However, they did not bottom until two months after the 1974–1975 recession ended and found their lowest levels in the middle of the 1990–1991 recession. This timing difference makes it a little difficult to use housing data to gauge the finality of recession.

The other interesting cyclical characteristic of starts and permits data is that permits are not a particularly good leading indicator of starts. The peaks and troughs occur roughly at the same time, often the same month. Starts have peaked before permits

TABLE 15–2   Building Permits

January 1960–May 1997, Units

Phase	Historic Low	Normal Bounds			Historic High	Series Characteristics	
		Normal Low	Average	Normal High		Standard Deviation	Share of Total Observations
Recession	709K in Mar 1975	920K	1,026K	1,131K	1,564K in Oct 1970	211.0K	14.9%
Recovery	866K in Apr 1975	1,199K	1,376K	1,554K	2,238K in Jan 1972	354.7K	20.7%
Expansion	736K in Nov 1966	1,286K	1,435K	1,585K	2,419K in Dec 1972	298.7K	64.4%
Slow Phase	736K in Nov 1966	1,258K	1,392K	1,526K	2,051K in Jun 1973	268.2K	30.5%
Rapid Phase	935K in Jul 1981	1,313K	1,477K	1,641K	2,419K in Dec 1972	328.0K	33.9%
All Phases	709K in Mar 1975	1,196K	1,362K	1,528K	2,419K in Dec 1972	331.9K	100.0%

(two months prior, before the 1973–1975 recession) and after (four months after, before the 1981–1982 recession). They bottomed in the same month in three of the last seven recessions, with starts bottoming one month before permits in three other cycles. (See Figures 15-1 and 15-2 and Tables 15-1 and 15-2.)

Chapter 16

Industrial Production and Capacity Utilization

General Description

The **Industrial Production Index** (IP), begun in 1919, is one of the oldest continuous economic statistics on the economy. Industrial production measures output in manufacturing, mining, and utility industries, and is released by the Federal Reserve together with capacity utilization data. In addition to those data, the statistical release also includes monthly indexes on electric power usage in manufacturing and mining. The production data are classified two ways: (1) by market grouping, such as consumer goods, equipment, intermediate products, and materials; and (2) by industry groups, such as two-digit Standard Industrial Classification (SIC) industries and major aggregates of these industries including durable and nondurable manufacturing, mining, and utilities.

Economic Indicator Information at a Glance

Market Significance	Moderate
Typical Release Time	9:15 AM Eastern Time About the 15th Day of the Month
Released By	Federal Reserve Board
Period Covered	Prior Month
Web Site	http://www.bog.frb.fed.us/ releases/G17/

Capacity utilization and **utilization rates** are calculated for the manufacturing, mining, and electric and gas utilities industries, as well. A capacity utilization rate for an industry is equal to a production index (output) divided by an index of capacity. These capacity utilization rates have been criticized in recent years as being "too high," given the unleashing of all the new productivity-improving technology. Nonetheless, the Federal Reserve notes that these "capacity indexes attempt to capture the concept of sustainable practical capacity, which is defined as the greatest level of output that a plant can maintain within the framework of a realistic work schedule, taking account of normal downtime, and assuming sufficient availability of inputs to operate the machinery and equipment in place. The 76 individual capacity indexes are based on a variety of data, including capacity data measured in physical units compiled by trade associations, surveys of utilization rates and investment, and estimates of growth of the capital input."

Analyzing the Data

A portion of the industrial production measure is derived from manufacturing hours data, which are provided to the Federal Reserve by the Bureau of Labor Statistics usually on the Wednesday prior to their official release by the Labor Department.[1] The practice of early transmittal of the hours data to the Federal Reserve has fueled speculation from time to time about when the Federal Reserve chairman knows this information. Moreover, for internal purposes only, the Federal Reserve staff (at the chairman's request) created a weekly production index (which is far less comprehensive than its monthly counterpart) for more timely updates. This weekly production measure is circulated to the Federal Reserve Board of Governors only and is not made available to the public.

From the period beginning in 1992, the monthly industrial production index has been compiled from 264 subindexes (pre-

---

1   This observation was made by Manuel Johnson, who was a former vice-chairman of the Federal Reserve Board.

viously there were 255 series) based on the 1987 SIC system and currently has a reference period base year of 1992 equals 100 for the index. As of early 1997, the SIC system is being replaced with the North American Industrial Classification System (NAICS), which is being phased in over time throughout all of the statistical data collection efforts. In the aggregate, however, the future industrial classification system change should have little impact. The major components of the production index are shown in Table 16-1.

TABLE 16–1   Major Industrial Production Categories and Their Shares

Industrial Production	1996 Share
Total Index	100.00
Major Market Groups:	
Products, Total	59.92
Consumer Goods	28.15
Business Equipment	13.81
Construction Supplies	5.72
Materials	40.08
SPECIAL AGGREGATES	
Total Excluding:	
Autos and Trucks	97.48
Motor Vehicles and Parts	95.20
Computers	97.55
Computers and Semiconductors	93.68
Consumer Goods Excluding:	
Autos and Trucks	26.76
Energy	24.65
Business equipment excluding:	
Autos and Trucks	12.67
Computer and Office Equipment	12.26
Materials Excluding:	
Energy	31.96

Industrial Production	1996 Share
Major Industry Groups:	
Manufacturing	86.34
Durable	46.79
Nondurable	39.55
Mining	5.59
Utilities	8.07
SPECIAL AGGREGATES	
Manufacturing Excluding:	
Motor Vehicles and Parts	81.54
Computer and Office Equipment	83.89
Computers and Semiconductors	80.02
Manufacturing	
Primary Processing	27.72
Advanced Processing	58.62

In early 1997, the Federal Reserve implemented a new aggregation method for the production index and capacity utilization. This change in the index formulation was to a Fisher-ideal (chain-type) index—one that was similar to the change sought by the Bureau of Labor Statistics for the CPI and used by the Commerce Department for GDP. This change allowed for updating of the weights every year instead of every five years, and the weights are estimated for the current year. The Federal Reserve's implementation of this new formula affected industrial production data from 1977 forward only.

The source data used by the Federal Reserve to calculate industrial production include various types of information pieced together. Two primary types of source data are used to construct the monthly industrial production indexes: (1) output measured in physical units (for example, steel production, aluminum output, vehicle production, etc.) and (2) data on inputs to the production process, namely hours worked data and electric power use, from which output is inferred.

The capacity utilization rate data are benchmarked for manufacturing to the *Survey of Plant Capacity*, which is collected every two years. Capacity is derived from an estimate of a capital service-flow measure, which is linked to capital stock data produced by the Commerce Department.

The keys to interpreting the production and capacity utilization report include:

- In addition to the total change in production, watch computers and motor vehicles. Look at the special aggregates included under the marketing groupings—especially, total production excluding motor vehicles and parts and total excluding computers and semiconductors. Since computers and vehicles are the big movers in the economy, it is useful to look at how the rest of the industrial sector is performing, as well. Other special aggregates worth watching are manufacturing excluding motor vehicles and parts and manufacturing excluding computers and semiconductors.

- Keep in mind that strike activity in major industries, such as motor vehicles or commercial aircraft, can have a noticeable impact on the overall production index. Motor vehicles and parts have a 4.8 percent weight in the total production index.

- Be aware that weather impacts on utility usage are common. Since utility output accounts for about 8 percent of the total index, a large weather-induced swing in this component also could have a noticeable impact on the overall production index.

- Use the analytical perspective provided in the summary table. The Federal Reserve reports historical highs and lows in capacity utilization in the summary table so as to judge how tight capacity is. For example, for May 1997, the capacity utilization rate was 83.7 percent, which is 1.6 percentage points higher than its 1967–1996 average use and also 1.6 percentage points below its 1988–1989 high. Alan Greenspan, the chairman of the Federal Reserve, correctly observed that capacity is "a somewhat elusive concept," since it is not clear whether a high rate of capacity utilization will lead to: (1) higher prices, (2) higher output, or (3) a pickup in foreign goods demand. In reality, all three events occur even though the financial markets generally focus only on the price implication. Moreover, the concept of capacity assumes a fixed labor and capital input. In the short run, however, new technologies have reduced the labor input and produced an improvement in manufacturing productivity, which makes the interpretation even more tricky. Statistically, one should not read too much into the "inflation implication" between a high capacity utilization rate and producer prices.

- Do not ignore the **diffusion indexes** of industrial production. Although these data are reported with a one-month lag relative to the overall output change, they provide a measure of how widespread changes are in the industrial sector. Theory and empirical studies suggest that the production diffusion index contains information that is not found in the industrial production series itself.[2] Indeed, former Federal Reserve Board Chairman Arthur Burns even developed a "theory of diffusion" in his academic years.

Over the Business Cycle

Industrial production follows a normal cyclical pattern, with the strongest gains found in the recovery period. (See Figure 16-1 and Table 16-2.) During recessions, production typically declines by 0.8 percent per month, which gives way to a recovery where the monthly gain is 0.9 percent. During the expansion phase, the pace moderates to a 0.4 percent average gain per month, with a 0.2 percent per month average during the slow-growth phase of the expansion and a 0.5 percent average rise during the high-growth phase of the cycle. The capacity utilization rate is weakest during the recovery phase since the cumulative effects of the recession are still being reversed. There is little difference in the capacity utilization rate during the high- and low-growth phases of the expansion. (See Figure 16-2 and Table 16-3.)

---

2   See James Kennedy, "Empirical Relationships between the Total Industrial Production Index and Its Diffusion Indexes," Finance and Economics Discussion Series, Working Paper No. 163, Board of Governors of the Federal Reserve, Washington, D.C., 1991.

FIGURE 16–1   Industrial Production

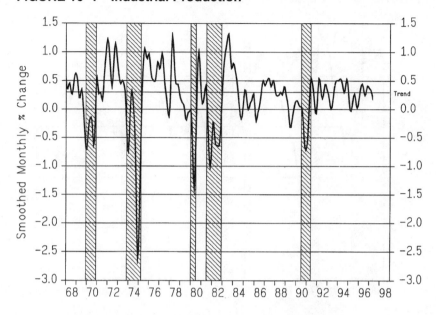

Special Factors, Limitations, and Other Data Issues

Numerous conceptual concerns have been raised about the industrial production index regarding the form and factor inputs used in an aggregate production function. For example, does electric power usage properly reflect capital use? Or should the electricity data be incorporated as a separate factor of production? These are some of the conceptual problems that regional

TABLE 16–2   Industrial Production Index
January 1948–May 1997, Month-to-Month Percentage Change

Phase	Historic Low	Normal Bounds			Historic High	Series Characteristics	
		Normal Low	Average	Normal High		Standard Deviation	Share of Total Observations
Recession	−4.2% in Dec 1974	−1.3%	−0.8%	−0.3%	2.2% in Feb 1982	1.0 pp.	16.2%
Recovery	−0.9% in Jan 1981	0.5%	0.9%	1.4%	3.3% in Apr 1950	0.9 pp.	20.9%
Expansion	−3.4% in Aug 1959	−0.1%	0.4%	0.8%	6.4% in Aug 1952	0.9 pp.	61.0%
Slow Phase	−3.1% in Jul 1956	−0.3%	0.2%	0.7%	6.4% in Aug 1952	1.0 pp.	29.5%
Rapid Phase	−3.4% in Aug 1959	0.1%	0.5%	0.9%	3.6% in Sep 1952	0.8 pp.	31.5%
All Phases	−4.2% in Dec 1974	−0.2%	0.3%	0.8%	6.4% in Aug 1952	1.1 pp.	100.0%

FIGURE 16–2   Capacity Utilization Rate

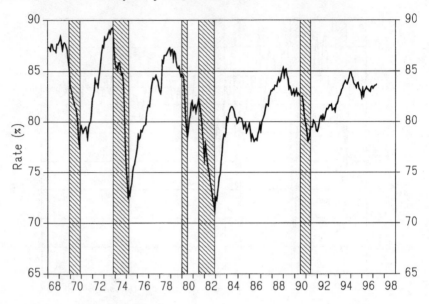

Federal Reserve Banks have wrestled with in their attempts to produce regional production indexes.

Other questions that have been raised include: Should the Federal Reserve produce a service production index, which would be the counterpart of the industrial production index? In fact, the Federal Reserve was doing just that for a while on an experimental basis. Although it was more heavily dependent on hours data than was desired, it was a "first step" toward a monthly service output measure.

TABLE 16–3   Capacity Utilization Rate
January 1967–May 1997, Percent

		Normal Bounds				Series Characteristics	
Phase	Historic Low	Normal Low	Average	Normal High	Historic High	Standard Deviation	Share of Total Observations
Recession	71.9% in Nov 1982	78.2%	80.2%	82.2%	87.4% in Dec 1973	4.1 pp.	15.6%
Recovery	71.1% in Dec 1982	77.4%	78.8%	80.2%	84.3% in Jun 1977	2.8 pp.	23.0%
Expansion	78.1% in Jun 1986	82.5%	83.9%	85.3%	89.4% in Jan 1967	2.7 pp.	61.4%
Slow Phase	78.1% in Jun 1986	82.4%	83.9%	85.5%	89.4% in Jan 1967	3.1 pp.	30.4%
Rapid Phase	79.1% in Nov 1986	82.7%	83.9%	85.1%	88.3% in Feb 1973	2.4 pp.	31.0%
All Phases	71.1% in Dec 1982	80.3%	82.1%	84.0%	89.4% in Jan 1967	3.7 pp.	100.0%

Relationship with Other Series

Employee hours directly account for 70 of the 264 industrial production component indexes (26.5 percent) and indirectly reflect monthly business conditions, which is why employment data are used to forecast the same month's industrial production change. Industrial production data are reported about 6 to 7 business days after employment, which has led to that standard forecasting practice.

Weekly production data are limited, and even composites of readily available weekly data, such as the *Business Week* production index, do not provide adequate information for forecasting the broader monthly production data.

Chapter 17

International Trade of Goods and Services

General Description

The monthly international trade report, issued by the Commerce Department's Census Bureau, details the level of exports and imports of goods and services of the United States. (Box 17-1 describes one other report issued by the Commerce Department that also covers capital flows.) The high degree of detail crisscrosses between seasonally adjusted and unadjusted data, nominal and real dollars, type of good or service, and country of origination or destination. The key breakdowns are as follows.

Major End-User Categories: The first breakdown is into goods and services. (See Tables 17-1 and 17-2.) On the export side of the ledger the balance is 73 percent goods and 27 percent services in

Economic Indicator Information at a Glance

Market Significance	Typically Moderate but Varies Considerably
Typical Release Time	8:30 AM Eastern Time Third Week of the Month
Released By	Commerce Department Census Bureau
Period Covered	Two Months Prior
Web Site	http://www.census.gov/foreign-trade/ http://www/press.html

---

BOX 17–1   Quarterly Current Account Data

One other report issued by the Commerce Department covers international flows. The *current account* data are issued in the final month of the quarter for the preceding quarter. These data present the most comprehensive picture of international flows, including capital flows as well as the goods and services data detailed in the monthly report. The capital flows cover government holdings of official reserve assets such as special drawing rights and foreign currency holdings as well as holdings of market assets such as U.S. Treasury securities. The capital flows also cover private financial flows such as direct investment and purchases of U.S. financial assets.

1996. On the import side it's about 84 percent goods and 16 percent services. The chronic deficit is entirely on the goods side. In 1995–1996 the goods averaged a deficit of $182 bn., while services averaged a surplus of $76 bn. (on a balance of payments basis). Furthermore, two product lines account for two-thirds of our goods deficit. The deficit on petroleum is approximately one-third of the total, while the deficit on motor vehicles and parts accounts for another third. The data are offered on both a balance of payments basis and a customs basis,[1] seasonally adjusted and not adjusted. Within this context the broadest breakdown is into six end-user categories for exports and seven end-user categories for imports.

Commodity: On the goods side the seven categories are delineated further by commodity type. The breakdown is highly detailed, including hundreds of categories ranging from civilian aircraft and computers to such items as rugs, shingles and wallboard, and nonmonetary gold. These data are available on a seasonally adjusted and unadjusted basis.

Country: The final key breakdown is by country. This is based only on total exports and imports of goods, and it's most impor-

---

1   Timing and definitions account for the difference. On the export side, the net adjustments to move from the customs to balance of payments basis result in a reduction in the level of exports of a little more than 1 percent. On the import side, the net adjustments add to the level of imports. They are more variable but average a little less than 1 percent.

TABLE 17–1 Goods: Exports and Imports
End-User Categories, 1996

	Exports %*	Imports %*
Foods, Feeds, and Beverages	7	4
Industrial Supplies	20	22
Capital Goods	49	36
Automotive	10	15
Consumer Goods	10	20
Other Goods	5	3

* Total may not add to 100% due to rounding.

tant to note that the data are only available on a seasonally un-adjusted basis. (See Tables 17-3 and 17-4.)

Analyzing the Data

There are numerous ways to interpret and analyze the trade data, and markets' reaction to the data can be extremely complicated. Strictly on fundamentals, the direction of the overall deficit compared with that of the previous month and its three-month average should have the strongest impact on the foreign exchange markets. Simply put, a rising deficit implies a growing supply of dollars and a falling deficit a declining stock of greenbacks. As to the extent to which the deficit actually affects the dol-

TABLE 17–2 Services: Exports and Imports
End-User Categories, 1996

	Exports %*	Imports %*
Travel	29	32
Passenger Fares	9	10
Other Transportation	13	19
Royalties and License Fees	13	5
Other Private Services	30	25
Transfers: U.S. Military Sales	6	7
U.S. Government: Misc. Services	0	2

* Total may not add to 100% due to rounding.

TABLE 17–3   GOODS: Exports and Imports
By Selected Country or Region, 1996

	Exports %	Imports %
Canada	22	20
Western Europe	23	20
Japan	11	17
Pacific NICs*	13	11
Mexico	8	8
South America	9	6
OPEC	3	5

* Hong Kong, Korea, Singapore, Taiwan.

lar's value, much can depend on perceived government attitudes toward exchange rates. When individual governments or the G-7[2] have voiced concern about exchange rate levels being overvalued or undervalued for a single currency or various currencies, the market effect can be exaggerated beyond what the fundamentals would imply.

The reaction of fixed-income markets to the trade data is more complex. The direction of the deficit can have an effect on interest rates if it is perceived that the dollar will be affected dramatically. Thus a widening trade gap would bring on a weaker dollar, which would then imply higher inflation. Fixed-income markets could respond by sending interest rates higher. However, the composition of the change in the trade balance can be more important if there are no overwhelming dollar concerns. For example, a deteriorating deficit that is due to rising imports indicates strong domestic growth. That implies higher interest rates. However, a deteriorating deficit fueled by declining exports implies a slowing economy and lower interest rates.

As a matter of fact, it is typically the export change that is most critical to fixed-income markets because of the inference about

---

2   The G-7 group of Western industrialized countries are the United States, Germany, France, Japan, United Kingdom, Canada, and Italy. Periodically these countries gather to discuss economic and political issues common to all. In the mid-1980s the group coordinated policy to significantly devalue the U.S. dollar, a key to that devaluation being coordinated interest rate cuts. In the 1990s there has been no coordinated economic policy stance regarding a single issue.

TABLE 17–4   Deficits and Surpluses
By Selected Country or Region, 1996

Deficits	
Total Deficit	–$111.0 bn.
Japan	–$26.6 bn.
China	–$19.5 bn.
Canada*	–$13.3 bn.
Mexico	–$9.5 bn.
OPEC	–$10.6 bn.
Surpluses	
Netherlands	+$5.2 bn.
Australia	+$5 bn.
Belgium	+$3 bn.

* Roughly 55 percent of Canadian imports are motor vehicles produced for U.S. manufacturers.

domestic economic growth and production. This is not to say that imports are not a sign of activity. Rather there is some ambiguity in an increase in imports. As much as it signals strong demand, it also infers that the demand is not being met by domestic producers. The result could be less income growth and less economic growth in the future.

As far as the specific data series, there are no particular subsets of exports or imports on which the markets focus. Analysts will look at the seven end-user categories of goods to gauge the breadth of any change, but this is standard practice for any series. If one could single out one category that can sometimes dominate month-to-month changes, especially of exports, it is aircraft. The high value of these exports, and the volatility of their shipment schedule, often causes this category to have a significant impact on export levels.

One other analytical point: Sometimes bilateral trade balances are particularly important to foreign exchange markets. In the mid-1990s the Japan/United States balance has been watched closely. In so doing it is important to remember that these data are not seasonally adjusted. Thus comparing one month's balance with the prior month's balance is improper. Rather, one should look at the change between the two months compared with the prior year's (or the average of the prior three years) change between the same two months to understand what the latest trade figure is telling the markets.

Finally, analysis of the trade in goods and services data includes translating them into a forecast of the net export component of gross domestic product. Although there are compositional and definitional differences between the two, general trends for the two are very similar on both the export and import side (see Figures 17-1 and 17-2). One has a choice of using the nominal trade data or the real data. The price index used to deflate the monthly trade data (see Box 17-2) is not the same as that used in the GDP data, but the series still provides a reasonably accurate picture of the direction and the extent of any change in imports and exports in a given quarter.

Trade over the Business Cycle

Unlike other economic sectors, there is no consistent relationship between the trade balance and the phases of the business cycle. During recessions net exports have run the gamut from de-

FIGURE 17–1   Merchandise Trade Flows: Monthly Real Exports and GDP Exports, Real Quarterly, Year-over-Year Growth Rates

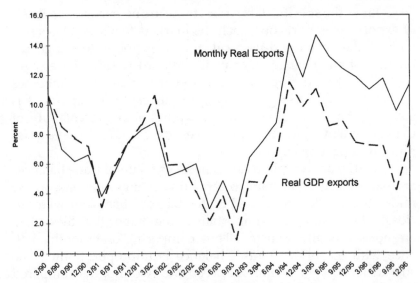

FIGURE 17–2 Trade Flows: Real Monthly Goods Imports and GDP Imports, Real Quarterly, Year-over-Year Growth Rates

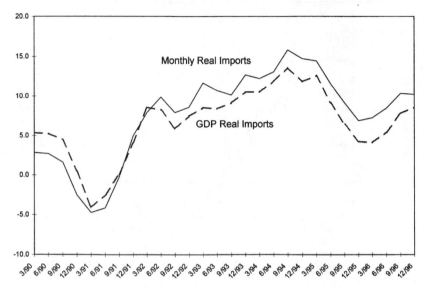

BOX 17–2   Import/Export Prices

The price indexes that are used to deflate the monthly trade data are released as a separate series. Import/export prices are released around the 20th of the month for the preceding month. Respondents to the BLS survey are asked to provide prices that include all discounts, allowances, and rebates. Export prices are measured on an f.a.s. basis (free alongside ship). Import prices are measured on an f.a.s. basis and an f.o.b. basis (free on board). The difference allows the BLS to measure the shipment cost to the export destination.

The export and import price series have fixed weights, set by shares of imports and exports, and are not seasonally adjusted. On the import side the series is broken down into petroleum import prices and nonpetroleum import prices, with the latter category conceptually useful for gauging the extent of imported price inflation.

For more information check the web site at the following: http://stats.bls.gov/news.release/ximpim.toc.htm.

FIGURE 17–3   International Trade Balance

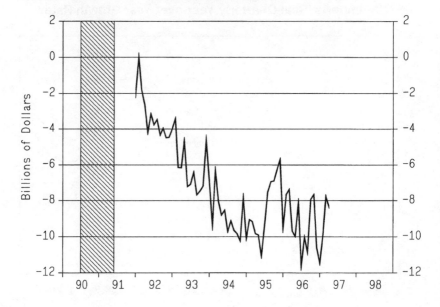

teriorating to showing little change to outright improvement. Clearly, a major reason is the different timing of business cycles here and abroad as well as the extent of the business cycle change here and abroad. Even imports, on a level basis, have not shown a clear relationship to the business cycle. The biggest factor accounting for this has been the secular deterioration of the United States's international deficit fueled by our secularly rising demand for imported goods. From 1960 to 1996, on a real basis, imports as a percentage of gross domestic product have risen from 4.9 percent to 13.8 percent, a trend that can obscure cyclical demand changes that would otherwise be plainly apparent. Exports have shown consistent growth during the expansionary phase of our business cycles, but the relationship goes awry during recessions and recoveries. (See Figure 17-3.)

Chapter 18

Manufacturing Orders, Inventories, and Shipments

General Description

The manufacturing sector report is an extension of the durable goods release. It includes orders, shipments, and unfilled orders data for the nondurable manufacturing sector and also incorporates inventory data, something not provided in the durable goods orders report, for all manufacturing. It is the most comprehensive picture of the manufacturing sector offered by government statistics, covering most manufacturing companies with 1,000 employees or more. Diversified companies must file separately for divisions that operate in different industrial areas.

Economic Indicator Information at a Glance

Market Significance	Low
Typical Release Time	10:00 AM Eastern Time Six Business Days after Durable Goods Orders
Released By	Commerce Department Census Bureau
Period Covered	Two Months Prior
Web Site	http://www.census.gov/ftp/pub/ indicator/ http://www/m3/index.htm

New Orders

New Orders are defined as the intent to purchase for immediate or future delivery. They must be supported by legal documents (i.e., purchase agreements, letters of intent), and they are the net nominal value between the current month's orders and cancellations of previous orders. Orders also are not directly accounted for in the survey. They are derived as the sum of shipments plus the change in unfilled orders. The key reason for this is that many companies supply new orders data only for those areas with an order backlog.

Durable goods orders account for roughly 50 percent of the total and 90 percent of the volatility. Although nondurable orders can show sharp changes, they cannot match the extremes of durable goods orders. In the period 1980 through 1996 durable goods orders had a maximum one-month increase of 12.1 percent and a maximum one-month decline of 10.7 percent. Nondurable orders' biggest one-month gain was 4.8 percent, and their sharpest one-month drop was 4 percent. Nondurable orders, item by item, just cannot match the size of durable orders for such items as aircraft, machinery, or military hardware, on a dollar basis.

Total manufacturing orders have a strong cyclical pattern, as one would expect. Their historic low is a drop of 6.6 percent during the 1974 recession, while the largest recorded increase was 7.3 percent in 1991. Their ability to lead the business cycle, particularly ahead of a recession, is historically obscured by the mid-1970s recession. Then there was a tremendous amount of inventory speculation that resulted in manufacturing orders rising until 10 months after the recession had begun. More accurate pictures of the series relationship with the business cycle are the 1970 and 1980–1982 recessions. Then orders peaked on a level basis, three months before the downturn.

Finally, it needs to be noted that the nature of the orders series allows for great volatility within stages of the business cycle. Orders have risen close to 5 percent during recessions and have dropped close to 4 percent during recoveries. Consistency is not the hallmark of manufacturing orders.

Shipments

Shipments, in these data, are sales. They are measured by the receipts, billings, or value of the product shipped. For nondurable goods, shipments are also orders. The lead production time is so short that they are interchangeable.

Inventories

Inventories are determined by the book value of stocks at the end of the month. They are broken into three categories: finished goods, work in progress, and materials and supplies. Each company uses its own method of valuation.

Manufacturing inventories account for approximately 45 percent of all inventories. During times of growth, the month-to-month variability is not particularly great; the normal range for both the recovery and expansion phases is only four-tenths of 1 percent for each growth phase. The breakdown into finished goods, work in progress, and materials and supplies does not offer much additional information. Superficially the three categories could tell a story about bottlenecks or production needs, but in reality the peaks and troughs of materials and supplies lead those of finished goods by only a few months if at all. This is not enough time to be of much use in forecasting inventory cycles.

Unfilled Orders

Industry backlog (unfilled orders) qualitatively works off two other series. The first is new orders. The other is production capacity. At the initial stages of a recovery, spare capacity is available to meet not only existing orders, but also new orders. Thus, unfilled orders usually decline as a recovery begins. It's only when new orders rise long enough to boost production near capacity limits (generally speaking, 83 percent for the economy as a whole) that orders "back up." This is best illustrated by the fact that the average increase in unfilled orders is greatest during the expansion phase of a business cycle, not during the recovery, as is the case for most real sector economic indicators. Suffice it to say that following orders matters much more than following unfilled orders.

Relationships to Other Series

The manufacturing inventory data go directly into the business inventory data, another monthly release. They are also one

FIGURE 18–1   Manufacturing Orders

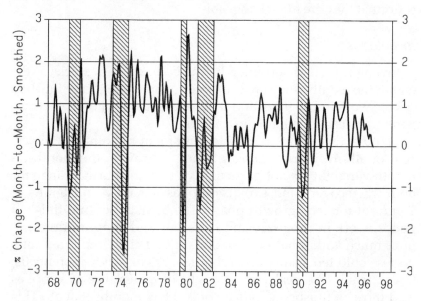

source for GDP inventory calculations. The shipments of nondefense capital durable goods other than aircraft also are used in
GDP calculations. They represent business spending on equipment.

Analyzing the Data

Given all the data, one might think that the markets would
show a fair amount of interest in this release. They don't. If there

TABLE 18–1   New Manufacturing Orders
March 1958–May 1997, Month-to-Month Percentage Change

Phase	Historic Low	Normal Bounds			Historic High	Series Characteristics	
		Normal Low	Average	Normal High		Standard Deviation	Share of Total Observations
Recession	−6.6% in Dec 1974	−1.6%	−0.4%	0.8%	4.7% in Jan 1974	2.4 pp.	14.6%
Recovery	−3.9% in Dec 1991	0.2%	1.3%	2.3%	7.3% in Jul 1991	2.2 pp.	22.3%
Expansion	−4.6% in Jan 1978	−0.4%	0.6%	1.5%	6.3% in Dec 1988	1.9 pp.	63.1%
Slow Phase	−4.4% in Apr 1979	−0.6%	0.4%	1.3%	6.3% in Dec 1988	1.9 pp.	29.7%
Rapid Phase	−4.6% in Jan 1978	−0.2%	0.7%	1.6%	5.5% in Jan 1964	1.8 pp.	33.4%
All Phases	−6.6% in Dec 1974	−0.5%	0.6%	1.6%	7.3% in Jul 1991	2.1 pp.	100.0%

TABLE 18–2   Unfilled Manufacturing Orders

February 1958–April 1997, Month-to-Month Percentage Change

Phase	Historic Low	Normal Bounds			Historic High	Series Characteristics	
		Normal Low	Average	Normal High		Standard Deviation	Share of Total Observations
Recession	−0.7% in Nov 1990	−0.1%	0.1%	0.4%	0.7% in Dec 1990	0.5 pp.	7.2%
Recovery	−0.9% in Jul 1992	−0.6%	−0.4%	−0.1%	1.5% in Jul 1991	0.6 pp.	16.2%
Expansion	−1.2% in Mar 1993	−0.0%	0.3%	0.6%	2.1% in Dec 1988	0.7 pp.	76.6%
Slow Phase	−0.6% in Aug 1989	0.2%	0.5%	0.8%	2.1% in Dec 1988	0.6 pp.	38.7%
Rapid Phase	−1.2% in Mar 1993	−0.3%	−0.0%	0.3%	1.2% in Feb 1988	0.6 pp.	37.9%
All Phases	−1.2% in Mar 1993	−0.2%	0.2%	0.5%	2.1% in Dec 1988	0.7 pp.	100.0%

is a focus, it is on orders, but the fact that durable orders have already been released about a week before lessens dramatically the importance of this orders series. Analysts pay more attention to the inventory component, in an effort to fine-tune GDP calculations, but even the story that comes out of this is usually not important enough for the market to pay this release much attention.

Manufacturing Orders over the Business Cycle

Manufacturing orders are a leading indicator of the business cycle; they peak before recessions begin (by an average of six months, although the deviation is wide) and bottom before recoveries take off (by an average of eight months). The average

TABLE 18–3   Manufacturing Inventories

February 1958–May 1997, Month-to-Month Percentage Change

Phase	Historic Low	Normal Bounds			Historic High	Series Characteristics	
		Normal Low	Average	Normal High		Standard Deviation	Share of Total Observations
Recession	−1.2% in Dec 1960	−0.3%	0.7%	1.6%	13.9% in Jan 1982	1.9 pp.	14.8%
Recovery	−1.2% in Jan 1983	−0.1%	0.2%	0.5%	1.3% in Mar 1984	0.5 pp.	22.2%
Expansion	−0.8% in Jan 1986	0.3%	0.5%	0.7%	1.6% in Jun 1979	0.5 pp.	62.9%
Slow Phase	−0.8% in Jan 1986	0.2%	0.5%	0.8%	1.6% in Jun 1979	0.5 pp.	29.7%
Rapid Phase	−0.6% in Nov 1992	0.3%	0.5%	0.7%	1.3% in May 1984	0.4 pp.	33.2%
All Phases	−1.2% in Dec 1960	0.0%	0.5%	0.9%	13.9% in Jan 1982	0.9 pp.	100.0%

rate of growth, however, follows the business cycle closely. Orders average a 0.4 percent drop during recessions and show a robust 1.3 percent gain during recoveries. In the expansion phase, orders grow at a more subdued 0.6 percent pace. (See Figure 18-1 and Tables 18-1 to 18-3.)

Chapter 19

NAPM Purchasing Managers' Index

General Description

The National Association of Purchasing Management (NAPM) survey was created out of a necessity to monitor the economy and, ultimately, the economy's impact on the pricing environment. In its early days, the NAPM survey provided information on national business trends that was unavailable elsewhere. However, since the initial days of the survey, government data sources have surfaced and provide more comprehensive and quantifiable measures for many of the concepts that are surveyed by NAPM. NAPM began to formally survey its membership to gauge business conditions in 1931. Today, the survey committee consists of over 300 persons selected from a cross section of 20 manufacturing industries to reflect each industry's contribution to gross domestic product. The trade association draws its survey participants primarily from a membership list of about 40,000 persons.

Economic Indicator Information at a Glance

Market Significance	High
Typical Release Time for Conference Board Measure	10:00 AM Eastern Time First Business Day of Month
Released By	National Association of Purchasing Management
Period Covered	Prior Month
Web Site	http://www.napm.org/rob/main.html

Analyzing the Data

The purchasing executive is asked in the questionnaire (see Table 19-1 for the survey form) to evaluate the change in his/her firm's:

- Employment
- Prices
- Supplier delivery time
- Production
- Inventories
- Lead times of purchased items
- New orders from customers
- New export and import orders
- Orders backlogs (a component that was introduced in 1993 at the suggestion of Federal Reserve Board Chairman Greenspan[1])

The survey participant's formal responses to the questions are limited to an evaluation of *higher, lower,* or *unchanged* compared with the prior month, yet the respondent also is encouraged to add voluntary comments. Each component of the survey is compiled into a *diffusion index* following the convention of adding the percentage of the sample rising (or falling) plus one-half of the percentage of the sample responding "same" or "no change." The diffusion index can range between 0 percent and 100 percent. A summary measure of business activity is formulated as a composite diffusion index, which is called the *Purchasing Managers' Index (PMI),*[2] based on a weighted average of new orders, production, employment, supplier delivery time, and inventories. The PMI summary measure is assigned the following weighting scheme:

$$PMI = 0.30 \times (New\ Orders) + 0.25 \times (Production) + 0.20 \times (Employment) +$$

$$0.15 \times (Supplier\ Deliveries) + 0.10 \times (Inventories)$$

---

1 The survey questions continually have evolved. A new export orders question was introduced in January 1988, and an import orders question began to be used in October 1989. Another new question on order backlogs is being contemplated.

2 This index, which was originally called the NAPM composite diffusion index, was formulated under the direction of Theodore Torda, who was a senior economist at the U.S. Department of Commerce.

TABLE 19–1   Business Survey Questionnaire
Report for NAPM Business Survey Committee

Answers should reflect the responsibility level of YOUR purchasing organization (plant, division, company) and essentially only for the SIC that you have indicated in the available space. It is essential that questions only have ONE answer, that ALL questions are answered, and that completed forms are returned or faxed no later than the date indicated. You are encouraged to consult others in your company in order to provide current and accurate answers to all the questions.

1. GENERAL REMARKS: Comment regarding any business condition, local, national, or international, that affects your purchasing operation or the outlook for your company or industry. Your opinion and comments are very important.

Remarks: _____

2. PRODUCTION—Check the ONE box that best expresses the current month's level compared to the previous month.

❑ Better than a month ago   ❑ Same as a month ago
❑ Worse than a month ago

Remarks: _____

3. NEW ORDERS—Check the ONE box that best expresses the current month's new orders compared to the previous month.

❑ Better than a month ago   ❑ Same as a month ago
❑ Worse than a month ago

Remarks: _____

4. NEW EXPORT ORDERS—Check the ONE box that best expresses the current month's new export orders compared to the previous month.

❑ Do Not Export   ❑ Higher than a month ago
❑ Same as a month ago   ❑ Lower than a month ago

Remarks: _____

5. ORDER BACKLOGS—Check the ONE box that best expresses the current month's order backlog compared to the previous month.

❑ Higher than a month ago   ❑ Same as a month ago
❑ Lower than a month ago

Remarks: _____

6. COMMODITY PRICES—Check the ONE box that best expresses the current month's change in approximate net weighted average prices of the commodities you buy compared to the previous month.

- ❏ Higher than a month ago   ❏ Same as a month ago
- ❏ Lower than a month ago

List, in the spaces provided, specific commodities (use generic names, not proprietary) which are up or down in price since the last report. This may or may not involve price changes.

Up in Price: _____

Down in Price: _____

7. INVENTORIES OF PURCHASED MATERIALS—Check the OVERALL inventory level (units, not dollars) including raw, MRO, intermediates, etc. (not finished goods unless purchased) compared to the previous month.

- ❏ Higher than a month ago   ❏ Same as a month ago
- ❏ Lower than a month ago

Reasons if higher or lower: _____

8. IMPORTS—Check the ONE box that best expresses the current month's overall imports (units, not dollars) including raw, MRO, components, intermediates, etc. (not finished goods unless purchased) compared to the previous month.

- ❏ Do Not Import   ❏ Higher than a month ago
- ❏ Same as a month ago   ❏ Lower than a month ago

Remarks: _____

9. EMPLOYMENT—Check the OVERALL level of employment compared to the previous month.

- ❏ Greater than a month ago   ❏ Same as a month ago
- ❏ Less than a month ago

Reasons if greater or less: _____

10. VENDOR DELIVERIES—Check the ONE box that best expresses the current month's OVERALL delivery performance compared to the previous month.

- ❏ Faster than a month ago   ❏ Same as a month ago
- ❏ Slower than a month ago

Reasons if faster or slower: _____

11. ITEMS IN SHORT SUPPLY—Report specific commodities (use generic names, not proprietary) you purchase that are in short supply, even if mentioned in previous reports.

---

12. BUYING POLICY—Indicate, by checking the ONE appropriate box for each category of purchases, the approximate weighted number of days ahead for which you are committed. Do not report hedging or speculative purchases.

	Hand to Mouth	30 Days	60 Days	90 Days	6 Months	Year+
Production Materials	—	—	—	—	—	—
MRO Supplies	—	—	—	—	—	—
Capital Expenditures	—	—	—	—	—	—

The formal results of the survey with commentary are published in the NAPM *Report on Business* issued monthly by the trade association. In May and December, NAPM issues a semiannual outlook survey, which addresses some longer-term issues.

The NAPM PMI generally is reported at 10:00 AM (Eastern Time) on the first business day of the month for the preceding month. This makes this indicator one of the earliest measures available for the prior month, and hence it has become a key focus for the financial markets. It also provides information that is not found in any other government statistic, such as data on supplier delivery times, items in short supply, and buying policy, which is the average number of days in advance that a company has made commitments to buy: (1) production materials, (2) maintenance, repair, and operating (MRO) supplies, and (3) capital expenditures. Typically, faster supplier delivery speed is associated with slower business conditions and vice versa.

Over the Business Cycle

The PMI (as shown in Figure 19-1) averages 54.5 percent during expansions, with the rapid phase averaging about 6 points stronger than the slow-growth expansion phase, which averages 51.7 percent. During recessions the PMI averages 43.4 percent, while during the recovery phase of the business cycle the PMI tends to be 54.0 percent, on average. (See Table 19-2.) The average PMI readings during the recovery and expansion phases are not significantly different.

FIGURE 19–1   NAPM Purchasing Managers' Index

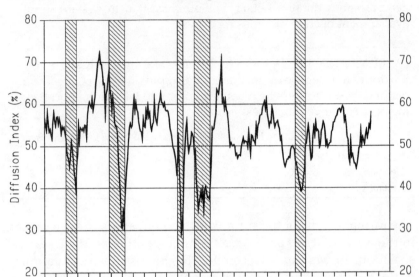

Analyzing the Data

The analysis of these data should be done on five levels: (1) business cycle turning-point implications, (2) the overall implication for economic growth, (3) the implication the price measure holds for inflation, (4) the theme of the components, and (5) the relationship between components of the report and other government indicators.

TABLE 19–2   NAPM Purchasing Managers' Index
January 1966–May 1997, Percent

| Phase | Historic Low | Normal Bounds | | | Historic High | Series Characteristics | |
		Normal Low	Average	Normal High		Standard Deviation	Share of Total Observations
Recession	29.2% in May 1980	39.2%	43.4%	47.6%	63.6% in Dec 1973	8.4 pp.	15.1%
Recovery	37.5% in Apr 1975	51.1%	54.0%	56.8%	69.9% in Dec 1983	5.7 pp.	22.3%
Expansion	42.8% in Apr 1967	51.7%	54.5%	57.3%	72.1% in Jan 1973	5.6 pp.	62.6%
Slow Phase	42.8% in Apr 1967	49.3%	51.7%	54.2%	68.1% in Nov 1973	4.9 pp.	31.6%
Rapid Phase	48.3% in Jul 1981	55.2%	57.6%	60.0%	72.1% in Jan 1973	4.8 pp.	31.0%
All Phases	29.2% in May 1980	49.1%	52.7%	56.3%	72.1% in Jan 1973	7.3 pp.	100.0%

1. *Tracking the NAPM PMI as a Turning-Point Indicator:* There are several critical threshold levels of the PMI that have significant implications for the economy. The key threshold levels in the PMI are: (1) the cyclical high, (2) 50 percent, (3) 44 percent, and (4) the cyclical low.

   History suggests that the NAPM PMI is a reliable forecasting indicator of a *growth cycle turning point.* Over the last 40 years, the NAPM PMI led growth cycle peaks by seven months, on average, and led growth cycle lows by three months. Hence, the PMI is a sensitive measure not only of business cycle turning points, but of a slowdown and acceleration in the expansion phase of the cycle.

   A reading of 50 percent or less is the second threshold level to watch for in tracking manufacturing activity. The 50 percent threshold is, by definition, the point at which an equal percentage of the respondents to the survey say business conditions are better as say they are worse. As such, the 50 percent point is significant for the financial markets from a *psychological* standpoint, as well as being a signal of potentially more weakness to come. On average, the PMI has fallen below 50 percent two months before recessions have begun (with a range of 14 months lead time in 1990 to a 10-month lag in 1973).

   When the PMI falls below 44 percent, that often has been a signal of an absolute decline in overall economic activity, though that signal, on average, occurred two months after the business cycle turning point. It is important to recognize that this index measures manufacturing activity only; hence, the PMI must fall below 44 percent (and not just 50 percent) in order for it to signal a widespread contraction in the economy. This is largely because service sector industries tend to be less cyclical and/or lag manufacturing activity, which could sustain the economy even if the manufacturing sector is deteriorating.

   During a recession, the PMI generally has continued to decline until it reaches 34.8 percent, on average (lowest 29.4 percent in 1980 and highest 43.6 percent in 1961). Once the PMI has turned around, it has taken an average of four months to cross above 44 percent, which generally has occurred simultaneously with a business cycle low.

Finally, the PMI has never declined below 44 percent without signaling a growth or business cycle. However, from these data alone it is very difficult to distinguish between the two types of national cycles.

2. *Using the NAPM PMI to Predict Real GNP and Industrial Production:* The relationship between industrial production (IP) and the NAPM PMI has become closer over time though the lead time of the PMI is rather short. On average, the PMI leads year-over-year changes in industrial production by two months. The estimated relationship between industrial production growth on a year-over-year basis and the PMI with a two-month lag is shown below.

$$\text{IP} = 0.519 \times \text{PMI}[-2] - 24.1$$

$$R^2 = 0.7452 \qquad \text{Sample Period: 1977–1997}$$

This relationship, which has been stable over time, suggests that the PMI must exceed 46.4 percent to be consistent with flat industrial production growth. Alternatively, when the PMI is at 50 percent, that has been consistent with 1.9 percent growth in production [that is, $(0.519 \times 50) - 24.1$].

Although it may be conceptually risky to associate the PMI with real GDP since GDP covers services and structures in addition to goods output, the fact is that the PMI anticipates real GDP growth (year over year) reasonably well with a lead time of one quarter.

$$\text{GDP} = 0.301 \times \text{PMI}[-1] - 12.8$$

$$R^2 = 0.7212 \qquad \text{Sample Period: 1977–1997}$$

The estimated quarterly GNP/PMI relationship suggests that a PMI reading of 42.5 percent has been consistent with no change in real GNP. Additionally, a 50 percent PMI reading has been consistent with 2.25 percent real GNP growth.

The key limitation of using the PMI to forecast some of the broader macroeconomic indicators is the short lead time. Nonetheless, the PMI provides an excellent guide to what is currently happening.

Although the PMI offers limited insight into longer-term growth prospects, it is still possible to use it to forecast beyond the near term. However, as is true of every forecast, the longer the forecast horizon, the more uncertainty associated with it. With this caveat in mind, the PMI could be used to project year-ahead growth using the following annual relationships:

$$IP = 0.529 \times (YEAREND[-1] - NAPM[-1]) + 2.8$$

$R^2 = 0.5842$ Sample Period: 1977–1996, Annual

where IP is annual industrial production growth, YEAR-END is the December NAPM PMI index for the prior year, and NAPM is the annual average PMI also for the prior year. The use of the December level of the NAPM PMI minus its annual average serves as a momentum indicator; that is, if the year ends higher than the annual average, that suggests positive momentum will continue, and vice versa. Similarly, an estimated equation also can be derived for real GDP:

$$GDP = 0.336 \times (YEAREND[-1] - NAPM[-1]) + 2.77$$

$R^2 = 0.6363$ Sample Period: 1977–1996, Annual

where GDP is annual real GDP growth. These two equations allow for a longer-term view.

3. *Prices Diffusion Index—A Leading Indicator of Inflation:* The members of the NAPM business survey committee are asked each month to judgmentally average the prices that they paid for commodities and to indicate whether prices rose, fell, or stayed the same compared with those of the prior month. A number of studies have shown that the diffusion index compiled from this question is a leading indicator of turning points in the inflation cycle.[3] (See

---

3   See, for example, Howard Roth, "Leading Indicators of Inflation," *Economic Review,* Federal Reserve Bank of Kansas City, November 1986, pp. 3–20. Also see Michael Niemira, "Updated PW Leading Indicator of Inflation," Paine Webber, December 26, 1986.

FIGURE 19–2   NAPM Price Diffusion Index

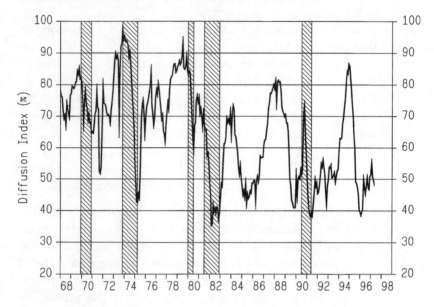

Figure 19-2 and Table 19-3.) However, the index does *not* provide a reliable indication of one-month changes in the Producer Price Index. Nonetheless, one study showed that the price diffusion index explained 59 percent of the fluctuation in one-month-ahead estimates of changes in the Producer Price Index for intermediate materials and supplies (SOP code 2100).[4]

4. *The Unfolding of the Business Cycle through the NAPM Business Survey:* The NAPM survey provides a relatively complete picture of manufacturing activity. Hence, at different stages of the business cycle, different measures are worth dwelling upon. For example, coming out of a recession, one would expect that the new orders diffusion index would perk up first, followed by production. Supplier lead times would tend to lengthen, suggesting that business activity is firming as well, though the greater adherence to just-in-time (JIT) inventories and the closer partnership of suppliers and customers are likely to limit the cyclical information from this measure in the future. As the economy continues to improve, employment and inventories

4   Lahiri and Dasgupta (1990).

TABLE 19–3   NAPM Price Diffusion Index
January 1966–May 1997, Percent

		Normal Bounds				Series Characteristics	
Phase	Historic Low	Normal Low	Average	Normal High	Historic High	Standard Deviation	Share of Total Observations
Recession	35.3% in Mar 1982	56.1%	65.1%	74.0%	95.3% in Jan 1974	18.0 pp.	15.1%
Recovery	38.2% in May 1991	56.7%	63.1%	69.5%	84.2% in Jul 1976	12.8 pp.	22.3%
Expansion	38.5% in Feb 1996	59.0%	66.5%	73.9%	97.6% in Nov 1973	15.0 pp.	62.6%
Slow Phase	38.5% in Feb 1996	55.0%	63.5%	71.9%	97.6% in Nov 1973	16.9 pp.	31.6%
Rapid Phase	42.1% in Nov 1992	65.3%	70.9%	76.6%	90.0% in Mar 1973	11.3 pp.	31.0%
All Phases	35.3% in Mar 1982	58.0%	65.5%	73.0%	97.6% in Nov 1973	15.1 pp.	100.0%

should notch higher. With a lag, prices will begin to reflect the strengthening economy. Similarly, the NAPM survey can be used to watch the unfolding of a slowdown or recession. New orders would be an early indicator to reflect weakness in the economy, which tends to spread to supplier delivery times, production, and prices. Generally, the economic weakness will show up in the employment and inventories diffusion indexes last.

5. *Other Links with Government Data:* There are government data series that conceptually match components of the NAPM survey. For example, the NAPM employment diffusion index is conceptually similar to the U.S. Bureau of Labor Statistics' manufacturing employment diffusion index. However, the government series tends to be more comprehensive, and the two measures often can move in different directions in the very near term. The NAPM price diffusion index is similar to the commodity price diffusion indexes that used to be calculated by the Commerce Department, and the NAPM production diffusion index is conceptually similar to the Federal Reserve's industrial production diffusion index calculated over one-month intervals. The Federal Reserve series also is more comprehensive than the NAPM measure, but it is reported with a one-month lag, which makes the NAPM series more timely.

Finally, one very near term barometer of future business conditions that is sometimes calculated from the purchasing manager survey detail is the difference of the new orders and inventories indexes, which conceptually is similar to a ratio of a leading indicator to a lagging indicator. The Purchasing Management Association of Oregon (PMAO), for example, presents such a monthly index with its monthly survey, which has been dubbed its monthly *forecasting index*. Statistically, the correlation between the PMI and the difference between the national measures of new orders and inventories is highest with a one-month lead time, which means that the same methodology used by PMAO can be applied to the national data. Based on this methodology, a simple one-month-ahead forecasting relationship can be derived as follows:

$$PMI = 0.833 \times PMI[-1] + 0.296 \times FCINDEX[-1] - 7.70$$

$$R^2 = 0.8638 \qquad \text{Sample Period: } 1980\text{--}1997$$

where FCINDEX is the forecast index, which is expressed in a similar fashion as the PMI and is calculated as: (New Orders minus Inventories) divided by 2 plus 50.

Special Factors, Limitations, and Other Data Issues

These data have been developed primarily to monitor the manufacturing sector. Hence, the *Report on Business* measures activity in about a fifth of the U.S. economy. As of 1997, NAPM has launched the testing phase of a *nonmanufacturing* purchasing manager survey. If the test is successful, this new survey is likely to be unveiled in May 1998.

The current manufacturing survey has been criticized for a sampling bias, its "backward-looking" nature, and its subjective responses.[5] But these findings view the survey simply as a *means*

---

5   Harris (1991). Harris concluded that his "results suggest that the index is flawed . . . it is a poor leading indicator and on its own it can be a misleading measure of short-run movements in the economy" (p. 13). One valid criticism of the construction of the summary measure that has been put forth by Klein and Moore (1988) is that the inventory component should enter the composite index as a change, not as a level. The parallel for this argument is how inventories are treated within the national income accounts. Gross domestic product (GDP) is the sum of final demand plus the *change* in inventories and not the stock of inventories (which is the concept measured by the NAPM survey question). As for the timing concern that Harris raises between, say, the NAPM PMI and industrial production, one way to statistically address this issue is to test for what is known as "Granger causality" between the two measures. A simple application of this test between 1980 and 1991 with one, three, and six lags suggests that there is *strong evidence* that the NAPM PMI "Granger-causes" changes

to an end, instead of as a separate and reasonably reliable barometer for purchasing managers. Clearly, these survey data provide an easy way to track the economy *without too much data intensity.* Furthermore, research suggests that the *breadth* of a recovery, expansion, or recession contains information on future growth prospects, which is another reason to monitor diffusion indexes.[6]

In addition to the national survey, numerous regional purchasing manager associations around the country survey local purchasing manager executives. Probably the best known of the regional surveys is the Chicago survey. National Association of Purchasing Management—Chicago generally releases its local area business conditions report on the last business day of the month at 10:00 (Eastern Time) for that same month. Consequently, the Chicago survey often is viewed as a *window* on the more comprehensive NAPM report. The typical question that financial market participants ask once the Chicago survey is released is: "What do the regional survey results mean for the NAPM report? In evaluating the Chicago survey for its national implication, it is important to keep in mind the following: (1) The *Chicago Business Barometer* (CBB), which is the summary measure released with the Chicago report, is compiled differently from the NAPM PMI. The CBB includes order backlogs (unfilled orders), while the NAPM index does not; the CBB does not include inventories, but the NAPM index does. (2) The weighting scheme also is different. The new orders component has a larger weight in the CBB than it does in the NAPM PMI, while the CBB employment component has half the importance as in the NAPM index. Both measures are seasonally adjusted, but the Chicago index is seasonally adjusted at the total level while the NAPM index is seasonally adjusted by component and summed. (See Table 19-4.)

Some other regional surveys also are released prior to the national survey, which focuses some attention on those surveys as well. The Detroit, New York, and Milwaukee reports tend to be released before the national report. To find out more about these

---

in industrial production. Essentially, this means that the Harris criticism is overstated.

6   Kennedy (1991). This idea that diffusion or the breadth of change is important for the unfolding of the business cycle is not new. Arthur Burns (the former Federal Reserve chairman) and William Fellner (a former member of the President's Council of Economic Advisors) were both advocates of that hypothesis. The Fellner hypothesis, which is known as the *law of diminishing offsets,* argued that business cycle recessions occurred as a result of prior diminution of dispersion of growth rates.

TABLE 19–4   A Comparison between the CBB and the NAPM PMI
(What Is Included and the Associated Weight)

	Production	New Orders	Employment	Deliveries	Inventories	Backlogs
CBB	0.25	0.35	0.10	0.15	Not Included	0.15
NAPM PMI	0.25	0.30	0.20	0.15	0.10	Not included

regional surveys, a summary of the regional reports can be found on the NAPM's Internet site and in its monthly magazine.

The American Production and Inventory Control Society (APICS) Business Outlook survey is yet another purchasing manager survey, which is currently based on about 100 manufacturing firms. The first APICS survey was taken in December 1992, and it first became available publicly beginning in September 1993. This nationwide measure tends to be released earlier than most other purchasing manager surveys, so it is watched by the financial markets for an indication of what the NAPM survey might show. A summary measure is compiled for this survey that is an arithmetic average of the current conditions component and a future conditions component. The current conditions subcomponent is an average of five components: (1) manufacturing shipments, (2) employment, (3) industrial production, (4) inventory stocks, and (5) unfilled orders. The future conditions subcomponent is an average of: (1) durable goods new orders (excluding aircraft and defense), (2) production plans, and (3) the actual-to-desired inventory/sales ratio. The society describes the compilation of the APICS indexes as follows:

First, we calculate the percentage change in any given series for each company. These are then weighted by the size of the company, and a total weighted percentage change is calculated. These figures are then seasonally adjusted. The result might show, for example, a 0.5% gain in industrial production, a 2.1% increase in shipments, or a 0.3% decline in employment. These percentage changes are then converted to an index number format for ease of comparability. A value of 50 for each individual component means that variable is unchanged from the previous month. A maximum value of 100 means the increase is as large as the biggest expected monthly gain; that figure is based in large part on the biggest gain that has occurred at any time since 1980. A minimum value of zero would mean the decline is as large as the biggest expected monthly drop.

For example, if the shipments' average increase was up 2.3 percent for the month and the maximum monthly increase was 3.8 percent over the historical period (based on government data), then the index value would be calculated as $50 \times (1 + 23/38)$, or 80.3. Despite the markets' view that these data provide a window on the NAPM PMI, the reality is that there is a low statistical correlation between the two series as measured on a level basis (correlation coefficient is 0.476) or in change form (correlation coefficient is 0.119, as measured between September 1993 and May 1997).

The Federal Reserve Bank of Philadelphia conducts a monthly survey of local manufacturers, which is called the *Business Outlook Survey* (BOS) and is very similar to the purchasing managers' surveys. The BOS also asks local manufacturers to provide a six-month-ahead forecast of various business barometers such as capital spending, prices, employment, etc. This survey collects information late in the prior month and early into the current month. It is reported at mid-month for the current month and is extremely timely information. Other regional surveys are conducted by Federal Reserve Banks such as Richmond and Atlanta, which release monthly surveys, while the Federal Reserve Bank of Kansas City compiles a quarterly survey of regional manufacturing conditions.

Unfortunately, there is little consistency between most of the purchasing managers' regional surveys and even the national survey, which is *conducted totally independently of the regional associations* and does not incorporate any survey input from the regional association surveys. Regional surveys are summarized in *NAPM Insights*, which is the official publication of NAPM.

In evaluating the regional surveys, it is important to note whether or not the data are seasonally adjusted (most regional surveys do not seasonally adjust their data) and be aware whether the survey is solely manufacturing based or whether it includes respondents from nonmanufacturing firms (for example, the Boston survey includes service establishments, and New York does as well). There is nothing wrong with including nonmanufacturing firms in the survey, but for cross-country comparisons, that distinction must be clear to the user. Because regional coverage and methodologies may differ widely across surveys, most regional surveys are more appropriate for historical comparisons within the region and may not be appropriate for geographic comparisons. Another practical concern with the regional surveys is that due to the generally smaller sample size than the national, the regional surveys can be more choppy even if the data are put on a consistent basis.

Finally, some regional surveys prefer to report their results as *net difference indexes* or *net percentage rising* (NPR). The NPR is simply the percentage of respondents reporting higher minus the percentage reporting lower. The net difference, which is bounded by +100 and −100, is related to the diffusion index as follows:

$$NPR = 2 \times (DI - 50)$$

where DI is the diffusion index. Similarly, the identity can be reformulated as:

$$DI = 50 + (NPR/2)$$

The choice of which formula to use for expressing the direction of survey change is arbitrary.

References

Ammer, Dean S., "The N.A.P.M. Business Survey: How It Works. How to Use It as a Purchasing Tool," National Association of Purchasing Management, 1983.

Bretz, Robert J., "Behind the Economic Indicators of the NAPM Report on Business," *Business Economics*, July 1990, pp. 42–47.

Bretz, Robert J., "Forecasting with the *Report on Business*," *NAPM Insights*, August 1990, pp. 22–25.

Harris, Ethan S., "Tracking the Economy with the Purchasing Managers Index," Research Paper No. 9124, Federal Reserve Bank of New York, August 1991.

Hoagland, John H., and Barbara E. Taylor. "Purchasing Business Surveys: Uses and Improvements," *Freedom of Choice: Presentations from the 72nd Annual International Purchasing Conference,* National Association of Purchasing Management, 1987.

Kennedy, James E. "Empirical Relationships between the Total Industrial Production Index and Its Diffusion Indexes," Finance and Economics Discussion Series 163, Board of Governors of the Federal Reserve System, Divisions of Research and Statistics and Monetary Affairs, July 1991.

Klein, Philip A., and Geoffrey H. Moore, "N.A.P.M. Business Survey Data: Their Value as Leading Indicators," *Journal of Purchasing and Materials Management*, Winter 1988, pp. 32–40.

Lahiri, Kajal, and Susmita Dasgupta, "A Comparative Study of Alternative Methods of Quantifying Qualitative Survey Responses Using NAPM Data," Working Paper, State University of New York at Albany, August 14, 1990.

"Purchasing Managers, Commerce Department Develop New Economic Index," U.S. Department of Commerce News, Office of Economic Affairs, February 4, 1982 (which was simultaneously issued as an NAPM press release).

Torda, Theodore, "Purchasing Management Index Provides Early Clue on Turning Points," *Business America*, Vol. 8, pp. 11–13.

Chapter 20

Personal Income and Consumption

General Description

Personal consumption expenditures (PCE) measure the value of goods and services purchased by the consumer, while personal income measures all sources of income to the household sector on a cash disbursement basis. These data are the monthly counterparts to the quarterly measures, which are part of the GDP report.

Economic Indicator Information at a Glance

Market Significance	Moderate
Typical Release Time	8:30 AM Eastern Time About 21st–22nd Business Day after End of Month First Business Day after GDP Report
Released By	U.S. Department of Commerce Bureau of Economic Analysis
Period Covered	Prior Month
Web Site	http://www.bea.doc.gov

Analyzing the Data

Personal consumption accounts for about two-thirds of real GDP. PCE measures consumer purchases of goods and services—including the net purchase of used goods—by individuals residing in the United States plus purchases made by the nonprofit sector (which account for about 4 percent of real GDP). These data cover three broad **product categories**—durable goods, non-durable goods, and services. The largest of those three groups is services, which currently account for slightly over 56 percent of total PCE. Nondurable goods expenditures are the next largest category, accounting for about 31 percent of the total, while the remaining 13 percent of expenditures are for durable goods such as furniture, cars and trucks, computers, etc. PCE does not include payments made to governments that are a result of administrative or regulatory functions; instead these are included under personal taxes and nontax payments on the income side. Portions of personal expenditures are "imputed" by the Commerce Department, which means that they are inferred by a statistical methodology from other data. Most of that imputation occurs in the service expenditure categories (such as for "homeowner rent" or, more formally, "owner occupied nonfarm space"—which alone accounts for almost 19 percent of total service spending).

The cyclical sensitivity of each of those types of purchases varies in reverse order to their size. Durable goods tend to be the most volatile and sensitive to the business cycle, followed by non-durables and then services. Because of the high degree of imputation and extrapolation, measured service spending appears much more steady than the reality. Between 1959 and 1997, the average absolute deviation of the month-to-month percentage change in consumer services spending was 0.29 percentage point; it was 0.59 percentage point for nondurable spending and a hefty 2.17 percentage points for durable goods spending.

Personal consumption data also can be viewed on an **expenditure basis,** in addition to the product basis—though many of the detailed monthly expenditure data are reported only as "unpublished data," which means the Commerce Department makes the data available with the caveat that they have a lower degree of accuracy than those published. On the expenditure side, consumption is the sum of spending for: (1) food and tobacco, (2) clothing and accessories, including jewelry, (3) personal care, (4) housing services, (5) household operation, (6) medical care, (7) personal business services, (8) transportation, (9) recreation, (10) education and research, (11) religion and welfare, and (12) foreign travel and other. Although this breakdown is not timely from a market perspective, it does provide a window on the underlying composition of spending.

On a monthly basis, personal consumption expenditures for durables and nondurable goods are based on or extrapolated using monthly data from the Census Bureau's retail sales report. About 85 percent of the goods consumption data are extrapolated using retail sales less auto dealer and building material store sales, while the remainder is based on unit vehicle sales.

Personal outlays are a slightly broader concept than personal consumption expenditures since that category includes interest paid by consumers to business (mortgage and consumer installment credit interest payments—but not the principal) and personal transfer payments to the rest of the world. In 1996, interest paid by persons accounted for 2.8 percent of personal outlays, and personal transfer payments (such as money sent to relatives abroad) accounted for 0.3 percent of total outlays. The personal outlay measure is used to calculate the **savings rate,** which is defined as disposable personal income (personal income less taxes) minus personal outlays and divided by disposable income.

Personal income accounted for a tad over 85 percent of nominal GDP in 1996, with 56 percent of personal income from wages and salaries. In addition to wages and salaries, the other components of personal income are the sum of other labor income, proprietors' income, rental income, dividend income, interest income, and transfer payments minus social insurance contributions by individuals. Personal income accounts for bonus payments and is adjusted for insurance loss. The adjustment for disaster loss or major storm loss is normally done through the rental income component. When the BEA identifies a major disaster impact, it adjusts rental income downward by the uninsured loss amount. Nonfarm proprietors' income also is likely to be adjusted downward to reflect uninsured loss to business property. But to the extent that there is insurance, personal consumption is adjusted downward. The BEA will lower property insurance services because this component of PCE is defined as the insurance premiums minus benefits. Although a major disaster adjustment will depress nominal consumption, real consumption—which is only based on premiums paid—will be unaffected, which will create an abnormal divergence between the real and nominal measures.

**BOX 20–1   Real Earnings—Combining Data
from Two Other Reports**

The real earnings data are derived from the Bureau of Labor Statistics monthly establishment survey of employment, payroll, and hours, inflation-adjusted using a deflator derived from the Consumer Price Index for Urban Wage Earners and Clerical Workers (CPI-W).

> The BLS defines these data as: arithmetic averages (means) of the hourly and weekly earnings of all production or nonsupervisory jobs in the private nonfarm sector of the economy. Average hourly earnings estimates are derived by dividing the estimated industry payroll—for all production or nonsupervisory jobs—by the corresponding paid hours. Average weekly hours estimates are similarly derived by dividing estimated aggregate hours by the corresponding number of production or nonsupervisory jobs. Average weekly earnings estimates are derived by multiplying the average hourly earnings and the average weekly hours estimates. This is equivalent to dividing the estimated payroll by the number of production or nonsupervisory jobs. The weekly and hourly earnings estimates for aggregate industries, such as the major industry division and the total private sector averages printed in this release, are derived by summing the corresponding payroll, hours, and employment estimates of the component industries. As a result, each industry receives a "weight" in the published averages that corresponds to its current level of activity (employment or total hours). This further implies that fluctuations and varying trends in employment in high-wage versus low-wage industries as well as wage rate changes influence the earnings averages.

The keys to interpreting the monthly income and consumption report include:

- Ask yourself, what is the indicated pace of real consumer spending for the current quarter as it is unfolding? That is the key value of these data for the markets, as a gauge of the current quarter's likely real GDP and real PCE pace. Hence, the market importance of these data varies over the given quarter. After the advance GDP report is released, the monthly consumption data tend to have the least market significance since the whole quarter is already known. But over the subsequent two months, the data take on more market importance, since they provide a timely estimate of the current quarter's real PCE and GDP pace.

- Be aware that unit vehicle sales, which are available prior to the consumption data, provide a guide to the volatile durable goods component, which is often dominated by swings in vehicle sales.

- Recognize that occasionally special factors impact the personal income tally. Personal income less special factors—which is a measure discussed in the Commerce Department's personal income and consumption press release but not shown in any data table—tends to have more market importance than the overall measure of personal income because it provides a more representative picture of the underlying income stream.

- Remember that in January any increases in social insurance contributions or base changes will show up as a "step-function" jump in that component. As a result, increased Social Security contributions will depress personal income. Another special factor to watch for is the COLA adjustment to Social Security and federal government retiree pensions. Finally, keep an eye on initial filings for unemployment insurance throughout the year. If the jobless claims pace is rising or falling sharply, it will impact transfer payments in a like fashion.

- Be alert to the trend in the personal savings rate, which could signal a liquidity problem or liquidity bulge facing the consumer.

Personal Consumption and Income over the Business Cycle

On a month-to-month basis, changes in personal consumption are difficult to interpret because of the high degree of noise. On a smoothed basis, however, the consumption dynamic and relationship with personal income becomes clearer. Although it is widely accepted in economic theory that consumption is dependent on income, the second part of that theoretical framework often is overlooked, which is that consumption determines income as well. This consumption-income link is considerably more important at cyclical turning points (both major and minor cycles). The rationale why consumption growth can lead income growth and with it the overall economy is tied to consumer credit. Consumers often supplement their income by charging purchases ("buy now, pay later"), which provides that extra boost to sales needed to turn the economy around after recessions. Even measures of consumer spending power can be misleading in the short term for assessing the consumers' spending ability, since big-ticket items leased or purchased on credit are paid off over a period of time, which does not concurrently drain savings in the period when the consumption is recorded, as is implied by the national income methodology. (See Figures 20-1 and 20-2 and Tables 20-1 to 20-3.)

Special Factors, Limitations, and Other Data Issues

One of the key conceptual limitations of the personal consumption data is the treatment of durable goods purchases, which are recorded as if they were fully paid for in the period in

FIGURE 20–1 Personal Consumption

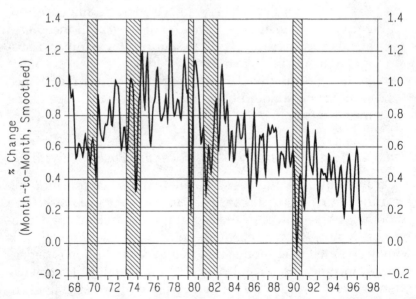

FIGURE 20–2 Personal Income

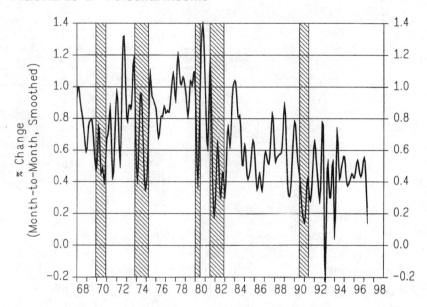

which they were purchased. Although a car can be paid off over several years, it is assumed to be bought and paid for all in the same time. As a result, the savings rate could look abnormally depressed if car and truck sales soar, for example. Indeed, only about 8 percent of vehicles are fully paid off at the time of purchase, while the remainder are leased or financed by conventional means. The flow-of-funds accounts, however, adjust for this and consequently develop a higher savings rate.

TABLE 20–1 Personal Consumption
February 1959–May 1997, Month-to-Month Percentage Change

Phase	Historic Low	Normal Bounds			Historic High	Series Characteristics	
		Normal Low	Average	Normal High		Standard Deviation	Share of Total Observations
Recession	−1.9% in May 1960	0.2%	0.5%	0.8%	1.8% in Aug 1974	0.7 pp.	14.6%
Recovery	−0.9% in Feb 1984	0.5%	0.8%	1.0%	2.5% in May 1975	0.6 pp.	20.9%
Expansion	−1.8% in Jan 1987	0.3%	0.6%	0.9%	2.5% in Sep 1986	0.6 pp.	64.6%
Slow Phase	−1.3% in Oct 1986	0.3%	0.6%	0.9%	2.5% in Sep 1986	0.6 pp.	30.4%
Rapid Phase	−1.8% in Jan 1987	0.4%	0.7%	1.0%	2.4% in Dec 1986	0.6 pp.	34.2%
All Phases	−1.9% in May 1960	0.3%	0.6%	0.9%	2.5% in Sep 1986	0.6 pp.	100.0%

TABLE 20–2   Personal Income
February 1959–May 1997, Month-to-Month Percentage Change

| | | Normal Bounds | | | | Series Characteristics | |
Phase	Historic Low	Normal Low	Average	Normal High	Historic High	Standard Deviation	Share of Total Observations
Recession	–0.5% in Dec 1960	0.2%	0.4%	0.7%	2.2% in Apr 1970	0.5 pp.	14.6%
Recovery	–1.0% in Jul 1971	0.5%	0.7%	1.0%	2.4% in Jun 1975	0.5 pp.	20.9%
Expansion	–3.8% in Jan 1993	0.3%	0.6%	0.9%	3.6% in Dec 1992	0.6 pp.	64.6%
Slow Phase	–0.5% in Feb 1963	0.4%	0.6%	0.8%	1.7% in Oct 1973	0.4 pp.	30.4%
Rapid Phase	–3.8% in Jan 1993	0.3%	0.7%	1.1%	3.6% in Dec 1992	0.8 pp.	34.2%
All Phases	–3.8% in Jan 1993	0.4%	0.6%	0.9%	3.6% in Dec 1992	0.6 pp.	100.0%

Relationship with Other Series

The monthly measure of personal income is calculated on a "cash" or "when paid" basis, while the quarterly measure is calculated on an "accrual" or "when earned" basis. This results in accounting differences in the wage and salary components between the personal income report and the GDP report. In the GDP report, there are two measures of wages—"wage and salary accruals" and "wage and salary disbursements," which differed by about a relatively small $3 billion in 1995.

A monthly measure of consumer prices is included within the income and consumption report, which is the **implicit price deflator of personal consumption.** Those data tend to track the pace of the CPI over the long haul, but between 1995 and early 1997 they have run about a 0.5–0.75 percentage point (at an annual rate) below the CPI pace. The question is, why? The BEA

TABLE 20–3   Personal Savings Rate
January 1970–May 1997, Percent

| | | Normal Bounds | | | | Series Characteristics | |
Phase	Historic Low	Normal Low	Average	Normal High	Historic High	Standard Deviation	Share of Total Observations
Recession	5.0% in Oct 1990	7.8%	8.6%	9.3%	11.3% in Dec 1973	1.5 pp.	17.4%
Recovery	5.3% in Feb 1977	7.0%	7.7%	8.4%	13.4% in May 1975	1.4 pp.	25.6%
Expansion	1.8% in Apr 1987	5.4%	6.3%	7.1%	10.8% in Nov 1973	1.7 pp.	57.0%
Slow Phase	3.5% in Apr 1996	5.5%	6.4%	7.2%	10.8% in Nov 1973	1.7 pp.	26.5%
Rapid Phase	1.8% in Apr 1987	5.4%	6.3%	7.2%	10.0% in Jul 1981	1.7 pp.	30.5%
All Phases	1.8% in Apr 1987	6.1%	7.0%	8.0%	13.4% in May 1975	1.9 pp.	100.0%

has examined that issue and concluded that one reason for the lower inflation pace was due to the difference in coverage—the PCE price deflator includes government health care reimbursement while the CPI does not. Another reason is that the PCE measure has different and varying weights compared with fixed weights for the CPI measure.

Finally, another measure of wages that is sometimes highlighted and compared to personal income is real earnings. These data are separately compiled by the BLS (see Box 20-1).

Chapter 21

Producer Price Index

General Description

The Producer Price Index (PPI) is a fixed-weight price index that measures the average domestic change in prices, less any discounts, received by producers of commodities at the whole-sale level. Imported goods prices are not directly measured in the PPI. However to the extent that they enter into producers' costs, they can affect what producers charge and receive for their goods. The PPI covers all three stages of processing: crude, intermediate, and finished goods.

Economic Indicator Information at a Glance

Market Significance	High
Typical Release Time	8:30 AM Eastern Time About the 10th Business Day of the Month
Released By	Labor Department Bureau of Labor Statistics
Period Covered	Prior Month
Web Site	http://stats.bls.gov/news.release/ ppi.toc.htm

The finished goods category covers products that will un-dergo no further processing. They will be bought and used as is. Machinery, computers, clothing, and household items such as flooring and kitchenware are representative of the category. Intermediate goods need additional processing or are used to create or complete a final product. Examples are plywood, concrete, paper and paperboard, leather, and plastic parts for manufacturing. Crude goods are the initial inputs, having undergone no processing. Basic commodities such as crude oil, raw cotton, iron ore, logs, and cattle hides are typical crude goods components. (See Table 21-1 and Box 21-1.)

The PPI surveys about 3,100 commodities via approximately 40,000 survey participants. The data are collected for the Tuesday of the week that includes the 13th of the month. Unlike the Consumer Price Index, all PPI data are subject to revision four months after the initial publication. Participation in the survey is voluntary, and sometimes not enough data for a particular component are available for the first calculation. Subsequent comprehensive price information can then result in revisions to the PPI. Similar to the CPI, annual seasonal factor adjustments are incorporated each February.

One of the basic differences between the PPI and the CPI is the PPI's exclusion of service prices; it is strictly a commodity-based index. The BLS has a separate price series on hospital costs but has yet to incorporate it in the PPI. Given the lack of services in the PPI, the first division of this series is into its food, energy, and all other, or core, components. All three stages of processing (crude, intermediate, and finished goods) are broken down into these three components (see Table 21-2).

One aspect of the PPI worth noting is its greater volatility compared with the CPI. The chief reason is that the most volatile sectors, food and energy, have a higher weighting in the PPI, their total being more than 36 percent compared with under 25 per-

TABLE 21–1   PPI Relative Importances*, 1996: Crude Goods, Intermediate Goods, and Finished Goods

	Crude	Intermediate	Finished
Food	38.0	5.0	23.6
Energy	42.4	13.8	14.7
Core	19.6	81.3	61.6

* For an understanding of relative importances versus weights, please see the Box 21-2 on page 200.

BOX 21–1   Agricultural Prices

One series that can be an input to forecasting the PPI and the CPI is the Department of Agriculture's agricultural price series. It's released at 3:00 PM, usually on the last business day of the month that the data cover. The data are broken into prices paid by farmers and prices received by farmers, with the latter being the series that is often utilized to help forecast the food component of the two price indexes. The data include, inter alia, livestock and product prices, dairy products, and fresh fruits and vegetables. These data are presented only on a nonseasonally adjusted basis for the total of all prices received. There are seasonally adjusted breakdowns for components such as fresh fruits and vegetables, dairy products, and poultry. The series' volatility greatly exceeds that of the food component of either the PPI or CPI. In fact, its relationship with the two food components is not very tight. Although it is not the norm, it certainly is not unusual for agricultural prices to decline (rise) while the two food components rise (decline).

---

cent, than in the Consumer Price Index. But even the core PPI is more volatile than the core CPI. The reason is that the higher up the processing chain, the less impact an initial price shock will have since a portion of the initial cost shock is absorbed at each level. This same reasoning applies to the three processing stages, crude, intermediate, and final, within the Producer Price Index. Second, we come back to the fact that the PPI does not include services. As discussed in the CPI section, service inflation is less volatile than goods inflation, and it also has run higher than goods inflation. For these reasons, outright declines occurred 19 times in the PPI, but never at the consumer price level, over the last ten years.

TABLE 21–2   PPI and CPI: Energy, Food, and Core Component Comparisons
Average Absolute Year-to-Year Changes in Inflation Rates; 1986–1996

	CPI	PPI
Energy Prices	3.5%	6.8%
Food Prices	0.9%	1.5%
Core Prices	0.4%	0.8%

In terms of breaking the PPI down into additional components, it is not as amenable to doing so as is the CPI. Only two
broad categories exist, consumer goods and capital goods, with
respective relative importances of 76% and 24%. From there one
is forced to go to individual components for information on the
sources of any unusual inflation news.

Analyzing the Data

One appraises the Producer Price Index as one does the CPI.
(See Box 21-2.) Focus is placed immediately upon the month-to-
month change in the overall PPI and the core PPI, with the core
rate change as important as, if not more so than, the overall PPI's
change. Annual inflation rates are not important at the time of release. A wide disparity between the overall PPI's change and the
core's change is the first thing to note. A much different than expected total PPI change that is matched with an as-expected core
rate change is much less likely to affect the markets than is an expected overall PPI change coupled with a core rate change that is
very different than expected. A reading two-tenths or more from
expectations would be considered a surprise, and would more

BOX 21–2   Measuring Price Change:
What Is a Relative Importance?

The BLS's Consumer and Producer Price Indexes are constructed
as a "weighted average of relatives," which means the index
shares are derived from the price of a specific commodity or service divided by the total value of purchases. The BLS publishes
these *relative importances* for December of the prior year, and they
are commonly—but incorrectly—referred to as weights. Relative
importances actually change every month and really are price-
adjusted quantity weights. But it is not necessary to update relative importances during the year since the last published relative
importance is generally close enough to approximate the contribution of any given component. The exception is when a price
moves sharply during a given year. Then the relative importance
can change enough to make a difference. In 1992 a huge increase
in the price of aircraft cut its relative importance from 4.118 in December 1991 to 1.912 in December 1992.

than likely generate a market response. The core intermediate and core crude changes are also surveyed. They matter most when the market sees the potential for a change in inflation's direction. Each is considered a leading indicator of finished goods inflation (see Figure 21-1) although much of the price pressures at these lower levels are passed immediately through to finished goods within the same quarter, if not the same month.

Once the two rates have been assimilated, the detailed categories are scoured for aberrations that might be causing the core and total rates to be masking a different inflation story. One must rummage through approximately 54 nonfood, nonenergy components such as tobacco, passenger cars, women's apparel, household appliances, and computers to discover the source(s) of any unexpected price change. Again, the focus is to determine whether or not one or two components can be isolated as the source of the surprise or whether or not it is a more broad-based change, one that may be signaling a change not only in one month's inflation rate, but in the trend inflation rate also.

Again, as is the case with the CPI, the financial markets can become accustomed to recurring inflationary pressures emanating from specific sectors and more readily dismiss them. The car

FIGURE 21–1 PPI: Stage of Processing Core Rate Increases, 4-Month Moving Average: Year-over-Year Percentage Change

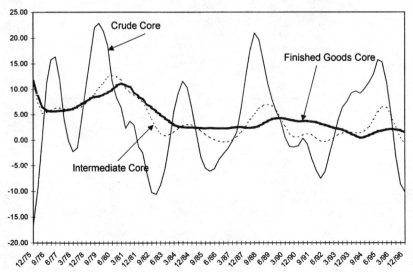

FIGURE 21–2   Producer Price Index

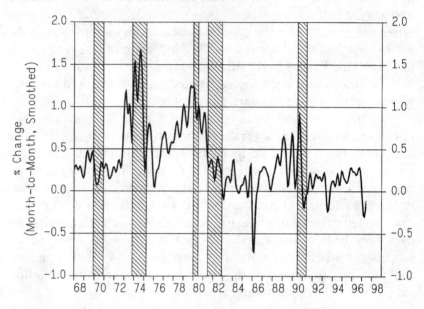

FIGURE 21–3   Producer Price Index Less Food and Energy

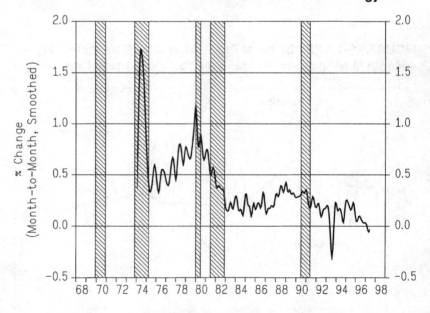

TABLE 21–3   Producer Price Index
January 1948–June 1997, Month-to-Month Percentage Change

| Phase | Historic Low | Normal Bounds | | | Historic High | Series Characteristics | |
		Normal Low	Average	Normal High		Standard Deviation	Share of Total Observations
Recession	-1.1% in Feb 1949	0.0%	0.4%	0.7%	2.7% in Jul 1974	0.7 pp.	16.2%
Recovery	-0.8% in Jan 1983	0.0%	0.2%	0.4%	1.2% in Mar 1981	0.4 pp.	20.9%
Expansion	-1.3% in Feb 1986	0.0%	0.3%	0.5%	3.5% in Aug 1973	0.5 pp.	61.1%
Slow Phase	-1.3% in Feb 1986	-0.0%	0.2%	0.5%	3.5% in Aug 1973	0.5 pp.	29.5%
Rapid Phase	-0.8% in Aug 1993	0.1%	0.3%	0.5%	2.1% in Aug 1950	0.5 pp.	31.6%
All Phases	-1.3% in Feb 1986	0.0%	0.3%	0.5%	3.5% in Aug 1973	0.5 pp.	100.0%

component is the most identifiable example of this phenomenon, but others, such as tobacco, have filled the bill in past years and others could do so in the future. The theme of this willingness to ignore specific price pressures is consistent with the markets' desire to focus on the underlying inflationary picture, not transitory blips.

Producer Prices over the Business Cycle

The cyclical attributes of the PPI can be analyzed in two ways: in terms of its own relationship to the business cycle and in terms of its cyclical relationship to the CPI. Producer prices' peaks and troughs (based on annual rates of inflation) lag the business cycle but by different spans of time. The peaks typically are reached within three to six months of the top of economic activity. The

TABLE 21–4   Producer Price Index Less Food and Energy
February 1974–June 1997, Month-to-Month Percentage Change

| Phase | Historic Low | Normal Bounds | | | Historic High | Series Characteristics | |
		Normal Low	Average	Normal High		Standard Deviation	Share of Total Observations
Recession	0.0% in Feb 1982	0.5%	0.7%	1.0%	2.2% in May 1974	0.5 pp.	15.7%
Recovery	-0.4% in Jan 1983	0.2%	0.4%	0.5%	1.1% in Jan 1981	0.3 pp.	24.9%
Expansion	-1.2% in Aug 1993	0.1%	0.3%	0.5%	2.0% in Jan 1980	0.3 pp.	59.4%
Slow Phase	-0.6% in Sep 1985	0.1%	0.3%	0.5%	2.0% in Jan 1980	0.3 pp.	28.5%
Rapid Phase	-1.2% in Aug 1993	0.1%	0.3%	0.5%	1.0% in Apr 1978	0.3 pp.	30.9%
All Phases	-1.2% in Aug 1993	0.2%	0.4%	0.6%	2.2% in May 1974	0.4 pp.	100.0%

troughs typically lag the bottom of the business cycle by about nine months. (See Figures 21-2 and 21-3 and Tables 21-3 and 21-4.) In terms of the CPI, the timing relationship between the two price indexes is closely linked. More often than not, peaks and troughs for each have occurred in the same quarter and almost certainly within one quarter of each other. The qualifiers for this indicate that there have been exceptions, but the general thrust of historical observation—that inflation lags the business cycle and the CPI and PPI have almost identical cyclical patterns—is the best rule of thumb.

Chapter 22

Productivity and Costs

General Description

Productivity measures the output of goods and services relative to its labor input or factor of production. Although the concept of productivity is well founded in economic theory and measurement, the growth of services and computerization of industry have made the estimation of output, and hence productivity, more difficult. Federal Reserve Chairman Alan Greenspan has said in numerous speeches that he believes that productivity is being understated because of the failure to properly account for output growth. But any shortfall with these data rests with the NIPA data and BLS employee hours data, which are the source data for the productivity and cost measures. Despite all the limitations of these data, they still are one of the most comprehensive sets of data to look at to understand the cyclical pressures in the economy.

Economic Indicator Information at a Glance

Market Significance	Moderate
Typical Release Time	10:00 AM Eastern Time About 6 weeks after End of Quarter
Released By	U.S. Department of Commerce Bureau of Economic Analysis
Period Covered	Prior Quarter
Web Site	http://stats.bls.gov/

Analyzing the Data

The productivity and cost data are reported about six weeks after the end of the quarter and about 10 days following the advanced estimate of real GDP. They are revised about one month later based on more complete estimates of output and hours worked. The market generally focuses upon the nonfarm component of this report, though the report is a comprehensive measure for the total business sector. With a one-month lag, data on the manufacturing and financial sectors are reported, but they tend to be ignored by the financial markets.

In essence, these data are a repackaging of previously reported data and, as such, command less market interest. The Labor Department calculates these data as follows:

Business sector output is an annual-weighted index constructed after excluding from gross domestic product (GDP) the following outputs: general government, nonprofit institutions, paid employees of private households, and the rental value of owner-occupied dwellings. Corresponding exclusions also are made in labor inputs. Business output accounted for about 76 percent of the value

FIGURE 22–1   Nonfarm Productivity

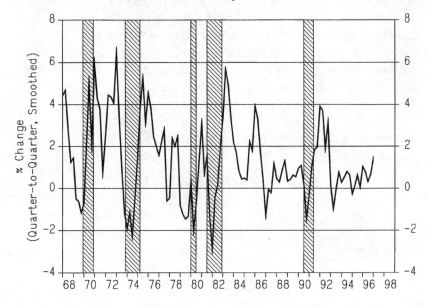

FIGURE 22–2   Nonfarm Unit Labor Costs

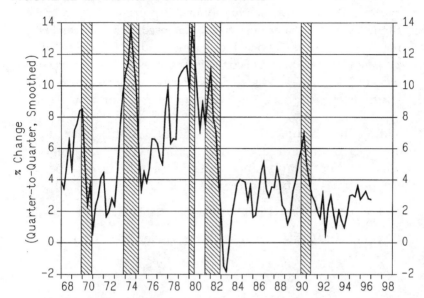

of GDP in 1992. Nonfarm business, which also excludes farming, accounted for about 75 percent of GDP in 1992.

The Labor Department goes on to say:

> Productivity measures describe the relationship between real output and the labor time involved in its production. They show the changes from period to period in the amount of goods and services produced per hour. Although these measures relate output to hours at work of all persons engaged in a sector, they do not measure the specific contribution of labor, capital, or any other factor of production. Rather, they reflect the joint effects of many influences, including changes in technology; capital investment; level of output; utilization of capacity, energy, and materials; the organization of production; managerial skill; and the characteristics and effort of the workforce.
>
> The primary source of hours and employment data is the BLS Current Employment Statistics (CES) program, which provides monthly survey data on total employment and average weekly paid hours of production and non-supervisory workers in non-agricultural establishments. Jobs rather than persons are counted.

Weekly paid hours are adjusted to hours at work using the BLS Hours at Work survey, conducted for this purpose. Data from the BLS Current Population Survey (CPS) are used for farm labor; in the nonfarm sector, the National Income and Product Accounts (NIPA) prepared by the Bureau of Economic Analysis (BEA) of the Department of Commerce and the CPS are used to measure labor input for government enterprises, proprietors, and unpaid family workers.

Within the productivity report, the BLS reports measures on output per hour, unit labor costs, compensation, and real compensation. The relationship—in growth rate terms—between these measures can be approximated as follows:

(1) Productivity Growth = Output Growth minus Hours Growth

(2) Unit Labor Cost Growth = Compensation Growth minus

Productivity Growth

or

Productivity Growth = Compensation Growth minus Unit

Labor Cost Growth

(3) Real Compensation Growth = Compensation Growth minus

Inflation Growth

It is important to recognize the definitional relationships, since all too often the markets seem to be surprised by, say, an upward revision to unit labor cost growth when the productivity is revised downward.

TABLE 22–1   Nonfarm Productivity
1960 Q1–1996 Q4, Two-Quarter Smoothed Annualized Percentage Change

| | | Normal Bounds | | | | Series Characteristics | |
Phase	Historic Low	Normal Low	Average	Normal High	Historic High	Standard Deviation	Share of Total Observations
Recession	−2.9% in 1982Q1	−1.0%	−0.1%	0.7%	5.0% in 1970Q3	1.7 pp.	17.6%
Recovery	−0.7% in 1980Q3	2.2%	3.1%	3.9%	6.3% in 1961Q4	1.7 pp.	23.6%
Expansion	−1.5% in 1979Q3	0.7%	1.7%	2.7%	6.8% in 1962Q1	2.0 pp.	58.8%
Slow Phase	−1.5% in 1979Q3	0.3%	1.1%	1.9%	4.8% in 1963Q3	1.6 pp.	33.1%
Rapid Phase	−1.3% in 1987Q1	1.1%	2.2%	3.2%	6.8% in 1962Q1	2.1 pp.	25.7%
All Phases	−2.9% in 1982Q1	0.7%	1.7%	2.8%	6.8% in 1962Q1	2.1 pp.	100.0%

TABLE 22–2   Nonfarm Unit Labor Costs

1960 Q1–1996 Q4, Two-Quarter Smoothed Annualized Percentage Change

Phase	Historic Low	Normal Bounds			Historic High	Series Characteristics	
		Normal Low	Average	Normal High		Standard Deviation	Share of Total Observations
Recession	2.4% in 1970Q3	6.1%	7.8%	9.5%	13.7% in 1974Q3	3.4 pp.	17.6%
Recovery	−2.6% in 1961Q4	1.7%	3.3%	4.8%	11.9% in 1980Q3	3.1 pp.	23.6%
Expansion	−2.6% in 1961Q4	2.1%	3.6%	5.1%	11.3% in 1979Q4	3.0 pp.	58.8%
Slow Phase	−1.5% in 1963Q3	2.8%	4.3%	5.8%	11.3% in 1979Q4	3.0 pp.	33.1%
Rapid Phase	−2.6% in 1961Q4	1.6%	3.0%	4.5%	10.5% in 1979Q1	2.8 pp.	25.7%
All Phases	−2.6% in 1961Q4	2.4%	4.1%	5.8%	13.7% in 1974Q3	3.4 pp.	100.0%

These data are often more important to assess the nation's health than is generally thought of in the financial markets. Most importantly, the **ratio of output prices to unit labor costs** has long been viewed as a leading indicator of the business cycle around the world. Ernst Boehm, for example, summarized the cyclical importance of these data as follows: "The price-cost cycle contributes appreciably to the explanation of the amplitude of business cycles as well as their duration. In particular, the empirical evidence shows that a major downswing in the price-cost cycle is generally associated with a classical recession. By contrast, the occasions when a growth slowdown does not lead to a classical recession are generally marked also by a relatively mild downturn in the price-cost cycle."[1] (See Figures 22-1 and 22-2 and Tables 22-1 and 22-2.)

Relationship with Other Series

Once a year, the BLS publishes data on multifactor manufacturing productivity in the United States and around the world. Those data, which have little market interest, allow for international comparisons and can often provide a window on the international competitiveness issue.

---

1   "Understanding Business Cycles Today: A Critical Review of Theory and Fact," *Analyzing Modern Business Cycles*, Philip A. Klein, ed., M. E. Sharpe, Armonk, N.Y., 1990, pp. 25–26.

Chapter 23

Retail Sales

General Description

The retail sales report, issued by the Bureau of the Census, is the first, but not the most comprehensive, picture of consumer spending for a given month. (The personal consumption expenditure data are a more exhaustive treatment of spending, its inclusion of service purchases being the chief difference between the two series.)

Economic Indicator Information at a Glance

Market Significance	High
Typical Release Time	8:30 AM Eastern Time Mid-Month
Released By	Commerce Department Census Bureau
Period Covered	Prior Month
Web Site	http://www.census.gov/svsd/www/advtable.html

The estimated value of total retail sales is determined by the user source of the sale—the establishment—and not the end user. Thus, regardless of the end user (i.e., a manufacturer or a wholesaler) a sale made by these establishments is considered a retail sale. On the other hand, a retail sale made by a wholesaler is not part of the retail sales series. For definitional purposes a retail establishment is defined as "a business that sells goods primarily for individual or household use."

The data include cash and credit sales, with discounts and refunds excluded. Excise taxes are included if paid by the manufacturer or wholesaler and passed on to the consumer. Excise taxes are excluded if paid directly by the purchaser and remitted to local, state, or federal authorities. This pertains to sales taxes as well.

It is not possible to say the number of retail establishments that are surveyed. A company's employer identification number is used for classification purposes, and some businesses will use one such number for the entire organization while others will use a separate number for each location within the selling enterprise.

In estimating retail sales volume, the Bureau of the Census breaks its universe into a sample of big companies and three samples of smaller business establishments. The big companies report every month. Each of the three small business samples reports once a quarter. Thus, the advance estimate of retail sales (the first estimate for a given month) consists of reports from big companies and one sample of small businesses. By the final report (the third month) all of the reporting establishments have supplied sales figures, and the data for that month are considered final (until once-a-year benchmark revisions). This reporting method certainly accounts for a part of the volatility of the retail sales series. But just as important is that when the Bureau of the Census requests data from the establishments, within the first week of the subsequent month, many still do not have hard figures for sales, especially smaller businesses.

The retail sales report is broken down by type of product sold by an establishment (see Table 23-1). The first cut is durable and nondurable goods. Within the durable goods sector, which accounts for approximately 35 percent of the total estimated volume of retail sales, there are three major categories reported: building materials; motor vehicles; and furniture, home furnishings, and appliance stores. These three categories account for over 80 percent of durable purchases. The remaining 20 percent are accounted for by such businesses as sporting goods stores and book and jewelry stores. The nondurable sector is dominated by the food store category, which represents approximately 20 percent of retail sales, with general merchandise stores

TABLE 23–1   Retail Sales Contribution by Major Type of Establishment, 1996*

Durable Goods	41%
Building Materials	5%
Automotive Dealers	25%
Furniture Dealers, Etc.	5%
Nondurable Goods	59%
General Merchandise Stores	13%
Food Stores	17%
Gasoline Stores	6%
Apparel Stores	4%
Eating and Drinking Establishments	10%
Drug and Proprietary	4%
Liquor Stores	1%
Mail Order Houses	2%

* Total will not add to 100. Categories present in retail sales report do not represent the total aggregate.

(discount, department, variety stores, etc.) the next largest contributor. (See Box 23-1.)

There is one key breakdown of retail sales, and it is in keeping with the recurring habit of analyzing data series with one or two components removed. In this instance it is automotive dealers that are "ex'ed" out. Much like the core CPI and PPI, this ex-auto component could be considered a "core" reading; and it's reported as a stand-alone number, just like the core CPI and PPI. As is the case with other economic series, the intent is to strip out volatile components, ones that can dominate the overall result to such an extent that the remaining information is obscured. In the case of retail sales another reason is that analysts and financial markets already have a reading on motor vehicle sales, the unit sales data reported by manufacturers in the first three business days of the month. In fact the unit data are a better series because their measurement is not obscured by changes in the price mix of purchases as the retail sales data can be. They are so much better that the GDP accounts use the unit sales data, not the retail sales component.

BOX 23–1   Weekly and Monthly Chain Store Sales

Since consumption accounts for two-thirds of real GDP, it is important to monitor the consumer closely. To this end, sales at the major retailers (such as Wal-mart, Kmart, JC Penney, Sears, Dayton Hudson, Federated Stores, etc.) provide a unique and timely window on consumer spending. Stock market participants have known this for years, and reports of stronger or weaker store sales have moved retail industry stock prices. However, the fixed-income markets now have become as responsive to these data, if not more so.

First, a little history is in order. Between the early 1960s and 1978, the Commerce Department compiled a weekly retail sales estimate for many of the sales categories currently available (e.g., food stores, furniture stores, etc.). Indeed, Federal Reserve Board Chairman Alan Greenspan was a big fan of that weekly series and once envisioned the day when a weekly GDP measure would be possible, with the centerpiece being the weekly retail sales. But in that era, the data commanded little market attention (as was the case with most economic data), and because of budget and statistical concerns, the collection of weekly retail sales data ceased in 1978.

Sometime after the Commerce Department stopped the publication of its series, Edward Johnson, a retail equity analyst, began a weekly sales survey of the major retailers. His survey was part of an equity research product called the Redbook Service (now known as the LJR Redbook Report). As might be expected, Johnson's estimate of chain store sales was less comprehensive than the Commerce Department series. And it was based on year-over-year growth rate indications from the major chain stores instead of their sales revenue (the basis of Commerce Department data). Regardless of the type of data, Ed Johnson filled a void for timely information on consumer spending.

Currently, two key weekly chain store sales surveys are followed by the financial markets: the **LJR Redbook** (released Tuesdays at 2:40 PM ET) and the **BTM/Schroders** retail chain store sales snapshot (released Tuesdays at 9:00 AM). However, during the Christmas season, other weekly sales surveys are available from **Telecheck, Visa,** and the **International Council on Shopping Centers.** Each of these Christmastime spending measures takes a certain perspective—check processing, charging, and shopping mall sales (excluding the anchor stores).

LJR Redbook estimates **total** industry sales weekly on a year-over-year percentage change basis using Commerce Department monthly department store sales data as its historical benchmark. LJR Redbook sales estimates are grossed up to the prior year's Commerce Department unadjusted dollar sales revenue, and then Commerce Department seasonal factors are used to estimate a seasonally adjusted change from the prior month. One source of bias, however, in this methodology is that the Commerce Department data are calendar-month sales while the retail industry and LJR Redbook report sales on a retail industry fiscal-month basis (that is, generally a 4-5-4 week calendar), which can extend across months. LJR Redbook highlights cumulative month-to-date changes compared with the prior month, which is the focus for the fixed-income markets, as well. The cumulative-to-date estimate assumes that if sales held at the current pace, then this is what it would mean for the full month. Finally, LJR Redbook also compiles a free-standing weekly same-store sales average.

The BTM/Schroders weekly index is constructed as a **comparable-store sales** measure and is not a total-store industry measure, which would account for industry store expansion and contraction. The BTM/Schroders weekly index is independent of the Commerce Department data and is compiled to be statistically consistent with (that is, "benchmarked" to) the more comprehensive Bank of Tokyo-Mitsubishi monthly chain store sales index, which extends back to 1969 and is a tally of aggregate comparable-store sales for 70 to 80 chain stores. Both measures—the weekly and the monthly sales barometers—are indexed to 1977 equals 100. The BTM/Schroders weekly series is seasonally adjusted using a propriety outlier-adjustment methodology. Outlier adjustment is a dynamic state-of-the-art method of adjusting a time series for its volatility, which may be a result of typical seasonal variation and irregular factors such as strikes and weather disruptions. The outlier correction uses standard deviations to determine the degree of adjustment. Because the BTM/Schroder weekly sales measure is a seasonally adjusted index, the report highlights—and the market focuses upon—week-to-week changes in sales. Some electronic sources of these data can be found at **http://www.lp-llc.com/cents/** and at **http://www.chainstoreage.com.**

In using these data, it is important to recognize the limitations of the weekly data, which may be subject to considerable volatility for numerous reasons. First, one must make an assumption about the market share of each retailer. Second, the stores provide only growth rate indications, sometimes couched in terms such as "high single digits," rather than explicit sales revenues. Third, some stores use unusual accounting periods. Fourth, sales promotions at single retailers can have a big effect on weekly numbers. Fifth, an implicit weight must be given to each week within the month, for the cumulative month-to-date change. This can be very tricky around major holidays.

Separately, at the beginning of each month a much wider array of retailers report actual sales revenue on a monthly basis, and various industry analysts issue their own tallies of these company reports. The company reports usually are available about a week before the Commerce Department releases its retail sales data for the comparable month. Their comprehensive nature makes them important to the financial markets, as their breadth sometimes can change the picture of consumer spending relative to what the weekly readings had inferred. Although the stores reporting are only publicly held companies, they account for 70 percent to 80 percent of nonauto durable sales and general merchandise and apparel sales.

Analyzing the Data

The breaking out of the automotive dealer component is as key to the analysis of retail sales data as the core price index is to the CPI and PPI reports. In fact, to the extent that unit motor vehicle sales are already known, sales ex-autos can be thought of as the only new piece of information, filling out the consumer spending picture for the month (ex-services). For this reason, if, when retail sales are reported, the total and the ex-auto month-to-month changes are extremely disparate, it typically will be the ex-auto number that determines market performance.

Once the two major categories are known, attention quickly focuses on possible revisions to the prior two months and then the details of the latest month's spending. *Revisions can play as important a role in the markets' interpretations of the retail sales data as the latest set of spending numbers,* if only because the revisions can be so large (for reasons outlined in the description of the series). Going one step further, it is not unusual for revisions to set the

FIGURE 23–1   Retail Sales

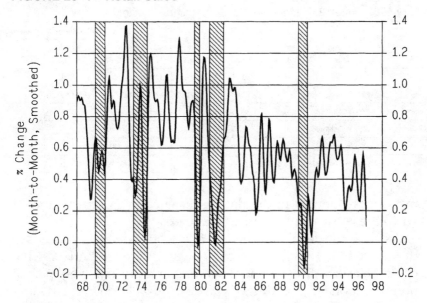

FIGURE 23–2   Retail Sales Less Auto Dealer Sales

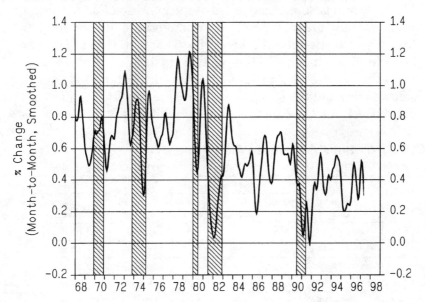

TABLE 23–2   Retail Sales
February 1967–June 1997, Month-to-Month Percentage Change

		Normal Bounds				Series Characteristics	
Phase	Historic Low	Normal Low	Average	Normal High	Historic High	Standard Deviation	Share of Total Observations
Recession	–2.6% in Dec 1973	–0.4%	0.3%	1.0%	3.7% in Jan 1975	1.4 pp.	15.6%
Recovery	–1.5% in Aug 1983	0.3%	0.8%	1.4%	4.6% in May 1975	1.1 pp.	23.0%
Expansion	–6.5% in Jan 1987	0.0%	0.6%	1.3%	5.9% in Sep 1986	1.3 pp.	61.4%
Slow Phase	–4.2% in Oct 1986	0.0%	0.6%	1.2%	5.9% in Sep 1986	1.2 pp.	30.1%
Rapid Phase	–6.5% in Jan 1987	0.0%	0.7%	1.4%	5.0% in Feb 1987	1.4 pp.	31.3%
All Phases	–6.5% in Jan 1987	0.0%	0.6%	1.2%	5.9% in Sep 1986	1.3 pp.	100.0%

markets' responses to the data, overwhelming (if they conflict with) the latest set of spending numbers.

As far as the detail of the latest report, one way to look at it is to differentiate between those components that are part of what could be called discretionary spending and those that are part of nondiscretionary spending. Typically, durable goods and non-durables such as general merchandise and apparel stores account for the former. If the spending is concentrated in these areas, then the directional change is considered that much more meaningful. The food and gasoline categories fit the nondiscretionary description. Not only are they purchases that tend to follow a trend, but they are also strongly influenced by what can be very large and volatile price changes of the goods purchased. This breakdown takes the "ex-ing"-out process one step further (and to some, one step too far), but the logic is that purchases of essentials are not a good benchmark of consumer buying attitudes.

TABLE 23–3   Retail Sales Less Auto Dealers
February 1967–June 1997, Month-to-Month Percentage Change

		Normal Bounds				Series Characteristics	
Phase	Historic Low	Normal Low	Average	Normal High	Historic High	Standard Deviation	Share of Total Observations
Recession	–1.6% in Dec 1974	0.0%	0.4%	0.9%	3.1% in Jan 1975	0.9 pp.	15.7%
Recovery	–1.7% in Feb 1976	0.2%	0.6%	1.1%	4.1% in May 1975	0.9 pp.	23.1%
Expansion	–2.1% in Jan 1968	0.2%	0.6%	1.1%	3.7% in Sep 1967	0.9 pp.	61.3%
Slow Phase	–2.0% in Oct 1967	0.2%	0.6%	1.0%	3.7% in Sep 1967	0.9 pp.	30.2%
Rapid Phase	–2.1% in Jan 1968	0.2%	0.6%	1.1%	2.6% in Nov 1968	0.9 pp.	31.1%
All Phases	–2.1% in Jan 1968	0.1%	0.6%	1.0%	4.1% in May 1975	0.9 pp.	100.0%

Retail Sales over the Business Cycle

In terms of the business cycle, the retail sales series is best termed a *coincident indicator*. However, its cyclical volatility is not great; consumer purchases on a nominal basis can often continue to rise even after a recession has begun because of the inflation effect on purchase prices. On an annual basis, retail sales have never declined. The smallest annual rise, +0.9 percent, came in 1991. Furthermore, monthly retail sales typically increase even during recessions. The best way to relate retail sales to the business cycle is in terms of the rate of growth of sales on a month-to-month basis. Most months will show increases, but during a recession they will be relatively small and the declines, although still an exception, will be more frequent. (See Figures 23-1 and 23-2 and Tables 23-2 and 23-3.)

Chapter 24

Unemployment Insurance Claims

General Description

The unemployment insurance (UI) program is a shared state and federal government-financed income-maintenance plan set up to help workers impacted by cyclical and temporary bouts of unemployment. The administration and eligibility requirements for collecting unemployment or jobless benefits are determined by each state. Consequently, coverage can vary by state. For example, some states, such as California, include agricultural workers, while most do not. Some states pay workers who are involved in work stoppages, while most do not. Over time, the unemployment insurance program has included special longer-term benefits, which have extended the duration of support for the unemployed up to twice the normal length of coverage.

Economic Indicator Information at a Glance

Market Significance	Moderate
Typical Release Time	8:30 AM Eastern Time Every Thursday
Released By	U.S. Department of Labor Employment and Training Administration
Period Covered	Prior Week Ending Saturday
Web Site	http://www.dol.gov/

These programs have generally been legislated by Congress during or shortly after recessions. In 1991, Congress passed such a program, called the Emergency Unemployment Compensation Act of 1991. That act was amended late in that same year, which established the Emergency Unemployment Compensation (EUC) Program, and those benefits were totally funded by the federal government. The EUC program was again amended in 1992 by Congress to increase the number of weeks of coverage. Much like the seven temporary and extended unemployment benefit programs that have preceded the EUC over the last 30 years, that one served a timely need and was allowed to phase out in April 1994. These special programs, when in place, will inflate the filing pace.

Analyzing the Data

An initial claim for state unemployment insurance or jobless claim includes two types of claimants: (1) the first-time claimant during a benefit year and (2) a repeat or "additional" claimant, who has filed previously and is again out of work. Some industries (such as the apparel industry) have an on/off work pattern at times, which might result in the same individual filing an initial claim every month for some "downtime." Once an individual files for benefits, the individual's eligibility is checked. (During the year some states have noted that the percentage of individuals filing for benefits but who are ineligible has been as high as 40 percent.) An individual out of work for a strike may or may not qualify for jobless benefits, depending on the state and whether the work stoppage is a lockout or a walkout. But once an individual qualifies for benefits, the unemployed individual enters the ranks of the *continuing claimant* roll. Both series—the initial and continuing claims—provide an ongoing view of the labor markets. The jobless claim level and change provides the first indication of worsening or improving job markets. As such, it is the key focus of the financial markets. However, the continuing claims data provide a window on how quickly the labor markets can absorb the newly unemployed. For example, if the jobless claims pace accelerates but the continuing claims level holds steady, it suggests that the duration of unemployment is rather short. However, the reverse is also true.

If the pace of jobless claims is relatively low but the continuing claims pace continues to rise, then the duration of unemployment is lengthening, which typically happens in the early stages of a business cycle expansion.

The keys to interpreting the jobless claims report include:

- Note whether there was a holiday during the given period since despite the best efforts of the BLS to seasonally adjust these data, holidays still could have a noticeable impact on the weekly change.
- Be aware of whether or not an emergency/extended benefit program is in effect since individuals filing under special programs are not counted in the regular program, which is the focus of the financial market's attention. Also many states require individuals claiming benefits under federal disaster relief programs to file first for regular state unemployment benefits.
- Keep an eye on the calendar week. If the week is the first or second week of a new quarter, there can be some "turn-of-the-quarter" upward blip in claims. This occurs because sometimes it benefits the individual, who is unemployed late in a given quarter, to wait until the beginning of the subsequent quarter to file for benefits in order to include the prior quarter's wages in the calculation used for determining the wage base for UI compensation.
- Recognize that adverse weather can impact these data, especially for construction and agricultural workers.
- Keep in mind one long-term factor, that legal changes to state eligibility rules can result in changes in the filing pace, which is a reason that is cited for the longer-term downward drift in the trend.

Because of the short-term "noise" in these data, a four-week moving average of the data is often more informative of the trends and should be looked at for confirmation of any nascent trend. Additionally, the states often provide explanatory comments on why their state's claims rose or fell. Although those comments are lagged one additional week from the aggregate data, they still can be useful for signs of sector and regional weakness or special factors.

FIGURE 24–1   Initial Jobless Claims

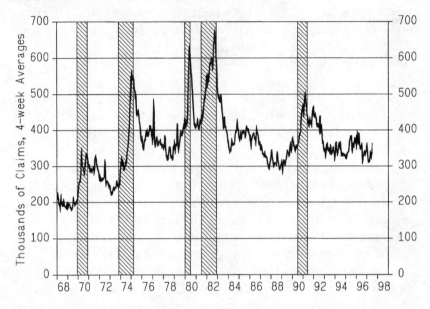

FIGURE 24–2   Continuing Claims

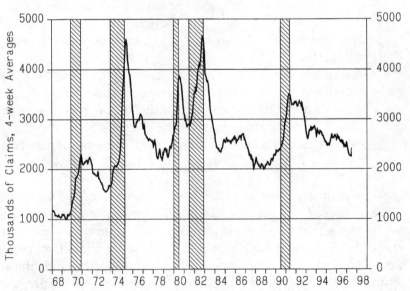

Jobless Claims over the Business Cycle

Jobless claims are a timely and sensitive measure of labor market conditions, and they are classified as a leading cyclical economic indicator of general business conditions. During recessions, the average pace of filings is about 425,000 claims (see Table 24-1), with an average increase of 14,500 per month. During recoveries the pace of filings tends to decline by about 8,500 per month and averages about 385,000 claims per week. During expansions, the improvement is slow—an average decline of about 100 claims per month, with an average filing rate of about 300,000. As might be expected, during the rapid phase of the expansion the improvement is more apparent, with an average monthly drop of 1,100 claims. (See Figures 24-1 and 24-2.)

Special Factors, Limitations, and Other Data Issues

Probably one of the key misunderstandings in using the initial claims data to project payroll employment changes is that in most states individuals must wait one week before filing a claim. This "waiting period" is often missed in relating the initial claims pace to monthly payroll employment changes.

Relationship with Other Series

Analysts often look to the weekly filings of unemployment claims and continuing jobless benefits as a guide to upcoming monthly employment and unemployment changes. But the sta-

TABLE 24–1   Average Weekly Initial Claims for Unemployment Insurance
January 1956–April 1997, Thousands

Phase	Historic Low	Normal Bounds			Historic High	Series Characteristics	
		Normal Low	Average	Normal High		Standard Deviation	Share of Total Observations
Recession	251K in Jan 1970	368K	424K	481K	672K in Sep 1982	112.9K	15.1%
Recovery	246K in Apr 1959	353K	385K	418K	518K in Dec 1982	64.9K	21.2%
Expansion	180K in Apr 1966	269K	301K	334K	435K in Jul 1981	65.0K	63.7%
Slow Phase	182K in May 1969	268K	304K	340K	431K in Dec 1979	71.5K	32.1%
Rapid Phase	180K in Apr 1966	268K	297K	327K	435K in Jul 1981	58.8K	31.6%
All Phases	180K in Apr 1966	293K	338K	382K	672K in Sep 1982	89.1K	100.0%

tistical relationships are less reliable than might be desired. For more discussion of this, see Chapter 10.

The monthly counterpart of these weekly jobless claims is a component of the Conference Board's composite index of leading indicators.

References

Burtless, Gary. "Unemployment Insurance and Labor Supply: A Survey," *Unemployment Insurance: The Second Half Century*, W. Lee Hanson and James F. Byers, eds., Madison, University of Wisconsin Press, 1990, pp. 69–107.

Employment and Training Administration, U.S. Department of Labor, *An Examination of Declining UI Claims during the 1980s*, Occasional Paper 88-3, 1988.

Price, Daniel. "Unemployment Insurance, Then and Now, 1935–85," *Social Security Bulletin*, Vol. 48, No. 10, October 1985, pp. 22–32.

Part 2

The Federal Reserve and the U.S. Treasury

Chapter 25

Overview

As important as it is to have a full understanding of business conditions indicators, the financial side of the equation plays just as crucial a role in the determination of financial market behavior, whether it's equities, foreign exchange, or the fixed-income markets. For as much as one may completely understand how the economy is performing, it will serve little purpose if that knowledge is not properly utilized to project possible policy actions, particularly those of the Federal Reserve. It is all too often that financial markets accurately interpret data that show a change in the economic fundamentals but react little (if any) because they believe (properly or otherwise) that regardless of what the numbers say about the economy, they will not lead to a change in monetary policy.

The following sections deal with money supply, the Federal Reserve, and the financing of the U.S. government's debt. The discussion of the money supply could just as easily come under the business conditions section. However, since it ostensibly serves, albeit ever so loosely, as a target variable for the Federal Reserve, and can be considered as the actual link between the Federal Reserve and the economy, it has been incorporated in this section. Needless to say, some market participants consider it the *only* economic variable worth watching. A view of the Federal Reserve is presented in two parts. The first is an overview of the Federal Reserve's decision-making process and the framework in which it conducts monetary policy. The second is a closer look at the mechanism by which the Fed controls the amount of reserves in the banking system. This discussion, in the past, had a heavy policy flavor. However, under the current policy disclosure system the discussion is merely technical. Finally, we present a general description of the U.S. Treasury's financing of the U.S. debt. A steady supply of government issues is a given in the current environment of huge government deficits. To the extent that supply of a commodity can affect its price, familiarity with the government's financing pattern is a necessary underpinning for understanding price changes of government securities.

Chapter 26

The Monetary Aggregates

General Description

Regardless of whether one is a monetarist or not, the fundamental premise that "money matters" is shared by all schools of economic thought. There are differences of opinion about such things as the magnitude of its impact and/or the channels through which it works, but one really cannot develop a macroeconomic model without money entering into the process.

Economic Indicator Information at a Glance

Market Significance	Low
Typical Release Time	4:30 PM Eastern Time Every Thursday
Released By	Federal Reserve Board
Period Covered	Week Ending Monday of Prior Week
Web Site	http://www.bog.frb.fed.us/releases/ h6/

Of course, that doesn't mean the issue is settled. One then has to define money. Thirty years ago, that was relatively simple; cash was cash, a check was drawn on a checking account at your commercial bank, and one earned interest by putting one's money in a local savings institution. The lines were drawn distinctly. But through the 1970s, the 1980s, and now the 1990s the lines became a blur and are now a burgeoning smudge. Legislative changes, financial innovation, and competition have spawned new deposit categories and investment channels, and increasingly sophisticated investors are constantly learning of new products and are willing to move their assets into investments that they didn't know existed six months before. Adding to the changes is the fact that over the last 15 years interest rates have changed dramatically. In the early 1980s the federal funds rate broke 19 percent, the 30-year bond yielded over 14.5 percent, and the spread between 30-year Treasury bonds and three-month Treasury bills reached –360 basis points. Through the ensuing decade, rates moved erratically to where at one point the federal funds rate was 3 percent, 30-year bonds fell to 5¾ percent, and the spread between the 30-year bond and the three-month bill was +425 basis points. The drop in yields and the almost 800 basis point swing in the yield spread created a plethora of changes in investment needs and options that had, and still are having, direct effects on the definition of money.

It is with consideration of this ever-changing environment that a rather straightforward presentation of the monetary aggregates will be made. Fundamental points about the longer-run viability of currently defined aggregates will highlight the problems created over the past 25 years. Although money may seem adequately defined at a given point in time, the existence of ongoing changes in the financial world makes it likely that such a situation will wind up having been temporary.

The Monetary Aggregates

The Federal Reserve currently defines three monetary aggregates. Theoretically, they are ranked in terms of liquidity, or the degree to which they are transactions oriented. Practically speaking, the aggregates are based also on how well various combinations of deposit categories have tracked economic activities or which deposit categories are deemed to be goods substitutes for each other.

M1: The narrowest aggregate is composed of actual hard currency held by the public (nondepository institutions), demand deposits, and traveler's checks. Demand deposits include normal checking accounts as well as interest-bearing checking accounts held at depository institutions, collectively called *other checkable deposits*. They are broken down into those held at commercial banks and at thrift institutions. (See Table 26-1.)

TABLE 26–1   M1 Compositional Breakdown: End of 1996

Demand Deposits	34.7%
Other checkable deposits	31.4%
Currency	33.1%
Traveler's Checks	0.8%

M1 is solely a transaction-oriented monetary aggregate; and in theory, it would look to be the aggregate most closely associated with economic activity. For this reason, the Federal Reserve chose M1 as its policy guideline when it moved from targeting bank reserves to targeting money supply in 1970. It held this preeminent position until 1983. During that period, due to financial deregulation and the high interest rate structure of the early 1980s, financial accounts such as money market funds greatly altered what could be considered transactions deposits and caused the relationship between M1 and economic activity and inflation to deteriorate sharply. (See Table 26-2.)

As a result the Federal Reserve demoted M1 as the prime policy focus and elevated the broader aggregate, M2—not because it was so much better as much as it was not so bad.

M2: It is a large step from M1 to M2 in terms of the size of each aggregate and the disparity of the components. M2 is more than three times the size of M1. In qualitative terms, M1's growth may or may not properly reflect economic activity at any given point, but its compositional nature is relatively pure (if not quite all encompassing). Such is not the case with M2. M2 enters that nebulous area of "near transactions" deposits. Its current formulation reflects the idea that an aggregate's composition should be based not only on similar characteristics but also on how well the aggregation of components, in total, shows a stable, long-term relationship with nominal economic activity.

TABLE 26–2   M1-GDP Correlation Matrix
Nominal GDP Growth and M1 Growth: 1960–1996

	1960–1969	**1970–1979**	**1980–1989**	**1990–1996**
GDP to M1	.720	.825	–.214	.195
GDP to M1 lag*	.613	.326	–.125	.255

* M1 growth lagged one year.

TABLE 26–3   M2 Compositional Breakdown: End of 1996

M1	31.4%
Savings Deposits	30.8%
Small Time Deposits	25.3%
Retail Money Market Funds	12.5%

The aggregates build on each other, so in addition to M1's components, M2 includes retail money market funds (balances less than $50,000), small time deposits (for less than $100,000), and savings deposits (which include money market deposit accounts, a bank's version of a money market fund). (See Table 26-3.)

M2 clearly includes deposits that possess varying degrees of liquidity. Check-writing privileges are granted money market funds and money market deposit accounts, and are very much akin to M1 deposits. From there, though, the degree of liquidity declines rapidly. Savings accounts are readily accessible but do not offer check-writing privileges. Small time deposits are plainly illiquid, with a fixed maturity and penalties for early withdrawal. But the Fed had a reason for including small time deposits in M2 even though their nature is far removed from the other components. The Fed found that these deposits were excellent substitutes for savings accounts, as a viable investment alternative. It was thought best to include deposit categories that could readily capture deposits from the more liquid categories, so as not to have an aggregate whose volatility greatly exaggerated and potentially misrepresented the underlying monetary flows.[1]

Until the 1980s, M2 exhibited a fairly stable relationship with nominal GDP (see Table 26-4). But that relationship broke down and essentially crumbled in 1991–1992.

Given the size and complexity of M2, it is important to stress the *long-term* nature of M2's statistical relationship to economic activity. Whereas one could make at least a theoretical case for M1 growth being closely related to nominal GDP growth over shorter periods of time, such a case cannot be made for M2. M2 is as

---

[1]   For a discussion of the role of small time deposits in M2, especially in light of the savings and loan crisis in the early 1990s, see John Wenninger and John Partian, "Small Time Deposits and the Recent Weakness in M2," *Federal Reserve Bank of New York Quarterly Review,* Spring 1992, pp. 21–35. There also is a discussion of how the definitions of the aggregates evolved.

TABLE 26–4 M2-GDP Correlation Matrix

Nominal GDP Growth and M2 Growth, 1960–1996

	1960–1969	1970–1979	1980–1989	1990–1996
GDP to M2 lag*	.703	.661	.232	−.496

* M2 growth lagged one year.

much, if not more so, a financial asset aggregate as it is a transactions aggregate. This point was brought home to policy makers in 1991 and 1992. At that time M2 growth was severely depressed by several factors. One was a significant shift out of lower-yielding short-term deposits into bond and equity mutual funds, neither of which is included in any monetary aggregate. Another was the halt in bank lending that made it unnecessary for financial institutions to attract funds into small time deposits (the building block of loans). Finally the savings and loan debacle resulted in the closing of thousands of thrifts. These institutions were the holders of significant amounts of small time deposits.[2]

TABLE 26–5 M3 Compositional Breakdown: End of 1996

M2	80.0%
Large Time Deposits	9.6%
Institutional Money Market Funds	5.3%
Repurchase Agreements	3.9%
Eurodollar Deposits	2.0%

Unfortunately even after banks resumed lending and the savings and loan crisis abated, the move by individuals into bond and equity mutual funds accelerated to such an extent that M2's relationship to activity never returned to its previous level.

M3: The broadest monetary aggregate builds on M2, including large time deposits (those over $100,000), repurchase agreements, eurodollar deposits, and institutional money market funds (over $100,000). It is roughly 20 percent larger than M2.

---

2   At the end of 1990 thrifts held $566 bn. of small time deposits, accounting for 49 percent of the total. By mid-1993 the total was $430 bn., only 36 percent of the total.

Since M2 constitutes the bulk of M3 (see Table 26-5), the additional informational value of M3 is limited. The behavior of M3 mirrors that of M2. The value added is limited to the information about large time deposits at commercial banks. These deposits have had a strong correlation to commercial and industrial loans made by banks because they are a major source of funding for such loans.

This lack of informational content is why M3 has never been the primary target of monetary policy. And even with volatile financial flows and the accompanying uncertainty about which aggregate is the best monetary policy indicator, it is unlikely M3 will ever attain primary status.

Other Monetary Policy Indicators

The monetary aggregates are the most obvious focal point of monetary policy. But some prefer other means to gauge the stance of monetary policy. The two most commonly used alternative measures are the monetary base and Federal Reserve bank credit.

Monetary Base

The Federal Reserve's monetary base is defined as "total reserves plus the currency component of the money stock plus the portion of the cash held in banks' vaults that is not applied toward reserve requirements." At the end of 1996 the currency component accounted for 86 percent of the monetary base, total reserves approximately 13 percent, and excess vault cash about 1 percent. As one can see, there should be a close relationship between M1 and the monetary base, since reserves are held primarily against M1 deposits and the currency component is common to both.

The rationale for focusing on the monetary base is that the components are considered the raw material from which money supply is created. The Fed, in theory, creates reserves and hard currency, so if one wants to ascertain what the Federal Reserve is up to, one should watch the monetary base, not the money supply. There are two problems with this approach, however. First the Fed creates reserves in response to the banking system's need for them. When a bank makes a loan and creates a deposit, it then is in need of additional reserves, and the Fed supplies them. The

FIGURE 26–1   Federal Reserve Board's Monetary Base

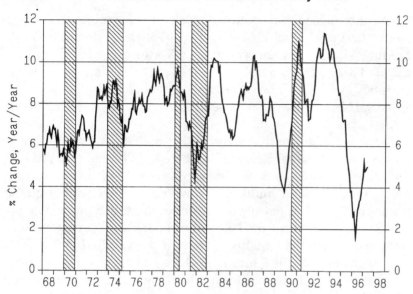

Fed does not provide the banking system with undesired re-serves, expecting it to make new loans from the new reserves. Essentially the Fed is reactive on the reserve creation front, not proactive as is often taught in Macroeconomics 101. Second, the growth of the currency component of M1 in recent years is due more to foreign hoarding of U.S. currency than it is to domestic money creation. Its growth greatly exaggerates the U.S. economy's use of currency as a transactions medium. (See Figure 26-1 and Table 26-6.)

TABLE 26–6   Federal Reserve Board's Monetary Base
February 1959–June 1997, Simple Annualized Percentage Change

Phase	Historic Low	Normal Bounds			Historic High	Series Characteristics	
		Normal Low	Average	Normal High		Standard Deviation	Share of Total Observations
Recession	−4.5% in Dec 1960	4.4%	6.3%	8.3%	19.2% in Jan 1991	3.9 pp.	14.5%
Recovery	−4.6% in Jan 1981	5.3%	7.1%	9.0%	16.2% in Jun 1975	3.7 pp.	20.8%
Expansion	−3.8% in Oct 1959	4.4%	6.1%	7.8%	16.7% in Dec 1986	3.4 pp.	64.6%
Slow Phase	−3.8% in Oct 1959	3.7%	5.5%	7.3%	13.0% in Oct 1973	3.6 pp.	30.4%
Rapid Phase	−1.5% in Feb 1962	5.3%	6.9%	8.5%	16.7% in Dec 1986	3.2 pp.	34.2%
All Phases	−4.6% in Jan 1981	4.6%	6.4%	8.2%	19.2% in Jan 1991	3.6 pp.	100.0%

Federal Reserve Bank Credit

Another measure of monetary policy is Federal Reserve bank credit. About 90 percent of this measure is the Federal Reserve's holdings of government securities, with the other 10 percent accounted for by the Federal Reserve's other assets such as foreign currency holdings. The data can be found in the Federal Reserve's H4.1 statistical release issued weekly at 4:30 PM on Thursdays.

For those who use this gauge, it is the first component that is critical, since Federal Reserve bank credit is considered the balance sheet manifestation of what is commonly called "monetizing the debt." Actually it could be characterized as such although the phrase carries ominous, negative connotations of a process that is strictly technical in nature. When the Fed needs to supply permanent reserves to the banking system, it does so by buying Treasury securities. But the timing and frequency and size of these purchases are determined by the banking system's demand for reserves. These purchases are not conducted arbitrarily as a means of "liquefying the system," and they do not reflect changes in monetary policy. (A further discussion of these purchases is

FIGURE 26–2   Federal Reserve Bank Credit

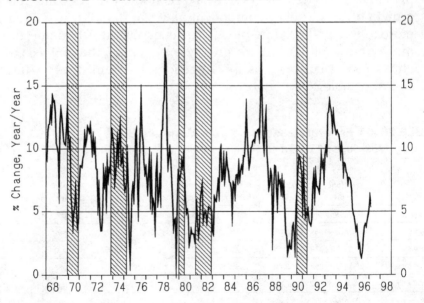

FIGURE 26–3   Money Supply: M1

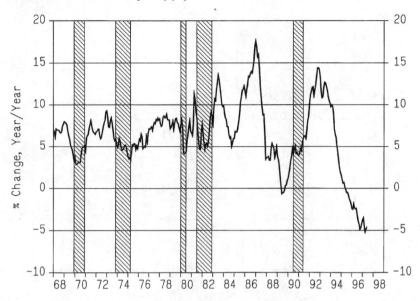

FIGURE 26–4   Money Supply: M2

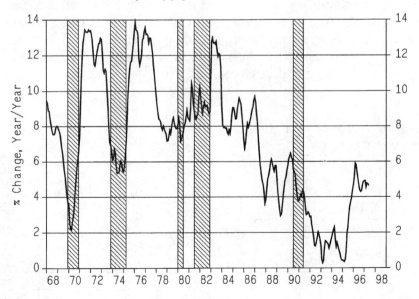

FIGURE 26–5   Money Supply: M3

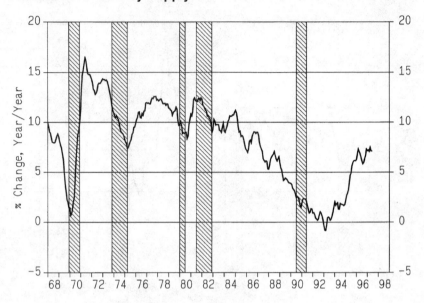

in Chapter 28.) Regardless, for some the monetization aspect of these purchases signifies underlying money creation, making Federal Reserve bank credit worth watching. The fact that the Federal Reserve's purchases of Treasury securities is due to reserve growth results in relatively close relationships between the growth of bank credit, reserves, and M1. (See Figure 26-2.)

TABLE 26–7   Monetary Aggregate: M1
February 1959–June 1997, Simple Annualized Percentage Change

		Normal Bounds				Series Characteristics	
Phase	Historic Low	Normal Low	Average	Normal High	Historic High	Standard Deviation	Share of Total Observations
Recession	−18.8% in Apr 1980	1.8%	5.0%	8.2%	22.8% in Oct 1982	6.4 pp.	14.5%
Recovery	−11.9% in Dec 1980	4.8%	7.4%	10.1%	22.0% in Aug 1980	5.3 pp.	20.8%
Expansion	−14.3% in Oct 1996	1.6%	4.7%	7.8%	30.4% in Dec 1986	6.2 pp.	64.6%
Slow Phase	−9.7% in Aug 1996	0.9%	4.0%	7.2%	20.6% in May 1986	6.3 pp.	30.4%
Rapid Phase	−7.6% in Sep 1959	3.2%	5.9%	8.7%	30.4% in Dec 1986	5.5 pp.	34.2%
All Phases	−18.8% in Apr 1980	2.3%	5.3%	8.4%	30.4% in Dec 1986	6.1 pp.	100.0%

TABLE 26–8   Monetary Aggregate: M2
February 1959–June 1997, Simple Annualized Percentage Change

		Normal Bounds				Series Characteristics	
Phase	Historic Low	Normal Low	Average	Normal High	Historic High	Standard Deviation	Share of Total Observations
Recession	−6.5% in Feb 1970	5.1%	6.9%	8.7%	15.1% in Mar 1975	3.6 pp.	14.5%
Recovery	−2.1% in Jun 1992	6.3%	9.0%	11.8%	34.3% in Jan 1983	5.5 pp.	20.8%
Expansion	−3.5% in Jun 1994	4.4%	6.1%	7.9%	16.0% in Apr 1981	3.5 pp.	64.6%
Slow Phase	−1.0% in Jul 1966	4.5%	6.1%	7.8%	13.2% in Dec 1984	3.3 pp.	30.4%
Rapid Phase	−3.5% in Jun 1994	4.3%	6.2%	8.1%	16.0% in Apr 1981	3.8 pp.	34.2%
All Phases	−6.5% in Feb 1970	4.7%	6.8%	8.9%	34.3% in Jan 1983	4.2 pp.	100.0%

TABLE 26–9   Monetary Aggregate: M3
February 1959–June 1997, Simple Annualized Percentage Change

		Normal Bounds				Series Characteristics	
Phase	Historic Low	Normal Low	Average	Normal High	Historic High	Standard Deviation	Share of Total Observations
Recession	−5.6% in Feb 1970	5.8%	8.0%	10.3%	17.7% in Sep 1970	4.5 pp.	14.5%
Recovery	−3.0% in Apr 1992	6.3%	8.7%	11.2%	18.6% in Mar 1971	4.9 pp.	20.8%
Expansion	−4.6% in Jan 1993	5.0%	7.0%	9.0%	15.9% in Aug 1972	4.0 pp.	64.6%
Slow Phase	−4.5% in Aug 1969	4.5%	6.4%	8.3%	15.8% in Sep 1979	3.8 pp.	30.4%
Rapid Phase	−4.6% in Jan 1993	5.5%	7.6%	9.7%	15.9% in Aug 1972	4.2 pp.	34.2%
All Phases	−5.6% in Feb 1970	5.4%	7.5%	9.7%	18.6% in Mar 1971	4.3 pp.	100.0%

Money Supply over the Business Cycle

There are more similarities than differences between the growth of the three monetary aggregates over the business cycle. All show peak growth rates prior to the onset of a recession and growth low points before the end of the recession. This characteristic has led to M2's inclusion in the leading indicator index. In terms of actual growth rates, all three aggregates experience that fastest growth during the recovery stage, with M2 actually averaging the same growth rate during recessions as during expansions. (See Figures 26-3 to 26-5 and Tables 26-7 to 26-9.)

Chapter 27

Monetary Policy:
The Decision-Making Process

The Decision-Making Bodies

Monetary policy is determined by two operational bodies: the Federal Open Market Committee (FOMC) and the Federal Reserve Board (FRB). The Federal Reserve Board is *the* monetary authority, although in practice the duties of each overlap when it comes to monetary policy. It's a point made apparent by the fact that the members of the FRB are automatically members of the FOMC. The FRB's decision-making and policy-making scope go beyond monetary policy into, inter alia, the areas of banking regulation and international banking, while the FOMC's jurisdiction is solely domestic monetary policy.

The Federal Reserve Board. The FRB is composed of seven members, appointed by the President of the United States. Terms run for 14 years, with the chairman and the vice chairman being appointed for four-year periods. If a member resigns, the replacement fulfills the remainder of the term rather than starting a new one. In making appointments the President is supposed to take into consideration the Federal Reserve districts in which existing members preside or were "elected from." In theory no two FRB members can be from the same district. The idea is to have diverse geographical representation on the board. The Senate must approve all FRB appointees.

The Federal Open Market Committee. Commonly referred to as the FOMC, the committee has 12 members, the seven members of the FRB and five presidents of the 12 Federal Reserve districts. The president of the New York Federal Reserve Bank is always one of the five. The four remaining seats rotate annually among the remaining 11 districts.

How Policy Is Made

Although there is no real "starting point" for monetary policy, one convenient place to begin is with the first installment of the chairman of the Federal Reserve's semiannual Humphrey-Hawkins testimony. It is then—the first testimony is presented to the House and Senate Banking Committees each February—that the FRB and the district presidents set forth their goals for growth in the money supply and their projections for inflation and economic activity. The chairman of the Federal Reserve Board also provides a picture of how the economy has performed and is performing, and what economic issues the Federal Reserve Board may need to address in the coming year.

It is a broad agenda, with the only policy specifics being monetary targets. The year's goals for money supply are set in accordance with the Full Employment and Balanced Budget Act of 1978, the legislation that mandated that the Federal Reserve chairman testify before Congress twice a year (Humphrey-Hawkins testimony). At the chairman's second appearance, typically in July, the monetary targets are reevaluated and altered if deemed prudent, and preliminary money supply growth targets are set for the coming year. All growth and inflation forecasts are just that, forecasts. They are not policy targets for inflation or growth.

The policy importance of the Humphrey-Hawkins testimonies varies according to what the Federal Reserve Board is using as its policy target. When money supply was the primary consideration, changes in its growth targets provided key information on how "easy" or "tight" the Federal Reserve was likely to be for much of the year. Recently, with Federal Reserve policy having no specific statistical guidelines, instead being guided by a more eclectic, more all-encompassing approach to growth and inflation, the effect is more short run. Comments by the chairman are analyzed for the effect on policy merely within the next month or two.

Macroeconomic Policy

For our purposes macroeconomic policy will be defined as "achieving growth within a stable or declining inflationary environment." How the Federal Reserve chooses to meet this goal varies over time. Prior to the late eighties the conduit for such policy was money supply growth (before that, it was reserve growth). In using money supply targets the Fed signaled its determination to bring about a stable to declining rate of inflation by setting lower and lower targets for money supply growth. In 1986 the target for M2 was 6 percent to 9 percent growth. By 1991, M2's target range was 2.5 percent to 6.5 percent growth. Without exploring fully the theoretical underpinnings, it is sufficient to say that the generally held belief "that inflation essentially is a monetary phenomenon" was the driving force behind this long-term policy position. In fact it is this belief that guides many Federal Reserve policy makers to deem that fighting inflation is the Federal Reserve's primary, and only, goal, since it controls only the money supply.

Currently, however, there are no explicit policy goals. Through the early 1990s the relationship between money supply growth and economic growth and inflation broke down (see Chapter 26). Technically, the velocity of money was no longer stable, making it difficult for the Fed to ascertain just what a given rate of money supply growth meant for economic growth and inflation. The Fed still set targets for money growth but did not base policy decisions upon such growth. Rather it began to base its policy decisions upon an eclectic assessment of growth, inflationary potential, and actual inflation—a practice it continues today. Such generic, nebulous policy guidelines are only possible when the Federal Reserve has the trust and confidence of financial markets.

Changing Policy: The Federal Open Market Committee and the Federal Reserve Board

Most of the operational details of monetary policy are conducted under the auspices of the Federal Open Market Committee. Formal meetings take place, currently, eight times a year, about every five to six weeks. Most meetings are one-day affairs, with two-day meetings the norm for the FOMC meetings immediately preceding the two Humphrey-Hawkins testimonies in February and July. The discussions are wide ranging, converging all aspects of economic activity. Fed staffers present forecasts for economic growth, inflation, and money supply growth. The committee members and the other Federal Reserve presidents discuss the current economic situation in detail, evaluating statistical and anecdotal evidence. Various issues can be brought to the fore (e.g., the U.S. dollar, bank lending restrictiveness). Given the size of the committee, disagreement is only natural; diverse opinions are held on most subjects. After the committee has discussed all macroeconomic issues, attention is turned to policy for the upcoming intermeeting period. After opinions are expressed, a consensus is developed on what policy should be—more restrictive, less restrictive, or an unchanged policy stance. A further nuance to this process is whether policy should have a symmetric or asymmetric bias during the intermeeting period. An asymmetric stance is one in which the committee is more likely to adopt a tighter (easier) stance during the intermeeting period than it is an easier (tighter) stance. The actual wording used to express such a bias would be the following (in the case of an asymmetric directive biased toward tightening): "slightly greater reserve restraint would be acceptable while slightly lesser reserve restraint might be acceptable. . . ." The key is the choice of *would* versus *might; would* is considered a stronger wording than *might.* If the Fed were to adopt a purely neutral stance, the symmetrical directive would say: "greater or lesser restraint *would* [both] be acceptable. . . ." A vote is then taken in support of the directive that outlines the consensus view. Votes against the directive are not uncommon, but usually are offered only by one or two FOMC members. Under current Federal Reserve procedures the decision arrived at is announced publicly around 2:15 PM. (See Box 27-1.)

If there has been no outright change in policy, the announcement typically reads, rather tersely:

The FOMC meeting has ended. There will be no further announcement.

Outright policy changes involve a change in the discount rate and/or a change in the federal funds rate. An example from the

BOX 27–1 The Fed Formalizes Policy Change Notification Procedure

From testimony by Alan Greenspan, chairman of the Federal Reserve Board, before the Committee on Banking, Housing, and Urban Affairs of the United States Senate, February 22, 1995:

To make our policy intent as transparent as possible to market participants without losing our flexibility or undermining our deliberative process, at its latest meeting, the FOMC decided to preserve the greater openness of its policy making that it established last year. To that end, all decisions to change reserve market conditions will be announced in a press release on the same day that the decision is made.

The debate surrounding each policy decision will be reported, as is currently the practice, in comprehensive minutes of the meeting that are released on the Friday following the next regularly scheduled meeting of the FOMC. For students of monetary policy making, those minutes will be supplemented by lightly edited transcripts of the discussion at each FOMC meeting. Transcripts for an entire year will be released with a five year lag. Continuing our current practice, the raw transcripts will be circulated to each participant shortly after an FOMC meeting to verify his or her comments, and only changes that clarify meaning, say to correct grammar or transcription errors, will be permitted. A limited amount of material will be redacted from these transcripts before they are released primarily to protect the confidentiality of foreign and domestic sources of intelligence that would dry up if their information were made public. A complete unedited version of the transcripts of each FOMC meeting will be turned over to the National Archives after thirty years have elapsed, as required by law.

After careful consideration, the FOMC believed that these steps, which essentially formalize the procedures that we have been using over the past year, strike the appropriate balance between making our decisions and deliberations accessible as soon as feasible and retaining flexibility in policy making while preserving an unfettered deliberative process.

August 16, 1994, decision to raise the discount rate 50 basis points and the federal funds rate 50 basis points is as follows:

> The Federal Reserve announced today the following monetary policy actions: The Board of Governors approved an increase in the discount rate from 3.5% to 4% effective immediately. The Federal Open Market Committee agreed that this increase would be allowed to show through completely into interest rates in reserve markets. . . .

The announcement then explains the basis for such a decision, citing such macroeconomic factors as the strength of the economic expansion and/or inflationary pressures. Public statements announcing a decision to change only the federal funds rate are shorter and provide no reasons for the decision (that is, such statements, so far, have not provided an explanation). An example from the April 18, 1994, decision to raise the federal funds rate 25 basis points is as follows:

> Chairman Greenspan announced today that the Federal Reserve will increase slightly the degree of pressure on reserve positions. This action is expected to be associated with a small increase in the short term money interest rates.

The decision as to whether the policy directive was symmetric or asymmetric for the upcoming intermeeting period is not announced. Discovery of such positions is made when the minutes of each meeting are released. On the Thursday immediately after an FOMC meeting, at 2:00 PM ET, the minutes of the meeting preceding the one that just occurred are released (that is, the minutes are released with a one-meeting lag). It is only through a thorough reading of these minutes that one can find the Fed's symmetric or asymmetric policy stance.

As can be seen, the Federal Reserve Board is responsible for changes in the discount rate, while the FOMC determines changes in the federal funds rate. The FRB can change the discount rate within the context of an FOMC meeting or independently. All but one policy change since the Fed instituted its "announcement rule" in February 1994 has occurred at an FOMC meeting, a predilection that may or may not be the rule of thumb in years to come.

Policy Changes: The Channel to the Market and the Economy

Whereas monetary policy is set in terms of broad inflation and growth goals and possibly specific monetary targets, an actual policy shift does not deal directly with these areas. As has just been documented, the main mechanism of change is short-term interest rates,[1] namely, the discount rate and the federal funds rate.

A change in the discount rate is considered a bolder, more overt move, signaling an aggressive policy action. For monetary policy makers it is a "sit up and take notice" change given to the public at large and the financial markets. A change in the federal funds rate is the more commonly employed policy tool. It is considered a quieter, albeit just as effective, means of affecting interest rates. In the past the fact that a change in the discount rate would make the front page of newspapers while a change in the federal funds rate typically was consigned to the business section offers a sense of the difference between the two, although the Fed's switch to announcing publicly all interest rate decisions has pushed even federal funds rate changes (and no changes) to the front page.

Once a policy change is effected, it is up to the financial markets to carry out the Fed's game plan (if they had not already in anticipation of a move). Though general market rates, Treasury bill, note, and bond rates, and all other short- and long-term interest rates are not tied directly to the federal funds rate, they are loosely linked via the term structure effect—overnight rates are implicitly built into one-month rates, which are built into three-month rates, and on and up the interest rate maturity chain.[2] (See Table 27-1.) As Table 27-2 indicates, the effect on market interest

---

1   A second tool, but historically one that has been used infrequently, is a change in reserve requirements. During the banking sector difficulties in the 1990–1992 period, this mechanism was employed twice. In December 1990, the FRB cut the reserve requirements on net eurodollar liabilities and nonpersonal time deposits with maturities of less than 1½ years from 3 percent to zero. In February 1992, the FRB cut the reserve requirement on transaction deposits from 12 percent to 10 percent. Ostensibly, both cuts were undertaken to increase bank lending and shore up bank profitability. Since this policy lever is not commonly employed, all future references to policy shifts will pertain strictly to interest rate changes.

2   For a discussion of the term structure of interest rates, refer to any standard monetary policy or financial market textbook, such as Frederick S. Mishkin, *Economics of Money, Banking and Financial Markets*, 2d ed., Scott Foresman, Glenview, Ill. 1989.

TABLE 27–1   The Interest Rate Chain

Discount > Federal Funds > Treasury Bill > Treasury Note > Treasury Bond
Rate   Rate   Rates   Rates   Rates

TABLE 27–2   Yield Curve Correlation: The Federal Funds Rate and Treasury Rates

	Three-Month Treasury Bill	One-Year Treasury Bill	Five-Year Treasury Note	Ten-Year Treasury Note	Thirty-Year Treasury Bond
	1980 to 1996, Quarterly				
Federal Funds Rate	.990	.971	.883	.849	.815
	1980 to 1996, Monthly				
Federal Funds Rate	.981	.953	.848	.805	.771

rates of a change in the federal funds rate is less and less the further one goes out the yield curve.

Be that as it may, the guiding principle of monetary policy as conducted by the Federal Reserve is to rely on interest rate changes to effect economic growth and subsequently inflation and money supply growth. And that effect can be quite strong. But again, the Federal Reserve has no control over the extent to which changes in the discount rate or federal funds rate are transferred to market interest rates, especially long-term interest rates. The ultimate effect can be either less or greater than would be expected given the actual change in the short-term rate. Another look at Figure 27-2 shows also that the correlation between the federal funds rate and Treasury bill rates falls with shorter periodicities (i.e., months versus quarters), especially as one moves further out the yield curve. A host of other factors, supply and demand and financial market psychology, have important effects on longer-term interest rates. Still, the rather high degree of correlation shows that the Fed's policy mechanism is by no means a hit or miss prospect. As imperfect as this mechanism is, it does work.

Chapter 28

Open Market Operations: Reserves and the Banking System

General Description

During 1994–1995, open market operations lost their policy importance. Prior to its decision to publicly announce policy changes, the Federal Reserve had used open market operations to transmit policy initiatives to the marketplace. It was then that "Fedwatchers" played an important role in fixed-income markets, analyzing the Federal Reserve's balance sheet and watching and interpreting daily open market operations for clues to a Fed move. The process could be murky or sparkling clear, depending upon whether the Fed wanted to make an overt statement or a covert nudge to interest rates.

Now, Fedwatching merely means keeping an eye on the newswires around 2:15 PM ET every four to six weeks (after each FOMC meeting). And now, open market operations are strictly technical in nature, the Federal Reserve's means of maintaining the proper amount of reserves in the banking system. Not that

Economic Indicator Information at a Glance

Market Significance	Low
Typical Release Time	4:30 PM Eastern Time Every Thursday
Released By	Federal Reserve Board
Period Covered	Week Ending Monday of Prior Week
Web Site	http://www.bog.frb.fed.us/releases/h41/

this is unimportant. Such actions help determine where the federal funds rate trades relative to its equilibrium level and in so doing affect the repo market. Open market operations can also take the form of the Fed buying for its own account $4 bn. or $5 bn. of Treasury bills or coupons. Such actions, especially the latter, can have a significant, even if only temporary, effect on fixed-income prices.

Beyond the market aspects of open market operations, an understanding of just how the Federal Reserve actually supplies reserves to the system will help clear up many misconceptions about the Fed's control of the money supply and its ability to liquefy the financial system.

Open Market Operations: The Technicals

The most basic tenet of economics, demand and supply, is the cornerstone of the Federal Reserve's open market operations. These operations are defined as the Fed's day-to-day management of bank reserves. As we shall see, this management effectively means trying to keep the supply of reserves in balance with demand around the desired federal funds rate. To some, these operations have an important macroeconomic aspect: the Fed's means of adding or draining liquidity from the financial system, and in so doing fueling or slowing economic activity. But this broader interpretation goes well beyond what is happening. As we shall see, the Federal Reserve's open market operations, under normal circumstances, are strictly a reactive procedure, not a proactive one. In keeping reserves in balance, the Fed responds to the system's needs; it does not create new ones.

Demand for Reserves

As you recall from Economics 101 or your first course in monetary theory, the U.S. banking system is subject to a fractional reserve system. That is, for every dollar a bank customer holds in certain accounts, the bank must hold a fraction of that dollar "in reserve." For the most part that fraction is 3 percent.[1] So for every

---

1   Net transaction accounts of zero to $46.8 mn. have a reserve requirement of 3 percent. Accounts of more than $46.8 mn. have a reserve requirement of 10 percent.

dollar on deposit, a bank must hold 3 cents in reserve. *In reserve* means either keeping 3 cents in its vaults, in cash, or keeping it on deposit at its district Federal Reserve Bank. These reserves, for obvious reasons, are called *required reserves,* and constitute the largest demand for reserves.

Required reserves are based on the average amount of deposits held by banks in a two-week period ending every other Monday, and they are held during the two-week period ending on the subsequent Wednesday. This 14-day Thursday-to-Wednesday period is called a "reserve," or "statement," or "maintenance" period. Thus if a bank had average deposits of $20 bn., in a particular statement period the bank would have to hold $600 mn., *on average,* over the course of the two-week period (assuming all accounts were less than $46.8 mn.). The bank does not have to hold 3 percent of each day's deposits, which can fluctuate wildly, on that day or hold $600 mn. on each day. All it has to do is make sure that its required reserves average $600 mn. for the two-week period. Thus a bank could hold $600 mn. per day or $8.4 bn. for one day and no reserves the other 13 days, and in each case it would meet its legal requirement.

The other source of demand for reserves is called *excess reserves.* Deposit flows are volatile and unpredictable. Furthermore, many smaller banks do not have the sophisticated systems necessary to monitor deposit flows extremely closely. As a result banks, in the aggregate, will hold more reserves than are necessary as a precaution against uncertain deposit changes. On an absolute scale, these reserves are a very small portion of the total demand for reserves, amounting to only about 2 percent.

These are the two sources of demand for reserves in the banking system and are so designated in the balance sheet shown in Table 28-1.

Supply of Reserves

Similar to the demand side of the ledger, there are two main sources of the "supply" of reserves. They are borrowed reserves and nonborrowed reserves. Banks can get reserves credited to their account at their district Fed by borrowing directly from their district Federal Reserve Bank. This is borrowing at the discount window, and the discount rate is the rate charged for this

TABLE 28–1   Sources of Demand

Reserves	
Demand	Supply
Required Reserves	
Excess Reserves	

privilege. All other sources of supply are called *nonborrowed reserves*, a catchall phrase for total reserves minus borrowed reserves. This source funds about 98 percent of the reserves in the system, and the federal funds market, or interbank market, is where these reserves are traded. The balance sheet is essentially complete, as shown in Table 28-2.

It can be summed up in equation form as:

Required reserves + excess reserves = TOTAL RESERVES =

borrowed reserves + nonborrowed reserves

For now, the focus will be on the nonborrowed reserve component. It is here that we find most of the factors that affect the supply of reserves, create the greatest imbalances in the equilibrium of reserves, and induce the Federal Reserve to conduct its open market operations. The nonborrowed reserve factors are listed in the Federal Reserve's H4.1 release (every Thursday at 4:30 PM). Many of these factors do not show significant movement from week to week or statement period to statement period. But there are a few that account for the greatest volatility in reserve flows and thereby create the need for open market operations. Chief among these more volatile factors are float, Treasury balances at the Federal Reserve, currency in circulation, and other assets.

TABLE 28–2   Sources of Supply

Reserves	
Demand	Supply
Required Reserves	Borrowed Reserves
Excess Reserves	Nonborrowed Reserves

Float

Float is the overlap in time between when a check is credited at the receiving bank and when it is finally debited at the paying bank. Essentially two banks are using the same dollar. A bank to which a check is presented for payment receives credit for the amount of the check from the Federal Reserve, within two days of its being presented. However, it can take more than two days for that check to be debited against the bank on which it is drawn. Usually inclement weather delays the processing of the check and creates "transportation float." Thus when processing is delayed, the paying bank still has the funds while the receiving bank is credited with the funds and can also use them to meet its required reserve need. Reserve-wise, note that an increase (decrease) in float increases (decreases) the supply of reserves within the banking system.

Treasury Balances at the Fed

The U.S. Treasury keeps its cash in two places, in tax and loan accounts (T&L) at depository institutions and in its account at the Federal Reserve. The former accounts must be collateralized, which effectively puts a cap on them, to the extent that the banks are willing to offer up collateral. Recently the most that the Treasury has deposited in T&L accounts is around $40 bn. But the amount in these accounts can vary widely, from the aforementioned $40 bn. to as low as a few hundred million.

The second depository for the government's funds is the Federal Reserve, the account from which the U.S. government pays its bills. The Treasury now attempts to keep its deposits at the Federal Reserve at around $5.5 bn. or around $7 bn. after significant tax dates. Try as it may though, the Treasury cannot always keep these balances stable. The Treasury's cash balances are subject to great volatility due to the unpredictability of tax receipts and government outlays. The fact that there is an approximate cap to the amount that can be held in T&L accounts also is critical. After important tax payment dates (January, April, June, and September), receipts can be so great that T&L limits are reached and all additional funds have to be deposited at Federal Reserve Banks. At these times Treasury deposits at the Fed can soar to over $25 bn.

How does all this affect the supply of reserves? When the Treasury processes a receipt and deposits it in a T&L account, all that happens is that the funds are transferred from a private sector account to a public account. Importantly the funds are still in the private banking system and the T&L accounts can be used to meet a bank's reserve requirements. However, when the Treasury transfers funds to its Federal Reserve account, the money is removed from the banking system and a bank cannot use it to meet its reserve requirement. From a reserve standpoint an increase (decrease) in Treasury balances at the Fed decreases (increases) the supply of reserves in the system.

Currency in Circulation

Currency in circulation is the amount of money actually held by the public in coin and paper. When cash and coin are held by a bank, it is called *vault cash*. As stated before, vault cash can be used to meet a bank's reserve requirements. When the public increases its demand for physical money (holiday periods typically show a large increase in currency in circulation), that reduces the amount of vault cash in the banking system and lessens the supply of reserves. Thus, the reserve impact is such that an increase (decrease) in currency in circulation decreases (increases) the supply of reserves.

Other Assets

Although it is not utilized in the following example, another important reserve category is worth mentioning—*other assets*. This component includes, among other things, the Federal Reserve's foreign currency holdings. It is through this category that foreign exchange interventions have an effect on open market operations. If the Fed is defending the dollar, it will buy dollars and sell foreign currencies. The dollars flow from the banking system to the Fed while foreign currencies will enter the world's financial system. As one can see, the action of supporting the dollar drains reserves from the system.

Balancing the Supply and Demand for Reserves

With an understanding of the main components of the reserve equation, the next step is to look at the connection between the balance sheet and open market operations. To do so, a more detailed balance sheet is constructed, with Treasury balances at the Fed, float, and currency in circulation representing the supply of nonborrowed reserves.

One way to look at each demand and supply component is to estimate the amount each factor changes from maintenance period to maintenance period. Thus if float was $500 mn. in period one and rose to $1.5 bn. in the subsequent period, $1 bn. more reserves are in the system in period two. This approach can be applied to each of the reserve factors. Similarly, if transactions deposits in the banking system rise from period one to period two, so will required reserves. For now we will assume that there is no change in the amount of reserves borrowed from the discount window and assign changes to each of the other balance sheet components, as shown in Table 28-3.

To make the analysis even easier, the balance sheet will be restructured such that one side will hold the factors that increase the supply of reserves (decreasing the demand for reserves has the same effect) and the other side will hold the factors that reduce the supply of reserves (or increase the demand). As the reserve factors are rearranged, remember that an increase in one factor, such as float, increases reserves in the system, while an increase in Treasury balances at the Fed decreases reserves in the system.

Table 28-4 shows that although float will rise and generate a surplus of reserves in the system, other factors will take reserves out of the system. Banks are expected to be holding more deposits, and thus will need to hold more required reserves. There also is forecasted a rise in banks' demand for excess reserves during the period. Furthermore, individuals are projected to desire

TABLE 28–3 Assigning Changes to Balance Sheet Components

Reserves			
Demand		**Supply**	
Required Reserves	+2,000	Borrowed Reserves	0
Excess Reserves	+500	Nonborrowed Reserves:	
		Treasury balances @ Fed	+1,000
		Currency in Circulation	+500
		Float	+1,000

TABLE 28–4   Rearranging Balance Sheet Components

Reserves			
Increase Supply/ Decrease Demand		**Decrease Supply/ Increase Demand**	
Float	1,000	Required Reserves	2,000
		Excess Reserves	500
		Treasury Balances at the Fed	1,000
		Currency in Circulation	500
SUM:	1,000	SUM:	4,000

more cash in hand, consequently reducing banks' holdings of vault cash (and therefore reserves). As one can see, whether demand increases or supply falls, the effect is the same: there is a shortage of reserves in the banking system.

Summing up each side, the net effect is that there is expected to be $3 bn. too few reserves in the system in the upcoming statement period due to either a reduction in supply or greater demand. If the situation were left unattended, demand would far exceed supply and the price of those reserves would have to rise. In this case, that means the federal funds rate would increase—if the situation were left unattended.

The existence of a reserve imbalance, something that occurs in just about every maintenance period, creates the need for open market operations. As stated before, these operations are the Federal Reserve's mechanism for maintaining the balance between the supply of and demand for reserves. In this instance the Fed would need to supply $3 bn. of reserves to the banking system to insure a smoothly functioning interbank market.

Need to Add Reserves

Taking a step back for a moment, it's important to remember that in the above example the reserve shortage exists only for that single two-week reserve period. In the previous and subsequent periods the reserve position can be very different. That means the Fed needs to supply the necessary reserves on a temporary basis.

The Fed's primary, if not sole, means of supplying reserves, temporarily, to the banking system is via a *system repo*.[2] System repos are repurchase agreements between the Federal Reserve and primary dealers. The Fed receives the securities, and the banking system gets the cash (reserves). The term of a system typically ranges from overnight to 14 days, although there is no limit to its length. There is no minimum or maximum size of a system repo although repos normally are not conducted for less than $1 bn. The average system repo, combining overnights and terms, in the first three months of 1996 was $3.6 bn. System repos for more than $10 bn. are not common but certainly are not unheard of. Term systems also can span two reserve periods.

The Fed announces its adding activity (and draining activity) between 10:30 AM and 10:45 AM. A short time later it announces the par value of the amount accepted for the reserve operation.

The Fed also adds reserves to the system permanently, by actually buying securities, either Treasury bills or coupons. These outright purchases are called *bill* or *coupon passes* and are conducted when the Fed perceives an extended add need of more than moderate size.

When the Fed purchases coupons, it does a portion of the coupon curve at a time, for example, securities with maturities of one year to 18 months, two years to five years, or five years to 10 years. It will then come back an hour or so later and announce the par value of the amount bought. Since the Fed started this new coupon pass procedure (the Fed used to buy all the securities at one time), purchases have been spread over two to three weeks.

The choice between a bill pass or coupon pass is based on such factors as the outstanding supply of bills and the type of pass the Fed has employed recently. In 1995 and 1996 the Fed conducted four bill passes and three coupon passes. The average size of the bill passes was $3.3 bn., while the average size of the coupon passes was $4.3 bn.

---

2   Prior to January 1, 1997, the Federal Reserve also conducted customer repos. These were repos that were already in place between the Federal Reserve and foreign central banks, for which the Fed holds a large pool of funds. To add reserves the Fed "passed through" the repo to primary dealers, such that the primary dealers received the cash instead of the Fed. Although the Fed said only that the current procedures (announced on December 18, 1996) make it *less likely* that customers will be used in the future, its current procedures offer little reason for the Fed to revert to their usage unless there were to be a wholesale change in Fed operating procedures.

Technically there is no difference between the type of pass—
the same amount of reserves is added. For fixed-income markets
though, a coupon pass is considered more bullish than a bill pass
since it is removing a supply of securities permanently.

Another means of adding reserves for the Fed, similar to a pass,
is to purchase Treasury securities, internally, from the foreign accounts that own a large pool of government securities. This could
be characterized as an under the table operation since it is not announced at the time of execution, but it can be discerned from the
Federal Reserve's H4.1 release for the week in which it was undertaken. The use of these internal purchases has diminished dramatically in recent years, but even before then the fact that these
purchases typically were for only a few hundred million dollars
meant they had no critical market or reserve impact.

Need to Drain Reserves

So far the only reserve position studied was one in which there
was a dearth of reserves. This is the situation in which the Fed
finds itself most weeks of the year. But there are also times when
there are too many reserves in the system. Remember that open
market operations are geared toward maintaining an equilibrium in the reserve market, so when the reserve factors move to
produce an overabundance of reserves, the Fed is forced to enter
the marketplace and conduct operations that take reserves out of
the system. In terms of the example above, all one would have to
do is flip the sign on each of the factors. They would move to opposite sides of the balance sheet and create a situation in which
there were $3 bn. too many reserves in the system.

The Fed reduces the supply of reserves in the banking system
via an operation that is the opposite of a procedure used to add
reserves. For all practical reserve-related purposes, a *matched
sale-repurchase agreement* is the opposite of a system repo. The Fed
receives cash from the banking system in exchange for securities.
Technically, though, it is not a reverse repo, but an agreement by
the Fed to literally sell the securities outright and then buy them
back on a specified date. The Fed is not allowed to enter into a repurchase agreement, an agreement in which it *lends* securities. A
matched sale is the same as a system repo in terms of the various
lengths, overnights to extended terms, and size—anywhere from

a few hundred million to over $10 bn. Most importantly the concept is the reverse as well. As the Fed receives cash for the securities, the money, or reserves, leaves the banking system. The supply of reserves is thereby reduced.

The use of matched sales has become the Fed's sole means of draining reserves through the marketplace. But that has not always been the case. Similar to a bill or coupon pass, the Fed also can drain reserves permanently, via a bill sale. Coupon sales are not utilized by the Fed. Again the motivation is the same, a large extended need—but a drain need this time. The most likely seasonal time to see a bill sale is in the January–February period.

There are two "internal means" of draining reserves from the system as well. The counterpart to buying securities from the pool held by foreign accounts, and kept at the Fed, is to sell securities to these accounts. The Fed receives cash (reserves), which reduces the supply of reserves. The second way is for the Federal Reserve to roll off a portion of its own holdings of Treasury securities at the Treasury's bill auctions. The Fed has large holdings of Treasury securities, some of which mature at every auction. Normally the Fed will replace its entire holdings of each bill with the bill being auctioned. But if it chooses, it can redeem a portion of those holdings for cash. In so doing the Treasury pays the Federal Reserve cash, and reserves move from the banking system to the Fed. This process has the same reserve effect as Treasury deposits at the Fed rising, although here the drain is permanent. There is nothing analogous to this on the add side because the Federal Reserve is not allowed legally to buy securities in the primary market, via the auction process. In recent years both of these draining techniques have been only infrequently used.

Summary

With the Federal Reserve Board systematically removing the mystery from policy decisions, the Federal Reserve's open market desk has done the same for open market operations. This process also has included an ongoing simplification of open market procedures. What had once been arcane is now mundane. Fixed-income markets no longer hold their collective breath waiting for "Fed time." It's only repo desks that have strong interest in the liquidity in the very short end of the Treasury market.

From a very broad perspective an understanding of the reserve process points to the inevitable conclusion that the Federal Reserve is not in the business of proactively using the supply of reserves to affect the system's liquidity, a common misconception (allowing for special circumstances such as the stock market plunge in October 1987). The Fed's reserve business is a reactive one; the Fed always supplies the amount of reserves the system needs, not more, not less (again, technical, day-to-day situations aside). Any proactive stance is via the policy route, and the tool is interest rates, not the supply of reserves.

Chapter 29

U.S. Treasury Financing

General Description and Recent History

With the U.S. government having run a deficit since 1970, the Treasury's need to issue debt is rather straightforward. (See Box 29-1.) To cover debt issuance of this magnitude the Treasury issues securities across the entire yield curve: from three-month bills to 30-year bonds, and it does so on a well-defined schedule.

Of course, that is not to say that there have not been changes over the years. Since 1980 the deficit has been as high as $290 bn. in fiscal 1992 and as low as $107 bn. in fiscal 1996. Such dramatic swings require changes in the Treasury's auction schedule and the sizes of particular securities. In 1982, for example, the Treasury issued $5 bn. three-month bills on a weekly basis, $7 bn. five-year notes once a quarter, and about $5 bn. 30-year bonds four times a year. At one point in 1996 the Treasury was issuing $27 bn. three-month bills on a weekly basis, $12.5 bn. five-year notes on a monthly basis, and an average of $11 bn. 10-year notes six times a year.

Such an example belies the fact that up through the 1980s the U.S. Treasury held to the principle that it should disturb its financing pattern as little as possible. The reasoning was that the marketplace could more easily absorb the government's huge financing needs if the debt schedule was well established and, in so doing, lower the Treasury's borrowing costs. Even in the late

---

BOX 29–1   The Debt Ceiling

The Treasury's authority to issue debt is based on congressional authority. Since the Second Liberty Bond Act of 1917 Congress, by statute, has set an overall limit for the amount of debt the Treasury can have outstanding. This debt includes marketable and nonmarketable debt (i.e., debt issued to state and local governments and debt issued to trust funds). Since the advent of large deficits in the early 1980s, Congress has had to increase the debt limit approximately 20 times. Sometimes it has delayed doing so. At those times the Treasury's financing schedule is thrown into disarray. The Treasury may delay auctions or reduce their size. Often it will pay down Treasury bills so it can continue issuing its coupon debt. The Treasury also may underinvest trust fund money, providing room to issue marketable debt.

Congress can legislate either a permanent debt ceiling increase or a temporary debt ceiling increase that expires on a given date. If the Treasury bumps up against the former, it can issue new debt but only to replace existing debt. Under the latter the Treasury has to literally let debt expire so as to get back under the lower debt cap.

1980s when the deficits grew dramatically, the Treasury was able to accommodate the ever-increasing funding needs merely by increasing the amounts of issues already in place.

As much as it was wanted, however, this commitment began to unravel in the early 1990s. Continued large deficits forced the Treasury to intermittently alter its financing pattern. First five-year notes were switched to a monthly auction schedule from a quarterly one in 1990. Then in 1993 the Treasury offered a slightly different twist in changing its financing pattern, all in theory, under the pretext of reducing borrowing costs. At that time the Treasury canceled the auction of seven-year notes, a relatively unpopular maturity, and cut the frequency of 30-year bond auctions from four to two. The objective was to concentrate more of its financing needs at the shorter end of the yield curve—three-month, six-month, and one-year bills and two- and three-year notes—in order to cut its financing costs. The rationale was that more often than not (historically speaking) the yield curve is positively sloped, so increasing the relative issuance of short-term debt versus long-term debt would lower the Treasury's borrowing costs. That yields on 30-year Treasury bonds were the lowest they had been since the security was introduced in 1977 and that corporations were lining up to issue long-term debt were not relevant issues. Neither, purportedly, was the pressure from congressional studies that had been championing such a change in the Treasury's financing pattern.

In 1996 additional changes were made. The years of deficit financing began catching up with the Treasury's financing cycle; as more securities matured, especially the monthly five-year notes, the Treasury had to find new ways to pay these securities down and also raise new cash. But instead of following the philosophy imposed three years earlier, of bulking up the calendar with shorter maturities, the Treasury reversed field. In May 1996 it announced 30-year bonds would now be auctioned three times a year instead of two, and 10-year notes would be auctioned six times a year instead of four times. A few weeks later, the Treasury then announced it was going to issue inflation-indexed securities (see Box 29-2) for the first time ever.

Just when the Treasury was pulling out all stops to finance the cumulative effects of its prior deficits, fiscal policy took a dramatic turn for the better. For fiscal years 1996 and 1997 the deficit fell dramatically, a two-year turnaround of $100 bn. Suddenly the Treasury was faced with the unusual prospect of finding ways to pare its debt issuance. Coupon auction sizes were reduced, and the issuance of 10-year notes was pared back to four times a year. Furthermore, faced with the potential for a balanced budget after the turn of the century, it's likely further changes in the Treasury's auction schedule will occur.

The Financing Pattern

The nature of the calendar makes it impossible to insure specific auction and settlement dates from month to month or year to year. The Treasury also tries to narrow the time between when a note or bond is auctioned and when it settles (called the *WI*, or *when issued*, period), and its ability to do so depends upon the calendar as well. Generally, if a settlement date falls on a weekend, the actual transaction takes place on the following business day. For example, two- and five-year notes always mature on the

BOX 29–2   Treasury Inflation Protection Securities (TIPS)

The U.S. Treasury's inflation-indexed securities are a new wrinkle in the Treasury's cash-raising arsenal. The indexed security pays a return in two ways. First, the rate of inflation will accrue to bondholders over the life of a bond (this portion is paid at final maturity). Thus a security purchased for $100, after a year in which inflation was 3 percent, will be worth $103. Second, a coupon rate is set on the security at the time of auction. This rate will be paid quarterly on all principal (including the inflation-adjustment increment). The first TIPS security, a 10-year maturity, was issued in February 1997. It had a coupon yield of 3⅜ percent. At that time, the 10-year note was offering a yield of 6.75 percent and inflation was running a little over 3 percent. For the Treasury the fact that the inflation rate plus the coupon rate added up to less than the coupon rate on a standard, nominal interest rate bond made the security less costly. Of course, inflation must remain low for this advantage to continue. In July 1997 the Treasury issued a TIPS security with a maturity of five years, and it plans to issue a 30-year TIPS bond in early 1998. The exact schedule of issuance for each TIPS security has not yet been set.

What is most interesting about the inflation-indexed concept is that it offers the best inflation protection when inflation is low. It is then that one wants insurance against rising inflation. Unfortunately investor psychology works in reverse. At times of low inflation investors perceive little risk of high inflation and thus have no appetite for inflation protection securities. It is only during periods of high inflation that investors desire inflation protection. However, buying them at that time prevents investors from achieving capital gains when inflation and interest rates ultimately fall, and the declining inflation rate cuts into the security's inflation accrual rate of return.

last day of the month, so the actual transaction often takes place on the first day of the following month. A settlement scheduled for a holiday, an infrequent occurrence, would also settle on the following business day. (See Table 29-1.)

Once a quarter the Treasury auctions three-year notes, 10-year notes, and (three times a year) 30-year bonds three days in a row.

TABLE 29–1   U.S. Treasury's Financing Pattern

Security	Frequency	Day Announced	Day Auctioned	Settlement Day
3-month bill	Weekly	Tuesday	Following Monday	Thursday
6-month bill	Weekly	Tuesday	Following Monday	Thursday
52-week bill	Every 4 weeks	Friday	Following Thursday	Following Thursday
2-year note	Monthly	Typically third Wednesday	Typically last or next to last Tuesday	Last day of month
3-year note	Quarterly: Feb., May, Aug., Nov.	First Wednesday of month	Tuesday following auction announcement	The 15th of the auction month
5-year note	Monthly	Typically third Wednesday	Typically last or next to last Wednesday of month	Last day of month
10-year note	Quarterly: Feb., May, Aug., Nov.	First Wednesday of month	Day after 3-year note auction/second Tuesday of month (July, Oct.)	The 15th of the auction month
30-year bond	Feb., Aug., Nov.	Last Wednesday of prior month/first Wednesday of month	Thursday following 10-year auction	The 15th of the auction month
TIPS	A fixed TIPS schedule will be set by end of 1998			The 15th of the auction month

Note: The web site for information on Treasury issuance of bills, notes, and bonds is www.publicdebt.treas.gov/sec/sec.htm. The web site for the Treasury's latest financing pattern is www.publicdebt.treas.gov/of/ofpatmth.htm.

267

This grouping is called *the refunding*. It is timed to coincide with the Treasury's largest ($25 bn. to $30 bn.) interest payments on its existing debt. For fixed-income markets, the refunding is a recurring hurdle, and the market's ability to absorb the debt is often a key sign of the fixed-income market's health.

Cash Management Bills

Another means of Treasury financing is cash management bills. Historically their purpose has been, and for the most part still is, to tide the Treasury over temporary cash low points before tax dates. Typical maturities are two to three weeks. But in the late eighties and into the nineties, cash management bills have begun to serve as a source of new cash for longer periods of time. Whereas cash management bills had always matured within a given quarter, the deficits of the 1980s forced the Treasury to extend the maturity of some bills to the point where they bridged fiscal years and had maturities close to one year. These longer-dated bills are not as frequent now, but they remain a source of new cash for the U.S. Treasury.

Unlike the regular bills, notes, and bonds, there is no set schedule for cash management bills. Nor is there a consistency of size. The volatility and unpredictability of the U.S. Treasury's cash position make it impossible to have any strict regularity in cash management bill issuance. But that having been said, there is a seasonality to the Treasury's cash low points and therefore when cash management bills are likely to be offered. The schedule shown in Table 29-2 indicates when these bills have typically been offered in the past, and it provides a reasonable estimate of

TABLE 29–2   Cash Management Bills

Issuance	Possible Maturity
Mid-March to Early April	Late April (After April 15)
Late May to Early June	Late June (After June 15)
Mid-August to Late August	Late September (After September 15)
Mid-November	Late December/Late January/Late March
Early December	Late December (After December 15)

when they could be issued in the future. The one thing that cannot be determined beforehand is the size. Still, in any given year, the Treasury could issue cash management bills at all, a few, or none of the times listed in the table.

Auction Sizes

In general, the sizes of the auctions are inversely related to maturity: the largest issues have a maturity of 52 weeks or less. The weekly auction of three- and six-month bills (officially 13- and 26-week bills) is announced in one combined size. Thus a $24 bn. weekly bill auction means the two bills are each $12 bn. in size. It isn't unusual for the year bill (officially a 52-week bill) to be of greater size than the weekly bills individually. Further exceptions to the "longer the maturity the smaller the size" unofficial rule are usually due to differing frequency of issuance, the most obvious example being the size of the 30-year bond relative to the 10-year note.

Auction sizes also depend upon the Treasury's financing needs, not only year to year, but quarter to quarter, within a fiscal year. For example the Treasury typically finds itself needing to raise large amounts of cash. But in the second calendar quarter, when individual tax payments are made, the Treasury cash needs are curtailed dramatically. In fact, the Treasury has actually retired debt in the April–June period (most recently in 1996 and 1997). At such times the Treasury might reduce the size of its weekly bill offerings by $3 bn. or more to help keep its cash balances from rising too rapidly. Cuts in coupon auctions have also been made in the past, but such reductions typically are limited to $500 mn.

The Treasury's announcements of the auction sizes presently are made at 2:30 PM. At the quarterly refunding announcement the Treasury also releases the schedule of auction dates for the subsequent three months (until the next quarterly refunding announcement). At 3:00 PM on the Monday immediately preceding the quarterly refunding announcement, the Treasury announces its estimates of the financing needs for the remainder of the current quarter and the following quarter. Such estimates are useful for gauging the potential size of upcoming auction amounts for

TABLE 29–3   Snapshot: Auction Sizes, August 1996

Three- and six-month bills	$29 bn. (combined)
One-year bill	$19.25 bn.
Two-year note	$19 bn.
Three-year note	$19 bn.
Five-year note	$12.75 bn.
Ten-year note	$12 bn.
Thirty-year bond	$12 bn.

bills and coupons. Analysts can compare their own estimates with those of the Treasury, knowing full well that the actual amounts of new cash raised, especially in the subsequent quarter, can vary significantly from their own and the Treasury's estimates. (See Table 29-3.)

Index

Page numbers in bold type refer to tables and figures.